John Calvin's Doctrine
of the Christian Life

John Calvin's Doctrine of the Christian Life

John H. Leith

Foreword by

Albert C. Outler

Westminster/John Knox Press
Louisville, Kentucky

Book design by Gene Harris

First edition

Published by Westminster/John Knox Press
Louisville, Kentucky

PRINTED IN THE UNITED STATES OF AMERICA

9 8 7 6 5 4 3 2 1

Library of Congress Cataloging-in-Publication Data

Leith, John H.
    John Calvin's doctrine of the Christian life / John H. Leith ;
foreword by Albert C. Outler. — 1st ed.
        p.   cm.
    ". . . published now as it was written [as Yale Ph.D. thesis] in
1947–1949 with minimal changes, for the most part reflecting current
language usage"—Pref.
    ISBN 0-664-21330-8

    1. Calvin, Jean, 1509–1564—Contributions in doctrine of Christian
life. 2. Spirituality—History of doctrines—16th century.
3. Reformed Church—Doctrines—16th century. I. Title.
BX9418.L43 1989
230′.4′20924—dc19   88-28058
                                                                              CIP

Contents

Foreword

The publication of this dissertation, four decades after its writing, on the occasion of the author's retirement and as part of the celebration of his eminent career as a great teacher, should be welcomed by a varied assortment of readers, and for several reasons.

To begin with, and *sine qua non* to all other considerations, it was and still is a good book, in its own right and on its own terms. This means that it was and still is very much worth reading by anyone interested in Calvin and in his contribution to Christian doctrine. It is a solid, balanced study of the mind and heart of one of the quite rare genius-level theologians in Western Christianity. Its constant focus is on Calvin's central concerns; its main achievement is a credible exposition of those concerns. It is, of course, based on the primary sources, including the Calvin corpus and its chief sources. And yet it is also in lively dialogue with the huge mass of secondary sources in Calvin studies, in their tumultuous dissonances over the past four centuries. In a field already worked over by many a diligent gleaner, Leith's results are neither tediously commonplace nor outrageously novel. Some readers may even find them more relevant now than they seemed to some in 1949. As a dissertation, it helped earn its author a Yale doctorate with honors; it eased his entrée into what has been an outstanding teaching career at Union Theological Seminary at Richmond, Virginia (1959–89). It was reproduced in facsimile in 1982 and has continued in this state of honorable obscurity until now.

Within this larger group of potential readers, there is also a smaller company (although still large and impressive in its own way) of Professor Leith's special students, who cherish him as mentor and friend. They will readily recognize here a rudimentary chart and compass for the theological orientation that has guided their teacher in his own development as a theologian, both as a scholar-teacher and as a scholar-statesman in the Reformed church family in Amer-

ica. They will thus understand more clearly why, if their teacher has
not been the most conspicuous among the Reformed theologians in
America in his time, he has nonetheless been one of the most influ-
ential, with an impact that continues to increase (as may be seen in
his recent Currie Lectures and in his forthcoming Warfield Lectures). The motifs in this early study still undergird his mature
theological position—and this, without contradiction, also includes
his social and political involvements over four decades.

For readers more particularly interested in questions about interpretation and methodology in the disorderly enterprise of historical
theology, this study will also have its special interests and rewards.
It is a careful, competent analysis of one of the most orderly minds
and impassioned hearts in the whole history of the Christian church.
And if, as should go without saying, such readers are also acquainted
with the bitter history of Calvin controversy, they can find here an
unexpectedly uncontentious summation of Calvin's central theological emphases, balanced out with quiet stipulations of what are
spoken of frankly as flaws in Calvin's ways of explaining and defending his speculative opinions. There is never a waver in Leith's basic
loyalty to the Reformed tradition, but neither is there any of the hero
worship that Calvin himself deplored. This is an important point, for
in 1949 there were still many survivors of the old theological *code
duello* and the deadly quarrels among Calvinists and between Calvinists and others. Some of these veterans were alive and well—and
defensive. Thus only newcomers to Calvin study will fail to realize
how far ahead of his time Leith was when he was wrestling with his
project, the project of mastering the vital essence of Calvin's Christian teaching and expounding this essence in a critical perspective
that reached beyond the older modernist-fundamentalist quarrelings
still rumbling in American religion in those days.

What really is bold here, and relatively new, is Leith's constructive
exposition of Calvin's essential message along with his calm critique
of Calvin's "inconsistencies" in explication. All this, be it noted, was
the work of a robust Calvinist, whose obvious aim was to get behind
historical stereotypes to the original intent of a second-generation
Reformer, unembarrassed to understand himself as a spiritual son of
Luther.

This is not, therefore, an eristic appraisal from "without" (Lutheran, Roman, Anglican, or otherwise). By the same token, there
is no interest in an easy harmonizing of the dissonant clashes of the
High Calvinists and their opponents (Remonstrants or Arminians).
Leith's positive thesis is that the force and power of Calvin's illumination of the Christian life came chiefly from its biblical base and less
from his admittedly great skills as a debater. The essence of Calvin's

central message can be seen, in a remarkable consistency, throughout the successive editions of *The Institutes* from 1536 to 1559–60, and in the commentaries and treatises along the way. Calvin's explications of this perennial message varied from context to context, however, in both their ordering and their nuancing. And this suggests a distinction (never crystal clear) between affirmation and explication. Leith's firm grasp of this distinction allows for an appropriate appreciation of the grandeur and simplicity of Calvin's affirmations, by contrast with the arguable status of his explications—since debates about the latter have generated so much more heat than light.

The heart of the matter for Calvin was the *sola gloria Dei.* This was echoed in his oft-repeated motto, "We are God's." From this it follows, and Calvin never tires of showing how it follows (as a theme and variations), that sovereign grace and redemptive grace are one and the same reality and that they are revealed in their full integrity, and supremely, in Jesus Christ. If there are difficulties in some of his explications of the problematics involved (as, for example, in that almost apologetic comment on "reprobation," *decretum quidem horrible, fateor* [*Inst.* 3.23.7]), these are to be grappled with rather than smoothed over by any compromise with his basic Christian convictions. In the Christian life so conceived, our first and last end as humans really is "to glorify God and to enjoy him forever." "We are consecrated and dedicated to God; therefore, we may not hereafter think, speak, meditate or do anything but with a view to his glory. . . . We are God's; to him, therefore, let us live and die" (*Inst.* 3.7.1).

But if the telos of Christian living is God's glory, the preeminent sign of that glory is God's grace and providence. And if Leith's exposition of grace seems to some of us as more gracious than some of the older pronouncements (e.g., the Lambeth Articles of 1595 or the Canons of Dort, 1619), they are shown here to be fully faithful to Calvin himself. The primal emphasis on grace is followed in close order by a constant stress on God's providence. Here, Leith's exposition of Calvin's flat-out rejection of all pagan notions of "fate" and "chance" is clear—and crucial. Moreover, Leith's insistence on Calvin's equal concern for faith *and* righteousness in the Christian life goes far toward refuting later charges (by anti-Calvinists) of antinomianism or, on the other hand, legalism. Leith is always clear about Calvin's primary stress on the authority of scripture as first and final; but his account of Calvin's biblical hermeneutics looks away from any of the later versions of uncritical inerrantism.

Despite all the virtues of Leith's positive expositions, his boldest passage still appears in his Conclusion, where he lists six alleged inconsistencies in the logical consequences of Calvin's theoretical explications of his vision of Christian existence. These inconsistencies are then spoken of as "fallacies which obscured [Calvin's] profounder insights." Finally, they are tagged as "contradictions which reveal the conflict between Calvin the exegete of scripture and Calvin the systematizer of scripture." Here, obviously, is the sticking point in Leith's case and, indeed, in his methodology as a whole. Instinctively, an older reader will wonder how such allegements would have struck the "Reformed veterans" whom we know so well in the ecumenical dialogues at mid-century (Wilhelm Niesel, Hermann Bauke, et al.). It could even have been that in those days a controversy might have been centered on Leith's critique of Calvin that would have overshadowed his *positive* aims in the essay. In any case, the informed reader will recognize in Leith's list of inconsistencies the juiciest bones of contention in all the old Calvinist–anti-Calvinist controversies (so fierce in their spirit and so tragic in their historical consequences). By now, happily, the climate of controversy has changed (and especially in the past half century). Even so, the issues that those old controversies posed (often *mal posé*) are still as relevant as ever. In Leith's perspicuous analysis of them there is much still to be probed and pondered, now more fruitfully than before.

If the crucial distinction between the *exegesis* of scripture and its *systematizing* is valid, even in a general sense, it provides a set of well-fitted interpretive keys for reading and rereading Calvin afresh. It also provides a fruitful way of viewing the entire succession of Christian theologians, in their continuities as well as their divergencies. It is a view that presumes, at the outset, that the chief aim of theological reflection is not an entire theological system (whole and intact) but an equal sense of at-homeness in both the biblical universe of discourse and that of the theologian's own world.

This, in turn, allows for a constructive alternative to literalism, on the one extreme, and emotivism on the other. God speaks to the faithful in and through scripture in such a way as to exclude a single and complete system, but also in such a way as to require a clear recognition of the integrity of canonical scripture, as canon. And this suggests, in its turn, that all theologians in every age be read with an eye to their ways of distinguishing between faithful exegesis and system-building.

This points to a difficulty inherent in the enterprise of historical theology as a discipline: How, then, are theologians to be read and evaluated? Almost by definition, all theologians are committed to some combination of exegesis and systematization, and simplistic answers from either side are unhelpful even when they are exciting. This is a dilemma with real horns, and we know many of the zealots and the unwary who have been gored by one horn or the other. A wiser way may be to ask whether, in whatever case, the concern of the theologian under review is more to edify the faithful than to conquer the naysayers—or, if the concern is to conquer, whether it is to do so by persuasion or by "demonstration." Leith's demonstration of Calvin's consistent concern for edification is convincing.

We know the eristic temper of the first historians of doctrine (the Magdeburg Centuriators, Baronius, et al.). We know the biases of the other epoch-makers in the field (Newman, Harnack, Seeberg, Pelikan, et al.). Leith's modest proposals in Calvin interpretation, however, carry some weighty implications that all historians could still learn from. They belong to the new atmosphere that we see in what is being called "ecumenical church history." History is a way of remembering; the positive function of memory is insight and edification in aid of wisdom. Leith's particular act of remembering Calvin makes him more accessible to current historians by its careful mix of exposition and criticism, both normed by Calvin's own primal orientation to the *sola gloria Dei.*

It goes without saying that honest history has to be critical. It forfeits its license when it settles for partisan goals or hires out as handmaiden to homiletics. The inconsistencies, fallacies, and contradictions that dog all theological systems remain as proper grist for competent historians. This irreducible residue of ambiguity should also be instructive to those who have begun to understand that the undecidability of most perennial perplexities is still no proper warrant for the sort of adolescent disrespect for orderly thought that we see in "deconstruction" (Derrida and De Man).

But by the same token, historians have no norms of their own by which theological controversies may be concluded so that one theological system may be preferred over any other, in any other *logical* sense than a comparative one. Leith is modest enough to resist all temptations to measure Calvin by any of the old polemical standards. On principles, therefore, his appeal is from Calvin's explications to Calvin's own prior norm: the word of God in scripture. This is not intended to preempt critical exegesis *and* interpretation; it is meant to set them in their right order. In so doing, however, Leith opens up some new horizons of ecumenical inquiry.

This open-ended historiography (open only at its far end, be it noted, since the front end must always be anchored in scripture and the apostolic faith) was an earnest of what actually has finally begun to happen in contemporary ecumenical interaction. Some of us remember how we began, fifty years ago, with such high hopes of achieving some sort of doctrinal consensus that would justify a cease-fire in the age-old tribal warfare among Christians. By now we know (as if it had not been obvious from the beginning) that Christian unity is not to be achieved with the displacement of all flawed church traditions by *the* perfect one. It is no longer even dreamed that arguable theological systems are about to be replaced by one that is unarguably true. The "better way" in the ecumenical movement is toward *convergence* (not *return*). Faith and Order is groping for that way in its current quest for a shared confession of the Apostolic Faith. And John Calvin, in his better moments, would have understood this, without any easement of his appeal to Jude 9 and its anchorage in canonical scripture.

That Leith did not have all these problems in view in 1948 makes it all the more interesting that his method and spirit, in this study of one of the truly great ones, look away from the older ways of using history in the service of denominational triumphalism and toward the more prescient motto from Lund (1952): "Our common history as Christians."

As a superannuated academic, Leith's senior by a decade, and also as one of the few lingering survivors from those present at this dissertation's creation, I plead a point of personal privilege for my final comment. In my rereading of this dissertation after all these years, what pleased me most was the sense of what new readers may discover here. But there were also insights that struck even me almost with surprise. At the very least, there are some open questions that should prompt some reconsiderations, but any thoughtful reader will be moved to reflection and further study. One of my earliest convictions was confirmed: Something like this is a better way of doing historical theology than most of the accustomed ways.

These are times of many radical new endings (of so many of the older either-ors) and of many new beginnings (some doubtful, some cautiously hopeful; none, however, a mere extrapolation of our Euro-centered past in any of its timebound forms). In such a time it is imperative for great Christian traditioners like Calvin to be repositioned, so that their enrichment of the Christian tradition in their own times may be appreciated more widely in the global Christian community that is emerging, and that the tradition's relevance for the Christian future may be appreciated in new ways. Professor Leith's book was a harbinger of this sort of thing, and in this sense it continues as a pointer reading toward a Christian future in which the *sola gloria Dei* may once more be cherished as the sign of the most truly *human* reality that ever can be.

If this much may be said of a forty-year-old exercise (with no more hyperbole in the saying of it than what may be allowed an old teacher of a good student, who has continued as a good friend), then this also may be said: Its publication, belated as it is, is very much more than a mere memorial.

ALBERT C. OUTLER

Preface

The publication of a dissertation written forty years ago calls for some explanation. The idea, I am told, arose in a gathering of some of my students with Albert C. Outler, my professor at Yale, who helped to supervise the writing of the dissertation. I am very grateful, especially as I near retirement, for the idea and the implementation of it by Presbyterian ministers who once studied Calvin with me.

The publication of the dissertation has symbolic and personal worth to me, whatever its theological value may be. It does explain in part why I developed as I did for eleven years as pastor of the First Presbyterian Church in Auburn, Alabama, and for the past thirty as a teacher of theology at Union Theological Seminary. It is published now as it was written in 1947–1949 with minimal changes, for the most part reflecting current language usage. The occasion of its publication calls for at least four brief comments and a statement of how, after these years, I would develop the conclusion of the dissertation.

First, let me state my gratitude for the privilege of having been at Yale University in 1946–1948. The faculty advisers and readers of the dissertation were Albert C. Outler, Roland H. Bainton, and Robert L. Calhoun. H. Richard Niebuhr gave me advice about the general arrangement of the dissertation and the specific suggestion for Chapter 4. Kenneth Scott Latourette was director of graduate studies and gave encouragement when spirits were low. No graduate student in theology ever had a more distinguished faculty, all of whom were personally committed to the mainstream of the Protestant tradition.

Many reasons can be given for writing a dissertation, not the least of which is the securing of a Ph.D. in an area of learning. This goal required a dissertation which would define a problem, investigate the problem, and bring critical judgment to bear on the resolution of the problem, if possible. This exercise, when properly done, has its own inherent worth. As a student who was also a Presbyterian minister, I had another purpose. I hoped that the writing of the dissertation would give me an understanding of the classic, seminal statement of Reformed faith which I had first learned partly by rote in reciting the Shorter Catechism the day before my tenth birthday, a goal which my mother and father had set, and which I achieved through their labors. With the intellectual understanding I hoped would come an internal empathy so that this way of doing theology would become my own, yet without becoming an external orthodoxy to be imposed on me.

Calvin's theology posed a problem for me in that I was aware that although this theology had been the occasion for personal, human greatness and had contributed to the development of free societies with high economic productivity, I also knew that the same theology had been associated with brutality and with the repression of human imagination and creativity. At the very time I was writing the dissertation, there was in the life of my own denomination a theological fundamentalism which denied freedom for theology and which imposed on those who took life in the church seriously a heteronomous system of structures, laws, and beliefs. Yale University provided freedom, and my professors were in theological development beyond the liberal-fundamentalist controversy. This was good; the dissertation could not become a way of dealing with that theological problem. As Robert Lowry Calhoun once suggested to me, fighting fundamentalists was not a very high theological purpose. Count your blessings, he said, they at least believe in God. Albert Outler had known fundamentalism firsthand, and he served the purposes of my education remarkably well, however painful at the time, by always suspecting that behind any use of new reformation theological language on my part, there may have lurked the seventeenth-century or fundamentalist theological reality. In any case, my professors at Yale tried to teach me to understand Calvin in Calvin's own terms and to appropriate this theology for the theological task today without becoming either positively or negatively dependent on the fundamentalist-liberal controversy.

The importance of studying Calvin to understand his theology rather than to resolve controversies or problems which he never faced or in which he was not interested is basic for good theology today. Yet such distinguished theologians as Charles Briggs and Benjamin Warfield resorted to this method in their controversies at the beginning of this century, and dissertations are still being written using Calvin to disparage the Westminster Confession and seventeenth-century Reformed theology.

The study of Calvin was more than an academic exercise. It enabled me to consolidate my own theological life in the Presbyterian Church and to find in the *Institutes of the Christian Religion* a statement of the Christian faith of great power, clarity, and persuasiveness. I am now even more convinced that the *Institutes of the Christian Religion* is one of the clearest and most persuasive statements of Christian faith ever written. I know of no contemporary statement which surpasses it, even for the contemporary reader who is prepared to make a few allowances and transitions from a sixteenth-century text to the contemporary situation. This judgment has some quantifiable documentation in the sales of the *Institutes* for at least the past three decades.

This concentration on the *Institutes* is justified by Calvin's explicit intention that his work as exegete, preacher, and pastor should be understood in the light of it. The commentaries, sermons, letters, ecclesiastical advices, and practical churchmanship are best interpreted as the way the theology of the *Institutes* is expressed and given concrete shape.

I hope I know Calvin and Reformed theology better and more critically now than when I wrote the dissertation, but what I know now was first clarified and consolidated in the writing of the dissertation.

In the light of further study, and in particular in the light of having taught the *Institutes* to the Presbyterian ministers who have made possible this publication, I would like to supplement the conclusion of the dissertation with some reflections of the past forty years.[1]

The diverse conclusions reached by Calvin research raise the question whether Calvin can be understood in terms of the methods and presuppositions most familiar to theologians of the last two centuries. Calvin himself regarded theology as a practical science designed for the edification of the church. He explicated the intensely personal relationship of God and man in the light of the scripture, and he did this "before God" and under a powerful awareness of the holy. Calvin's *Institutes* is more a practical achievement than a theoretical work. The recognition of Calvin's intense sense of the holy and the practical determination of his theological work opens up new possibilities for understanding his theology.

The key to understanding Calvin's theology is to be found in the opening words of the *Institutes:* "Nearly all the wisdom we possess, that is to say, true and sound wisdom, consists of two parts: the knowledge of God and of ourselves. But, while joined by many

---

[1]Some of the following material appears in an essay, "Calvin's Awareness of the Holy, and the Enigma of His Theology," in *In Honor of John Calvin 1509–1564, Papers from the 1986 International Calvin Symposium, McGill University*, ed. E. J. Furcha, 1987.

bonds, which one precedes and brings forth the other is not easy to discern" (1.1.1). Calvin then goes on to say that "it is certain that man never achieves a clear knowledge of himself unless he has first looked upon God's face" (1.1.2). Here Calvin's words suggest that the theme which holds together his theology is God's relationship to humankind and humankind's relationship to God. In theology everything has to do with God and with God's relationship to humankind. This rubric, appearing in every edition of the *Institutes,* sets the limits and the conditions for understanding Calvin's theology. The particular formula that true wisdom consists of knowledge of God and knowledge of humankind and their interrelationship had been used by other theologians, but Calvin gives it a decisive place at the very beginning of his theological work.

Calvin's theology may be compared to a wagon wheel without the rim. There is a center hub of the wheel which holds it together and from which spokes extend, but there is no outer rim which brings the spokes into a self-contained order.[2] As the explication of the intensely personal relationship of God and humankind, the hub of the wheel is the personal relationship, or, to put it more theologically, faith. The spokes represent the various attempts to explicate this relationship according to particular themes which are developed as far as Calvin can take them, but which are never fully related to other particular truths. Hence the unity of Calvin's theology is in the relationship of God and humankind which is explicated in numerous ways.

The unity consists in the fact that theology explicates the relationship of humankind and God as God has revealed himself in Jesus Christ. The various explications are not systematized. For example, Calvin says all he can on human responsibility and on God's Lordship in the world. But he does not put them together in systematic unity.

Calvin's explication of the personal, existential relationship of God and humankind must also be interpreted in the light of Calvin's intense and vivid awareness of the holy or the presence of the living God. The church is a community of faith which stands in the presence of the Wholly Other, creator of heaven and earth. In the church and in all of its activities there is a sense of the numinous, of the *mysterium tremendum,* at once frightening and fascinating but in whose presence we stand in awe and devotion. The writing and teaching of theology in the church begins with this awareness and with this sensitivity.

One difficulty all modern interpreters have in understanding Cal-

---

[2]I first heard the model of the wheel with spokes but no rim used by John Dillenberger.

vin arises at this point. Everything Calvin wrote presupposes the presence and activity of the living God in immediacy and power. This awareness now has grown dim for those who are heirs of the Enlightenment.

We are all children of the Enlightenment. The dogmas of a post-Enlightenment culture, though not the spirit of the Enlightenment, may hinder our understanding of Calvin more than the complexities of his theology. Calvin's awareness of the immediacy of the divine presence and activity cannot be translated without remainder into the language and experience, of our time. Yet a recovery of an awareness of the Holy God who works personally in the created order, without doing violence to facts or the mind's integrity, is the precondition for understanding Calvin.

Calvin's theological work is not consistently an exposition of the personal relationship between God and humankind. He continually allows the Bible, the law, the ecclesiastical structure, or theological speculation, as for example about predestination, to become substitutes for the divine presence. This inconsistency in Calvin's work runs throughout his theological endeavors and the practice of the faith, yet it does not seem to be intentional. It derives in part at least from Calvin's intense concern to maintain the glory of God in Geneva and the temptation which every churchman has known to use the force of structures, of morals, or of theological orthodoxy to achieve what can only come as a gift of the Holy Spirit.

Calvin does not indicate much concern about what would today be regarded as theological method. The method grew out of his work, though there is his own testimony that he struggled with the arrangement of the *Institutes,* a concern which, as William Bouwsma points out, is more pedagogical and practical than systematic.[3] His theology was a commentary on scripture, directed to Christian experience and living, in the light of the theological reflection of the Christian community. Calvin wrote his theology to persuade, to transform human life, and to this end he endeavored to write with transparent clarity. He also wrote out of the intensity of his own personal experience and theological commitment. For this reason the method of his theology is finally hidden from us in the mystery of his own Christian experience.

The central unity in Calvin's theology is in the explication of the personal relation between God and humankind. Yet within this explication there are, first, ways of doing theology (methods) and, second, theological perspectives which give a coherence to all of

---

[3]William Bouwsma, *John Calvin, a Sixteenth-Century Portrait* (New York: Oxford University Press, 1988), ch. 9.

Calvin's writings and which frequently have deceived people into finding in the *Institutes* a logical unity it does not have.

Calvin's theology is unified by certain ways of theologizing.

1. All of Calvin's conscious theological activity was subordinate to the authority of the Bible as the revelation of God. Theology is the coherent explication of scripture in the language of ordinary discourse. This involved bringing the disparate texts and themes of scripture into some coherent whole. Calvin never elaborated the point, but it is clear he had a ground plan of the Bible in the light of which he organized his theology. (It is worth noting that Calvin never wrote a chapter on the interpretation of scripture as Bullinger did in the *Decades.*)

Calvin read scripture at least in part as the church had read it before him. He counted it theological wisdom to take seriously the judgment of great theologians and more particularly the great church councils, however subordinate they were to the authority of scripture.

The most important perspective which governs Calvin's theology is the authority of scripture as the norm of all theological thinking and speaking.[4]

2. A second concern which governs Calvin's theological work is the role of experience and the concreteness of the situation in which he wrote. Over and over again Calvin subjects what he has written theologically to the commonsense wisdom of experience. Revelation may go beyond human experience, but it cannot and does not contradict the clear facts of human experience or common sense. Calvin's theology is not an explication of Christian experience, but it never takes place apart from it and from the demands of the concrete situation. Calvin intends to explicate the relationship of God and humankind in light of the Word of God, always with reference to experience and to the concrete situation.

Calvin's theology has the quality of wisdom as a consequence of this experiential reference. Technical and scientific knowledge may come from intellectual endeavors, but theological wisdom comes from receiving in faith and in reflecting upon Jesus Christ, the wisdom and power of God, amid the complexities, the heights and depths of human experience. A person must live deeply, broadly, and for many years facing the challenges and crises of life to be a theologian. A Calvinist theologian comes to be, as John Calvin did, not in a school of religious studies, but in the church as a worshiping, believing community. Theological wisdom is personal, not frigid; of the affections as well as the mind.

---

[4]*Institutes* 1.13.3.

3. For Calvin, theology is a practical not a theoretical science. When Thomas Aquinas raised the question of whether theology was a practical or theoretical science, he answered that it was both, but he gave the greater weight to theory. For Calvin, theology was overwhelmingly a practical science, and he shows little interest or concern for theoretical questions. The purpose of theology is to glorify God, to save human souls, to transform human life and society. Questions and issues which do not directly bear on these practical concerns receive scant attention from Calvin. One significant test of the authenticity of any doctrine is the power of that doctrine to edify.

William Bouwsma speaks of Calvin's "rhetorical theology," directed to practical results rather than to a systematic theology intended for the ages.[5] Calvin understood the Reformation as a great effort, mediated by language, to transfuse the power of the Spirit into human beings. Bouwsma finds the most succinct statement of the principle that governs Calvin's theology in his commentary on Matthew 3:7. "It would be really a frigid way of teaching if the teachers did not determine carefully the needs of the times and sense the people concerned, for in this regard nothing is more unbalanced than absolute balance." This means that in a particular situation, theology must be expressed in an unbalanced way to be balanced.

In a very remarkable passage Calvin expressed his desire for an ecumenical council. However, he believed that an ecumenical council was an impossibility, and therefore he dismissed it from his mind. "In regard to the whole body of the church, we commend it to the care of its Lord! Meanwhile, let us not be either slothful or secure. Let each do his best. Let us contribute whatever is in us of counsel, learning and abilities, to build up the ruins of the church."[6] Theoretical interests or ideal possibilities must not be allowed to undermine what is possible and close at hand.

4. Calvin's theological work is also unified by style of expression. He attempted to write and to express theology simply without ostentation, with transparent clarity, and in the language of ordinary discourse. He despised the pompous, the artificial, the contrived, and the frigid.

Another set of themes unify Calvin's work which are more directly theological; they are theological perspectives, basic theological decisions which govern Calvin's thinking.

---

[5] William Bouwsma, "Calvinism as a Renaissance Artifact," *Calvin Studies,* Papers Presented at a Colloquium on Calvin Studies at Davidson College Presbyterian Church, 1984.
[6] Final paragraph of "Canons and Decrees of the Council of Trent with the Antidote," *Calvin's Tracts* (Edinburgh, 1951), 3:188.

1. One theological perspective is Calvin's way of relating the transcendence and immanence of God. His profound awareness of the sharp distinction between Creator and creature reflects itself in his doctrine of the person of Christ, which is Antiochene rather than Alexandrian; also in his doctrine of the presence of Christ in the sacrament, however concerned he was to emphasize the genuineness of our participation in the reality of Christ; in his doctrine of the church, which he never confused with an extension of the incarnation; and in his insistence on the transcendence of God's justice, truth, and love. Calvin radically desacralized created existence, as the contemporary idiom puts it. He emphasized the immediacy of God's presence and activity in the world, but he always jealously guarded the integrity of the Creator and the creature, allowing for no confusion or mixture.

2. A second unifying theme in Calvin's theology is his understanding of God primarily in terms of energy, activity, power, moral purpose, intentionality. God is the sovereign Lord of heaven and earth. Every doctrine in the *Institutes* reflects Calvin's insistence on the immediacy of the divine presence and on the activity of God in his creation. David Wiley has persuasively argued in a Duke University dissertation on Calvin's doctrine of predestination that although predestination is not the central dogma in Calvin, it impinges on everything Calvin wrote, emphasizing the immediacy of God's activity and the initiative of Divine Grace.

3. A third unifying theological perspective is Calvin's way of putting together nature and grace, or the way knowledge of God the Creator and God the Redeemer are related to each other. Creation and redemption cannot be opposed to each other. Yet they cannot be identified, for redemption is more than creation, not simply as its completion but, in the light of sin, as its transformer. The practical priority is on redemption. Calvin refused to discuss the possibility whether the Word would have become flesh if humankind had not sinned (2.12.4).

4. A fourth unifying theological perspective is Calvin's way of relating gospel and law, justification and sanctification. Gospel and law cannot be separated, for the gospel is in the law and the law is in the gospel. Yet they are different and must not be confused. Likewise, salvation as God's mercy (justification by grace through faith) and salvation as God's power (sanctification) must never be separated or confused. Calvin knew that justification is the "principal hinge" on which religion depends, but he also knew that it is the presupposition of sanctification which is the end toward which salvation moves on the human level.

5. Calvin's theology is also unified by a vision of the human

community under the authority of God. Calvin wished to maintain the distinction and independence of church and state. He was not (at least intentionally) a theocrat in the sense that he gave divine authority to any human personage. Yet he had a profound awareness that the world is God's creation, and he saw it as the theater in which God's glory is revealed and where God's people received the divine blessing and lived together as the Christian community. In his preaching Calvin sought—as he said in a sermon on 2 Timothy 2:16–19—"to draw the world to God and to build a kingdom of our Lord Jesus Christ that he may rule among us." He never defined the Christian life simply in terms of personal piety.

In summary, I have come to three conclusions about Calvin's theology: (1) Calvin's theology can best be understood as the explication of the very personal, existential relationship of God to humankind and humankind to God; (2) it finds its unity in this relationship, and the various facets of the relationship are explicated to the best of Calvin's ability without a final attempt to bring them in a unity on the circumference; (3) although Calvin's explication does not issue in a theology that is fully unified as to details, there is a unity and a distinctive character provided by certain ways of doing theology and certain theological perspectives. These ways of doing theology and these theological perspectives give an easily recognizable identity to Calvin's theological writings in sermons, letters, church polity, and theological tracts as well as the *Institutes.* They also leave their identifying imprint on the style and way of life of every congregation and every person who is Christian in the Reformed way.

Finally, a word of appreciation must be expressed to Presbyterian ministers and congregations who made this book possible; to the Westminster staff; to Ann White Leith, who typed the original dissertation with meticulous care on a manual typewriter; to Benjamin Farley, John Newton Thomas, Hobbie Bryant, and Katharina Kopplin, who helped translate the French and German footnotes into English; to Sally Hicks, who retyped the footnotes; and to Elizabeth Ayscue, Samuel Warner, Daniel Griswold, and Mary Catherine Miller, who helped read the proof.

John Calvin's Doctrine of the Christian Life

Introduction

In 1909 William Adams Brown, one of the most competent of recent American theologians, undertook to speak on Calvin's influence on theology and was embarrassed for lack of anything original to say. He found it impossible to approach Calvin's theology in the spirit of an explorer, for the latter's teachings were already commonplace knowledge. Further study of the Reformer's theology, he felt, offered no chance of new discovery.[1] Times have changed, however, in the forty years which have elapsed since Brown delivered this judgment; and now at least two factors make this an opportune time for a new study of Calvin's theology. The first is the theological renaissance which has sought to find in the heritage of the church an aid in solving the problems that human beings face today. A considerable number of contemporary theologians regard the Reformers as teachers who have a real message for modern times and not merely as objects of historical study. Many are convinced that Calvin's theology has much light to shed on the human situation today.

Furthermore, it is now apparent that Calvin research has not reached any simple agreement as to the content or nature of his theology. Actually, the disagreements are both numerous and important. There are conflicts between the strict Barthians and the followers of Brunner,[2] between the traditional Calvinists and the Crisis

---

[1] William Adams Brown, "Calvin's Influence Upon Theology," *Three Addresses Delivered by Professors in Union Theological Seminary* (New York, 1909), p. 20: "It is difficult to say anything original about Calvin. . . . There are certain great thinkers whose systems it is possible to approach in the spirit of the explorer, conscious as one turns each page, of the chance of some new discovery, but with Calvin it is not so. What he believed and what he taught has long been a matter of common knowledge."

[2] Karl Barth, *Nein! Antwort an Emil Brunner* (*Theologische Existenz heute,* no. 14; Munich: Chr. Kaiser, 1934); Peter Barth, *Das Problem der natürlichen Theologie bei Calvin* (*Theologische Existenz heute,* no. 18; Munich: Chr. Kaiser, 1935); Günter Gloede, *Theologia naturalis bei Calvin* (Stuttgart: W. Kohlhammer, 1935).

theologians,[3] between the French and the Germans,[4] between the historian of dogma Reinhold Seeberg and the Calvin scholar Peter Barth.[5] In contrast to the Calvin scholars who have taken the Reformer seriously as a teacher of this generation, the liberals have labeled him a fundamentalist.[6]

The real need in the field of Calvin research is a critical study of Calvin's theology which will indicate the relevance of this theology to the contemporary theological revival but which, at the same time, will critically appraise its actual sixteenth-century content and form. The problem is to hold in balance the fact that Calvin is a teacher of this generation with the equally important fact that his interpretation of the gospel is subject to human limitations which must be noted and corrected in the context of the total Christian tradition. Only when these two facts are held in balance can Calvin's position as a teacher of this generation be secured or the problems of Calvin research in a measure be solved. The nemesis of Calvin research, as I think will be indicated in this study, has been the prevalent assumption that the Reformer's thought was entirely coherent and consistent. Calvin's fame for logical clarity has obscured the underlying complexities and ambiguities of his doctrine.

A number of factors, it seems to me, indicate the advantage of a study of Calvin's doctrine of the Christian life. In the first place, the whole of his theology comes to a focus in the Christian life. Calvin understood this to be far more than a code of morals or a pattern of conduct.[7] It was his purpose, as will be demonstrated in this study,

---

[3]D. Kromminga, "And the Barthians," *The Sovereignty of God,* ed. Jacob Hoogstra (Grand Rapids: Zondervan Publishing House, 1941), pp. 79–81. I use the word "traditional" to designate in particular the Calvinism of B. B. Warfield and of the American Calvinistic Congress. In *God-Centered Religion* (Grand Rapids: Zondervan Publishing House, 1942), pp. 19–20, Paul T. Fuhrmann uses the word "classical" to designate not only American Calvinism of the above type but also the French Calvinism of Doumergue and Pannier. While these types of Calvinism have many similarities, it is also true that the French interpretation has been more liberal than that of the American Calvinistic Congress.

[4]Jacques Pannier, *Recherches sur la formation intellectuelle de Calvin* (Paris: Alcan, 1931); Wilhelm Niesel, "Calvin und Luther," *Reformierte Kirchenzeitung* 81 (1931), 195ff.

[5]Reinhold Seeberg, *Lehrbuch der Dogmengeschichte* IV/2 (Leipzig: A. Deichert, 1920), p. 613. Peter Barth, "Calvin," *Die Religion in Geschichte und Gegenwart* (Tübingen: J. C. B. Mohr [Paul Siebeck], 1927). This work is cited hereafter as *RGG.*

Also cf. Eugène Choisy, *La théocratie à Genève au temps de Calvin* (Geneva: C. Eggimann & Cie, 1897), with Wilhelm Niesel, *Die Theologie Calvins* (Munich: Chr. Kaiser, 1938) [E.T. *The Theology of Calvin;* Philadelphia: Westminster Press, 1956].

[6]Georgia Harkness, *John Calvin, the Man and His Ethics* (New York: Henry Holt & Co., 1931), pp. 66, 87.

[7]The inadequacy of any moralistic interpretation is confirmed by this passage from a sermon on Galatians 6:14–19: "To what end ought we to direct our lives, except that the Son of God reign in the midst of us, that we be ruled by the word of his gospel, and that we know his power,

to interpret the Christian life in terms of the personal response of human beings to the gracious and personal activity of God on their lives. The Christian life is a dynamic concept and cannot be separated from the living, personal, and mutual relationship which is its source. Insofar as the Christian life can be abstracted as ethics, it remains organically related to theology, flowing from it as a stream from a fountain. It is the concrete and actual expression of theological belief.[8] The extent to which Calvin succeeded in maintaining the existential quality of the Christian life in his theological writings and in his work as a pastor in Geneva is a question which will have to be answered in the course of this study. The fact that Calvin does lapse into nonexistential interpretations of the Christian life raises a crucial problem for Calvin research and requires an explanation.

The decisive character of the Christian life is revealed by the very fact that Calvin added the section on the Christian life as a conclusion to the *Institutes* of 1539. Apparently he felt that the extensive sections on the law and civil government which the *Institutes* already contained did not satisfy the thoroughgoing demands of the New Testament teaching about the Christian life. The study of Romans had taught him that the Pauline ethic is not contained in the demands of the Ten Commandments.

> The divine law contains a most excellent and well-arranged plan for the regulation of life, yet it has pleased the heavenly Teacher to conform men by a more accurate doctrine to the rule which he had prescribed in the law. . . . It is the duty of believers to "present their bodies a living sacrifice, holy, acceptable unto God. . . ." We are God's; to him, therefore, let us live and die.[9]

---

so that both great and small place all their confidence in him? And also that we might be reformed in all our life, to the end that we obey God and be ruled by his word. The spiritual temple of God is faith and newness of life. Faith means that we render thanks to God for all his goodness, that we take refuge in him, that we proclaim his praises so that his holy name will be invoked in the midst of us. In this way we shall become more and more the temple of God. Furthermore, it is necessary that we be renewed in our life and that we learn through patience to renounce ourselves and to dedicate ourselves to God. Let us learn to renounce all, even this world, and to be dedicated to that One who has bought us. In this way we shall be truly free. For there is good reason that Jesus Christ, who has bought us so dearly, should possess us and have us fully in his service. He is not able so to possess us if each one does not renounce himself and all that keeps him from Jesus Christ." (*Corpus Reformatorum: Joannis Calvini Opera Quae Supersunt Omnia,* ed. Guilielmus Baum, Eduardus Cunitz, and Eduardus Reuss [Brunswick: C. A. Schwetschke et Filium, 1863–1897], vol. 51, cols. 128–129.) This work is cited hereafter as *CR,* followed by volume number and column number; e.g., *CR* 51:128–129.

[8]Cross bearing, for example, is wholly unintelligible apart from the doctrine of providence.

[9]John Calvin, *Institutes of the Christian Religion,* tr. John Allen (Philadelphia: Presbyterian Board of Publication, 1936), book 3, chap. 7, para. 1. For the sake of brevity, this work is cited hereafter by book, chapter, and paragraph number; e.g., 3.7.1.

The high regard in which this section of the *Institutes* was held is seen in the fact that it was translated and published separately in English in 1549, and French and Latin editions were published in Geneva in 1550.[10] However, the independent publication of this section does not mean that it can be read apart from the remainder of the *Institutes;* for Calvin presupposes what was said in other places about humankind's relation to God. He states in a summary sentence what is the end of the Christian life, and he then devotes almost the whole of the section to the method by which the goal is to be attained—self-denial, cross bearing, and meditation on the future life. The fact that Calvin moved this section from the conclusion of the *Institutes* of 1539 to the middle of the section on soteriology in the 1559 edition reveals its close relation to the whole of his theology.

Calvin's avowed interest in theology was practical. Moreover, he regarded theology as a practical science. The original purpose of the *Institutes of the Christian Religion* was to provide a handbook which would be an aid to piety.[11] The true task of theology was not to give an answer to speculative questions, but to contribute to the edification of Christians.[12] The conduct of the Christian, not verbal assent

---

[10]*CR* 59:467–468. The French edition had this title page: "Excellent treatise on Christian life, which is like an instruction and formula to all those who profess to be Christians, for guiding their life and maintaining obedience to God here below, according to the ordinance of our master and ruler Jesus Christ, by Jean Calvin in Geneva 1550." (From facsimile published in *Revue d'histoire et de philosophie religieuses* 14 [1934], 211.)

[11]*Opera Selecta Joannis Calvini,* ed. Petrus Barth and Guilielmus Niesel (Munich: Chr. Kaiser, 1926), vol. 3, p. 6. This work is cited hereafter as *OS* with volume number and page number; e.g., *OS* 3:6.

[12]*CR* 33:709: "As we see in all papacy, what is called theology is nothing more than the swelling of an eastern breeze which dessicates and has no substance to feed and nourish poor souls. Now a general distinction can be made on two points. Papists have as a part of their theology questions and arguments which bear no fruit. In the first place, they torment themselves throughout their life and can't find any resolution. Why? They want to inquire about that which God has never revealed, and even about those things which he wants to be hidden. Now we know when he has not spoken, he wants us to remain silent, nor does he want us to greet him to ask what will be—but rather that we remain uninformed when he does not teach us. This is our real wisdom—that of not wanting to know more than that which God shows us in his instruction. Therefore, there are papist theologians who question things about which God wishes us to be ignorant. They debate in vain—it will never be resolved; because there are only conjectures. But let's take a case which can have a certain resolution, and about which it can be said: It is thus. There is no edification or profit when what they debate in schools is resolved. It will not be asked if we are saved by God's grace alone. It will not be shown that, being assured of the remission of our sins, we must have that much greater an occasion to praise and magnify his goodness toward us. It is not stated what consolation we should take in our afflictions. No—not at all. It is not the question, unless it's to flutter about, and those who are the most useless are the most esteemed as the most knowledgeable. They are clever people because they are speculative, that is to say, they carry themselves in the air and have no steadiness."

CR 53:467: "And furthermore, we should not give in to ambition to follow what pleases

to doctrine and ceremony, is the decisive test of religious convictions.[13] The Geneva Catechism opened with the question, What is the chief end of human life? The answer to this question was the burning mission of Calvin's whole theology. The fact that certain portions of the answer which he gave reveal a speculative bent, as will be pointed out in this study, must be ascribed to faulty execution rather than to avowed intention.

A second advantage of a study of Calvin's doctrine of the Christian life is the contemporary relevance of the subject itself. While this is primarily a historical study and is not to be distorted by current interests, all historical study has justification only insofar as it has bearing on our present course. The Christian life is a perennial concern of the Christian, and this is particularly true in our time. The course of recent events has shattered the optimism of the nineteenth and early twentieth centuries about the problems of human conduct. The kingdom of God or the ideal society appears to be less and less a realizable objective of human endeavor. Human beings are increasingly faced with the possibility that their own deeds may destroy civilization. In 1932 Reinhold Niebuhr wrote:

> His [man's] concern for some centuries to come is not the creation of an ideal society in which there will be uncoerced and perfect peace and justice, but a society in which there will be enough justice and in which coercion will be sufficiently non-violent to prevent his common enterprise from issuing into complete disaster.[14]

Furthermore, sinister ideologies have raised anew not only the question, What is the good? but also, Why be good at all, if being good

---

men as many do, who, seeing that they are applauded, always want to have some lively doctrine in which to take pleasure. On the contrary, let's look at what is useful to edify people in the fear of God. And also those who wish to profit from the word of God put away all curiosity. And when they come to a sermon, let it not be to have some doctrine which pleases them according to the flesh, but that they look to be taught to profit, that is, that they be incited to serve God better, to put their confidence in him."

CR 53:477: "We see then that the word of God does not have such an impact on us as it is to be wished. We have the doctrine of it, but the practice of it must be looked for much more."

CR 54:287: "It [the scripture] is given to us not only to show us the majesty of God but to edify us to our salvation. . . . Furthermore, we have been warned not to read the Holy Scripture to make it serve our fantasies or to draw from it vain questions."

[13]*CR* 37:294. Cf. *CR* 26:301, 309; 28:163; 36:44, 45; 40:674; 42:462–463; 43:394; 45:119, 325, 539; 51:19, 47; 55:340, 338, 228.

[14]*Moral Man and Immoral Society,* 1947 ed. (New York: Charles Scribner's Sons, 1932), p. 22. Not everyone agreed with Niebuhr's diagnosis. In 1934 John Dewey published *A Common Faith* (New Haven, Conn.: Yale University Press), which revealed an optimistic confidence in humankind's capacities and deliberately rejected the help of religion, which was regarded as not merely irrelevant but definitely harmful.

costs life itself? Even churches are in confusion as to their responsibility for the affairs of society as a whole.[15] Although Calvin's answers to these problems cannot be repeated verbatim today, they may provide creative insights which will stimulate a genuinely relevant answer for some of our present-day difficulties.

A third consideration which indicates the advantage of studying the Christian life is its relevance to the current status of Calvin research. Every new study must avoid slavish dependence on previous research, but it would be equally disastrous to ignore the conclusions of earlier studies and the problems they have raised. A brief review of the Calvin research of the past century will serve to point out not only some of the problems for which no satisfactory answer has been found, but also some of the more important conclusions which are now generally held about Calvin's theology.

Modern Calvin research received its initial impetus from the efforts to unite the Reformed and the Lutheran Churches in Germany in the first part of the nineteenth century. This effort toward church union naturally raised the question of Calvin's place in the history of Christian doctrine and especially of his relation to Martin Luther. The first studies sought to point out the importance of the personalities and cultural backgrounds of the first Reformers in accounting for the differences which arose in the various theologies of the Reformation.[16]

A more fruitful type of research approached the problem of Calvin's theology from the viewpoint of a system and asked what is the fundamental dogma from which the system is deduced. A well-known effort in this direction was made by Alexander Schweizer. He found that the feeling *(Bewusstsein)* of the absolute dependence of all creatures on God is the peculiar material principle of Reformed theology.[17] This principle is reflected in the strong protest of the Reformed Church against all paganism in the Medieval Church, whereas the Lutheran Church protested primarily against Judaistic relapses into Pelagian work-righteousness.

Baur, who defended the superiority of the Lutheran Church against Schweizer, saw value in Schweizer's designation of the material principle of Reformed theology. According to Baur, the distinguishing feature of Reformed theology is the idea of the absolute

---

[15] A notable example is the former Presbyterian Church U.S. [now part of the Presbyterian Church (U.S.A.)], where divergent opinions as to the role of the church in society were maintained.

[16] E. G. Ullmann, "Zur Charakteristik der reformirten Kirche. Mit Beziehung auf neuere litterarische Erscheinungen," *Theologische Studien und Kritiken* 16 (1843), 749ff.

[17] Alexander Schweizer, *Die Glaubenslehre der evangelisch-reformirten Kirche dargestellt und aus den Quellen belegt* (Zurich: Orell, Füssli & Co., 1844), 1:45.

causality of God.[18] Schneckenburger took issue with Baur as well as with Schweizer and vigorously maintained that Calvin did not deduce his theology from any objective idea of God.[19] The distinction between Lutheran and Reformed theology, according to Schneckenburger, lies in a difference of religious and ethical psychology. For the Lutheran, the decisive point is faith's experience of justification. For Reformed theology, the decisive point is the origin of faith itself.[20]

F. W. Kampschulte, who made a real contribution to Calvin scholarship by his biography of the Reformer, also regarded Calvin's theology as a system which was deduced from Divine Predestination.[21] Still another notable attempt to interpret Calvin in terms of one doctrine was made by Martin Schulze.[22] He found that an eschatology of an otherworldly sort is the central doctrine and the basis for the interpretation of the whole of Calvinism.

Studies on Calvin and his theology received a tremendous impetus from the publication of the *Opera Calvini* in the *Corpus Reformatorum,* which began in 1863, and they reached a climax in 1909 when the four hundredth anniversary of Calvin's birth was celebrated.[23] By no means do all of these studies follow the pattern of the

---

[18]F. C. Baur, "Über Princip und Charakter des Lehrbegriffs der reformirten Kirche in seinem Unterschied von dem der lutherischen, mit Rücksicht auf A. Schweizer's Darstellung der reformirten Glaubenslehre," *Theologische Jahrbücher* 6 (1847), 333.

[19]Matthias Schneckenburger, "Die neueren Verhandlungen, betreffend das Prinzip des reformirten Lehrbegriffs," *Theologische Jahrbücher* 7 (1848), 74.

[20]Matthias Schneckenburger, "Recensionen: Schweizer, *Die Glaubenslehre der evangelisch-reformirten Kirche,*" *Theologische Studien und Kritiken* 20 (1847), 960–961.

[21]F. W. Kampschulte, *Johann Calvin, seine Kirche und sein Staat in Genf* (Leipzig: Duncker & Humbolt, 1869), p. 263: "The teaching of divine predestination is the basic thought which dominates the whole Calvinistic system. One may say: The structure of Calvin's teaching in all its parts is based on it and receives from it character and color. The total conception of the divine economy of salvation is penetrated by the idea of predestination. The appearance of Christ on earth is, as it were, only the historical attestation of the divine decree of mercy. All individual teachings . . . are set in relation to the eternal decree and receive from it their peculiar impression."

[22]Martin Schulze, *Meditatio futurae vitae: ihr Begriff und ihre beherrschende Stellung im System Calvins* (Leipzig: T. Weicher, 1901).

[23]Among the more important works were the following: Ellis Gauteron, *L'autorité de la Bible d'après Calvin* (Montauban, 1902); Williston Walker, *John Calvin* (New York: G. P. Putnam's Sons, 1906); *Calvinreden aus dem Jubiläumsjahr 1909* (Tübingen: J. C. B. Mohr [Paul Siebeck], 1909); *Calvinstudien,* ed. J. Bohatec (Leipzig: Rudolf Haupt, 1909); Schulze, op. cit.; Willy Lüttge, *Die Rechtfertigungslehre Calvins und ihre Bedeutung für seine Frömmigkeit* (Berlin: Reuther & Reichard, 1909); A. Lang, *Johannes Calvin* (Leipzig: Verein für Reformations-geschichte, 1909); Abel Lefranc, *La jeunesse de Calvin* (Paris: Librairie Fischbacher, 1888); Hermann Strathmann, *Calvins Lehre von der Busse in ihrer späteren Gestalt* (Gotha, 1909); Max Scheibe, *Calvins Prädestinationslehre* (Halle: M. Niemeyer, 1897); Gisbert Beyerhaus, *Studien zur Staatsanschauung Calvins, mit besonderer Berücksichtigung seines Souveränitätsbegriffs* (Berlin: Trowitzsch & Sohn, 1910).

central dogma research. In a study published as early as 1868, Köstlin maintained that Calvin's theology can be regarded as a system only if the word is duly qualified. Although the *Institutes* reveal a tendency toward systematization, there is an increasing hesitancy in the various editions to draw the conclusions which the systematic approach demands.[24] The most exhaustive work on Calvin was done by Émile Doumergue, who incorporated a lifetime of research in his *Jean Calvin, les hommes et les choses de son temps.* This collection of material is monumental, but it is marred by the hagiographic tendency of the author. In his study of Calvin's theology, Doumergue underscores the importance of the honor of God; but at the same time he rejects the thesis that Calvin's theology is a system deduced from one or two material principles. Doumergue describes Calvin's procedure as the *méthode des contrariétés.*[25]

B. B. Warfield of Princeton Theological Seminary published a number of articles during this period which were characterized by able scholarship and thorough approval of the Reformer's theology.[26] In general, his interpretation was less liberal than Doumergue's and less existential than that of the Crisis theologians today. The American Calvinistic Congress preserves this tradition of Calvin research. Another important study was Choisy's *La théocratie à Genève au temps de Calvin,* which claimed that Calvin's administration in Geneva substituted a codebook of laws and doctrines for the living authority of Jesus Christ, and a legal institution for the body of Christ.

In 1922 Hermann Bauke published an important analysis of Calvin's theology.[27] The Calvin research of the previous century had produced a confusing medley of contradictory interpretations and evaluations, and Bauke asked the question: What is the peculiar character of the theology which makes all of these contradictory opinions possible? He was convinced that the experience of the preceding century had proved the inadequacy of every attempt to solve these problems by the study of any one doctrine or even of the content of the whole theology. The solution of the problem, he felt,

---

[24]D. J. Köstlin, "Calvins Institutio nach Form und Inhalt," *Theologische Studien und Kritiken* 41 (1868), 475: "For Calvin, obviously his striving for strict consequence and for unity of the system remain characteristic. Yet it is no less characteristic for him that he bows with simple renunciation before the divine majesty at the limits which he sees set for himself here, and that he makes the same renunciation a duty for everyone, since finally he does not feel called to draw the last consequences, nor does he achieve a real inner unity of the various sides, motives, and interests of the evangelical principle. And especially in the progressive development of the *Institutes* this peculiarity of his finds more and more expression."
[25]Émile Doumergue, *Le caractère de Calvin* (Paris: Éditions de Foi et Vie, 1921), p. 47.
[26]Cf. B. B. Warfield, *Calvin and Calvinism* (London: Oxford University Press, 1931).
[27]Hermann Bauke, *Die Probleme der Theologie Calvins* (Leipzig: J. C. Hinrichs, 1922).

lay in the study of the *Formgestaltung* and not of the content of the theology. Three characteristics of the *Formgestaltung* provide an explanation of the contradictory conclusions of Calvin research and offer a key for a true interpretation of his theology.

The first is a formal, dialectical rationalism. This does not mean that Calvin's theology is rationalistic in the Stoic or eighteenth-century sense. It is not a rationalism of material but of form, of the form in which the dogmatic materials appear, by which they are bound together, and in which they are expressed and systematized. This fact accounts for the difference between the theologies of Calvin and Luther, which, in regard to content, are very much the same. It also accounts for the fact that the German who thinks in terms of content rather than form has difficulty understanding Calvin's theology.

The second characteristic of the form of Calvin's theology, according to Burke, is the *complexio oppositorum*. Calvin's theological method is not the deduction of a system from one or two central doctrines. He does not seek to find some *Diagonale* or *Stammlehre* or central doctrine or material principle from which individual dogmatic teachings can be deduced and developed. On the contrary, he seeks to bind existing individual dogmatic teachings which are even in logical and metaphysical contradiction into a systematic coherence. This characteristic explains the existence of many contradictory interpretations, for interpreters have concentrated on one doctrine and neglected others which are equally important. Martin Schulze's studies are good examples of this fallacy.

The third characteristic is biblicism, by which Bauke meant a law which governed the pattern of Calvin's thought. The Reformer sought not merely to take the materials of his theology out of the Bible, but also to make his theology a complete and consistent representation of the Bible.

Bauke's study was a genuine step forward, for it made plain that every attempt to interpret the *Institutes* must consider the form as well as the content. He dealt a devastating blow to the notion that Calvin was a speculative systematizer who deduced a system of theology from one or two principles. Most of the recent Calvin scholars are in agreement with Bauke's conclusion in this regard; however, his study did not put an end to contradictory interpretations.[28]

---

[28]E.g., disagreement concerning Lutheran origins of Calvin's faith. Cf. Wilhelm Niesel, "Calvin und Luther," *Reformierte Kirchenzeitung* 81 (1931), 81–82, and Jacques Pannier, *Recherches sur la formation intellectuelle de Calvin* (Paris: Alcan, 1931).

Also, disagreement concerning doctrine of God. Cf. Erwin Mülhaupt, *Die Predigt Calvins, ihre Geschichte, ihre Form, und ihre religiösen Grundgedanken* (Berlin: Walter de Gruyter &

Although Bauke's study has much to contribute to the understanding of the particular aspect of Calvin's thought which constitutes this study, at least three tentative objections must be raised to his conclusions. First, his emphasis on the paradoxical character of Calvin's theology obscures its inner unity. It gives the impression that his theology is merely a collection of individual teachings formally and dialectically thrown together. Second, the question must be raised whether it is possible to separate fully form and content. For example, is the content of the definitions of predestination and reprobation completely free from their rationalistic form? Finally, the question must be asked as to whether the formal character of Calvin's thought is consistently the same. If the formal character varies, then Bauke's thesis is inadequate.

In recent years a considerable amount of Calvin research has accompanied the development of the Crisis theology.[29] Although the studies which have come out of this movement by no means agree in their conclusions, they have one characteristic in common. They regard Calvin not merely as an interesting object of research but also as a teacher who has much to say to the problems of the present day.[30] The studies of the Barthians in particular have been predicated on the thesis that Calvin's theology can only be correctly interpreted as a theology which stands under the sovereignty of the divine word.[31] In general, this group have been so concerned to point out the positive value of Calvin for contemporary theology that they have almost completely neglected those aspects of his thought which create real difficulties for the Christian conscience of today. They have rightly emphasized the Lutheran character of Calvin's theology, but they have ignored the differences between the two theologians.[32] Peter Barth has insisted that Seeberg's interpretation of Calvin

Co., 1931), pp. 169ff., and Otto Ritschl, *Dogmengeschichte des Protestantismus* (Leipzig: J. C. Hinrichs, 1908–27), 3:175ff.

[29] Among the more important are the following: Peter Barth, *Das Problem der natürlichen Theologie bei Calvin* (*Theologische Existenz heute*, no. 18; Munich: Chr. Kaiser, 1935); Peter Barth, "Was ist reformierte Ethik?" *Zwischen den Zeiten* 10 (1932); Alfred de Quervain, *Calvin, sein Lehren und Kämpfen* (Berlin: Furche, 1926); Alfred Göhler, *Calvins Lehre von der Heiligung* (Munich: Chr. Kaiser, 1934); Günter Gloede, *Theologia naturalis bei Calvin* (Stuttgart: W. Kohlhammer, 1935); Wilhelm Niesel, *Die Theologie Calvins* (Munich: Chr. Kaiser, 1938); Paul Jacobs, *Prädestination und Verantwortlichkeit bei Calvin* (Kassel: J. G. Oncken Nachf., 1937).

[30] Cf. Peter Barth, "Fünfundzwanzig Jahre Calvinforschung 1909–1934," *Theologische Rundschau* (1934).

[31] Cf. Karl Barth, *The Word of God and the Word of Man,* tr. Douglas Horton (Grand Rapids: Zondervan Publishing House, 1935), pp. 240ff.

[32] H. Strohl, in a review of Quervain's *Calvin, sein Lehren und Kämpfen,* a book described by P. Barth in 1934 as the best exposition from the Barthian point of view, claims that Quervain leaves wholly unintelligible the divergent historical developments of Calvinism and Lutheran-

leaves the active and vital role which Calvinism has played in history unintelligible,[33] but Barth's own interpretation leaves unexplained the fact that competent theologians like Warfield have found in Calvin's writings a theology which is different from the Barthian interpretation. Even the Crisis theologians are not in agreement among themselves as to the true interpretation of Calvin's theology. Brunner accuses the Barthians of reading Karl Barth's thought into Calvin's,[34] while the Barthians are dissatisfied with the Calvin scholarship of Brunner and his followers.[35] The opposition between the traditional Calvinists and the Crisis theologians has been clear-cut in the Calvinistic congresses.[36]

The most comprehensive treatment of Calvin's theology which the Crisis theology has produced is Wilhelm Niesel's *Die Theologie Calvins.* Niesel rejects Bauke's thesis that the problem of Calvin's theology can be solved by the study of the *Formgestaltung.* The true genius of this theology is found in the recognition of its Christocentric character. Calvin has but one subject in all of his teaching, which is God made flesh.[37] "Jesus Christ rules not only the content but also the form of Calvin's thought."[38] In regard to form, Niesel points out two predominant characteristics. The first is Calvin's use of the Chalcedonian formulae as a guide for his thought on many important doctrines.[39] The second characteristic is that the activities of God in all their diversity must in their execution be considered as a unit.[40] Although Niesel's study is suggestive, it completely ignores those aspects of Calvin's thought which are not Christocentric. This means that a good amount of material in Calvin's writings cannot be accounted for on the basis of Niesel's thesis.

This brief review of Calvin research points out at least two important facts which every new study of Calvin must take into considera-

---

ism. ("Récentes études sur la théologie de Calvin," *Revue d'Histoire et de Philosophie Religieuses* 6 [1926], 544–552.)

[33]"Fünfundswanzig Jahre Calvinforschung 1909–1934," *Theologische Rundschau* (1934).

[34]Conference with a student who was at Zurich in the spring of 1948; Emil Brunner, "Nature and Grace," *Natural Theology,* tr. Peter Fraenkel (London: Geoffrey Bles, Centenary Press, 1946).

[35]Peter Barth, *Das Problem der natürlichen Theologie bei Calvin;* Wilhelm Niesel, *Die Theologie Calvins,* p. 14, n. 6.

[36]*The Sovereignty of God,* ed. Jacob Hoogstra (Grand Rapids: Zondervan Publishing House, 1941); *De l'élection éternelle de Dieu,* ed. Martinus Nijhoff (Geneva: Éditions Labor et Fides, 1936).

[37]Niesel, *Die Theologie Calvins,* p. 234. See above, note 5.

[38]Ibid., p. 235.

[39]E.g., the relation between "written Word" and "Word made flesh" is similar to the relation between the human nature of Christ and the Logos. Also, between sign and thing signified in the sacrament; between justification and sanctification; union of the believer with Christ.

[40]Niesel, *Die Theologie Calvins,* p. 237.

tion. The first is the necessity of studying any aspect of Calvin's thought in the total context of his theology and work. No fact is more patent in the past century of Calvin study than the inadequacy of every attempt to understand Calvin's theology in terms of one isolated doctrine or in terms of one doctrine considered as a material principle from which the whole is deduced. Every individual doctrine is part of a complex whole.

Furthermore, a study of Calvin's thought must take into consideration the actual situation in Geneva. Calvin was a pastor and an administrator of church affairs not only in Geneva but also, to a considerable extent, in the whole of western Europe. The concerns of the actual ecclesiastical situation almost inevitably reflect themselves in theological and ethical interpretations.

Calvin research has also pointed out that any serious study of Calvin must take into consideration the problems which inconsistencies in Calvin's thought create. This has an important effect on methodology and procedure. Generalizations are exceedingly difficult to make with any real basis in fact; and even when possible, they must be duly qualified before they can serve as an adequate representation of the Reformer's thought. Failure to recognize the variegated character of Calvin's thought has proved to be the nemesis of a considerable amount of Calvin research in the past.[41] These failures must serve as a warning to every new study.

The inconsistencies in Calvin's thought are complex and cannot be reduced to any one type. For the sake of a satisfactory methodology, at least three types of inconsistency must be distinguished.

The first is the conscious and deliberate paradox. Calvin frequently sets one truth over against another truth and does not attempt to force a synthesis. A notable example of this type of paradox is found in the following sentence: "Man falls . . . according to the appointment of Divine Providence; but he falls by his own fault."[42] The importance of this kind of paradox has become almost axiomatic for recent Calvin research. Bauke has called this characteristic of Calvin's theology the *complexio oppositorum,* and Doumergue calls it "la méthode des contrariétés. . . . J'appelle 'contrariété' une contradiction apparente."[43]

A second type of inconsistency results from Calvin's failure to integrate the various strands of thought which went into his theological development. An example can be found in the confusion between

---

[41]E.g., Schulze, *Meditatio futurae vitae.* Cf. Bauke, *Die Probleme der Theologie Calvins,* p. 4; Doumergue, *Jean Calvin, les hommes et les choses de son temps* (Lausanne: Georges Bridel et Cie, 1899–1927), vol. 4, pp. 305ff.

[42]3.23.8.

[43]Bauke, op. cit., p. 16; Doumergue, *Le caractère de Calvin,* p. 47.

Hebraic and Platonic interpretations of the relationship of soul and body which is apparent in Calvin's writings.[44] The Platonic emphasis is strongest in the early writings, but it is never wholly eliminated. A similar inconsistency can be observed in Calvin's various treatments of the respective functions of the will and the understanding in the human personality.[45] This type of inconsistency has probably not received justice from Calvin research, possibly because it is so difficult to pin down with exactness except in the case of a few notable examples.

The identification of a third type of inconsistency is demanded, it seems to me, by an important cleavage in Calvin research. Why is it that some scholars conclude that Calvin's theology is dominated by its emphasis on the personal and living claim of God on every person,[46] and other scholars, who are equally competent, find that he substitutes a codebook for the living claim of God and a legal institution for the body of Christ?[47] As a hypothesis to be confirmed or rejected in the course of this study, we may tentatively affirm that this cleavage is due to the fact that Calvin's theological method vacillates between the existential interests of a participant in the Christian community and the demands of the systematic rationalism of a spectator or the temptations of a churchman to establish by force, structures, laws, or orthodoxy what can only come as a gift of the Holy Spirit.

If the evidence justifies this hypothesis, then considerable light will be thrown on numerous contradictions in Calvin's thought and on the cleavage which exists between the Crisis theologians' interpretation and the more classical picture of Calvinism.

In sum, the problem of this dissertation is to define what is Calvin's doctrine of the Christian life; to place it, as far as is possible, in the total context of his theology; and to see what light, if any, it has to shed on the contemporary status of Calvin research.

---

[44]E.g., cf. *CR* 5:196; 23:26–27; 49:560; 3.25.1.
[45]1.15.7; 1.15.8.
[46]E.g., Niesel, *Die Theologie Calvins.*
[47]Choisy, op. cit.; Seeberg, op. cit., p. 613.

Chapter **1**

The Christian Life

A. The Glory of God

The end of the Christian life is the glory of God, which, as the highest human goal, is of far greater importance than all corporal good and even the salvation of one's own soul.[1] In his reply to Cardinal Sadolet, Calvin wrote:

> It is not very sound theology to confine a man's thought so much to himself, and not to set before him, as the prime motive for his existence, zeal to illustrate the glory of God. For we are born first of all for God, and not for ourselves. As all things flowed from him, and subsist in him, so, says Paul (Rom. 11:36), they ought to be referred to him. I acknowledge, indeed, that the Lord, the better to recommend the glory of his name to men, has tempered zeal for the promotion and extension of it by uniting it indissolubly with our salvation. But since he has taught that this zeal ought to exceed all thought and care for our own good and advantage, and since natural equity also teaches that God does not receive what is his own, unless he is preferred to all things, it certainly is the part of a Christian man to ascend higher than merely to seek and secure the salvation of his own soul. I am persuaded, therefore, that there is no man imbued with true piety who will not consider as insipid that long and labored exhortation to zeal for heavenly life, a zeal which keeps a man entirely devoted to himself and does not, even by one expression, arouse him to sanctify the name of God.[2]

This doctrine has a twofold basis. In the first place we were created for no other end and to live for no other cause than that God may be glorified in us.[3]

---

[1] *CR* 26:693.
[2] *OS* 1:363–364. Translations from the tracts and commentaries are taken when available from the Calvin Translation Society edition.
[3] *CR* 24:362; 26:270; 32:170.

We are not our own; therefore neither our reason nor our will should predominate in our deliberations. . . . We are not our own; therefore let us, as far as possible, forget ourselves and all things that are ours. On the contrary, we are God's; to him, therefore, let us live and die. We are God's; therefore let his wisdom and will preside in all our actions.[4]

The doctrine is also based on the fact of redemption. "This is the end for which God has chosen us by gratuitous goodness; this is why he maintains and continues his grace toward us, that we might glorify him not only with our mouths but in the whole of our life."[5] God has adopted us that his glory might shine in us.[6] Sanctification is subordinated to the glory of God,[7] and the "final" cause of salvation is the demonstration of the divine righteousness and the praise of the divine goodness.[8]

This emphasis on the *sola gloria Dei* undercuts every act which is tainted with self-seeking. True morality is directed toward God alone.[9] As will be seen in the process of this study, the Christian life is the human response to the gracious activity of God on life. It is not, according to Calvin's interpretation, the imitation of a pattern of conduct or the achievement of an ideal, but a living and deeply mutual relationship to the living God which reveals itself in self-denial, cross bearing, and meditation on the future life. The fact that Calvin does not consistently maintain this position constitutes one of the problems of this dissertation.

An accurate understanding of the meaning of "the glory of God" is clearly of decisive importance for any interpretation of Calvin's thought and practice.[10] The significance of the concept centers in three questions: (1) What is the glory of God? (2) What is the relation of human welfare to the glory of God? (3) How do human beings glorify God?

A great variety of answers is given to the first question. In the first

---

[4]3.7.1. Cf. *CR* 33:570.

[5]*CR* 26:225.

[6]*CR* 29:5. Cf. *CR* 26:490.

[7]*CR* 51:147.

[8]3.14.17; 3.15.21.

[9]*CR* 45:191; Karlfried Fröhlich, *Gottesreich, Welt und Kirche bei Calvin* (Munich: E. Reinhardt, 1930), p. 30: "Calvin's deepest concern is neither the world nor its history, neither the worldly orders nor the social life, neither the formation of economy nor conduct of life. His main concern is (only) God and God alone, God's Word, God's authority, God's truth, God's gospel."

[10]Peter Barth, "Calvin," *RGG* 1:1431–1432: "Only a grotesque misunderstanding of the innermost motives of Calvinistic thinking can make any connection between the ideal of the 'glory of God' in Calvin and the homage paid by devoted subjects to monarchs thirsting for glory."

place, the glory of God shines in the structure of the world.[11] "God has not darkly shadowed his glory in the creation of the world, but he has everywhere engraved such manifest marks that even blind men may know them by groping."[12] God's glory consists partly in his wisdom and his power.[13] It also consists in his authority[14] and his righteousness.[15] It is manifested in the many proofs of his fatherly love which one finds in the world.[16]

The glory of God, however, principally shines forth in Christ and in the gospel he proclaimed. In him God's perfect glory and majesty are revealed.[17]

> The glory of God principally shines in this—that he is reconcilable and that he forgives our sins. God indeed manifests his glory both by his power and his wisdom, and by all the judgments which he daily executes; his glory, at the same time, shines forth chiefly in this, that he is propitious to sinners and suffers himself to be pacified; yea, that he not only allows miserable sinners to be reconciled to him but also of his own will invites and anticipates them.[18]

The glory of God is revealed even in the cross of Christ,

> for in the cross of Christ, as in a magnificent theater, the inestimable goodness of God is displayed before the whole world. In all the creatures, indeed, both high and low, the glory of God shines, but nowhere has it shone more brightly than in the cross, in which there has been an astonishing change of things, the condemnation of all men has been manifested, sin has been blotted out, salvation has been restored to men; and, in short, the whole world has been renewed, and everything restored to good order.[19]

The fact that God's glory shines principally in his redemptive grace means that this glory is not some hard, brutal fact in the universe which crushes human beings into servile obeisance. Rather, it signifies that the ultimate fact in the universe is redemptive grace as well as power.

Calvin, however, did not stop with the assertion that God's glory

---

[11]*CR* 33:570; 49:514.
[12]*CR* 48:415.
[13]*CR* 43:428–429.
[14]*CR* 36:89.
[15]*CR* 40:84.
[16]*CR* 36:129.
[17]3.2.1; *CR* 31:43, 50; *CR* 43:550; *CR* 44:160; *CR* 44:163; *CR* 48:88; *CR* 49:272; *CR* 52:256, 424.
[18]*CR* 43:428.
[19]*CR* 47:316.

is principally revealed in his forgiving love. He introduces the analogy of an earthly king's glory as a means of impressing on his readers and hearers the significance of the glory of God.[20] Yet an earthly king's glory frequently stands in irreconcilable contradiction to the forgiving love which was manifest in the cross of Christ,[21] and this false analogy of God's glory led Calvin to make statements which are incompatible with his assertions that the glory of God shines most brightly in the cross of Jesus Christ.[22]

The second question which is asked concerning the significance of this concept is the relation of the glory of God to human welfare. Does the *sola gloria Dei* mean the neglect of humankind? The Westminster Assembly did not think so. In answer to the question What is man's chief end? it said that "man's chief end is to glorify God, and to enjoy him forever."[23]

Calvin was certain that the highest human good was comprehended in communion with God. "The chief good of man is nothing else but union with God; this is attained when we are formed according to him as our exemplar."[24] The ultimate end of a happy life is to be loved by God.[25] Those who have God for their portion are destitute of nothing which is requisite for a happy life.[26] Sometimes Calvin defined a happy life in terms of a person's relation to Christ, but the result is essentially the same.[27] Other definitions say that it consists in obedience to God's word or the fixing of our gaze beyond this present life.[28] However, these are but facets of the central idea that true human happiness consists in union with God. The miseries which surround us result from the fact that we are banished from the kingdom of God. "We are miserable when we are separated from God."[29] By the sin of Adam, we are alienated from God; and the result is that our faculties are corrupted.[30]

Human beings achieve their highest good only in fellowship with God. Consequently, human welfare is served by the *sola gloria Dei.* "God does not require any honor from us because he needs it or

---

[20]*CR* 27:244–245, 250, 434.

[21]*CR* 27:247.

[22]E.g., *CR* 27:251, 263; 29:143.

[23]Westminster Shorter Catechism [*The Constitution of the Presbyterian Church (U.S.A.), Part I, Book of Confessions* (New York and Atlanta: Office of the General Assembly, 1983)].

[24]*CR* 55:48.

[25]2.1.4.

[26]*CR* 31:154. Cf. *CR* 27:135; 28:367; 29:5; 31:238–239; 34:468.

[27]*CR* 50:443, 623–624; 55:299, 327.

[28]*CR* 27:135; 46:81; 50:363.

[29]*CR* 33:662.

[30]*CR* 28:488.

because it profits him but for the sake of our salvation."[31] God has need of nothing, but it is to our profit that we serve him.[32]

> He so joins his glory with our salvation that we cannot procure the one without the other. We ourselves bring neither gain nor loss to God, and even when we fight for him with the greatest devotion, he has no necessity for us. He does not have to borrow our aid, but he constitutes us his magistrates. And for what purpose? That each of us may seek his good not in the world, not in corruptible things, but in the eternal salvation of our souls.[33]

Nevertheless, the glory of God can easily become the denial of human welfare. Calvin himself did not consistently maintain his teaching that the glory of God is supremely revealed in the salvation of humankind. On the contrary, he sometimes asserted in vigorous fashion the very opposite:

> Why is such implacable severity demanded unless to show us that . . . as often as his glory is involved our mutual humanity is erased almost from memory?[34]

> For in that you show that you are truly zealots in the service of God if you kill your own brothers and stop at nothing, scorning the order of nature, in order to show that God rules above all and that his decree is sovereign.[35]

These may be overstatements of the fact that God is the Creator and that human beings in themselves are not significant, but they are certainly dangerous overstatements. However high Calvin's motives may have been in such statements, they were the justification of deeds which have the appearance of brutality and inhumanity. They explain how Calvin could desire the death penalty for Servetus without any apparent emotional disturbance,[36] though he was fully capable of feeling the poignancy of death.[37]

Calvin himself was unaware of any inconsistency between the

---

[31] *CR* 26:309.

[32] *CR* 26:102; 27:78–79.

[33] *CR* 51:13. Cf. *CR* 28:588: "Now Moses once again declares that the people will not love God if not for their profit and salvation: as he said: Although God requires, rightly so, that we love him, he does not derive any profit or advantage from our doing so. What then? He looks for and procures our salvation. For he sees that we are quite miserable when we turn away from him. He therefore wants to win us over, but not just to have anything for himself, but that all the gain of it will come back to us."

[34] *CR* 8:476.

[35] *CR* 29:143. Cf. 27:263; 44:348.

[36] *CR* 14:590.

[37] *CR* 11:188ff.

foregoing statements and his assertion that the glory of God was principally revealed in his redemptive love redeeming humankind. This very fact makes these aberrations all the more dangerous even for those who seek to learn from Calvin today. Although it is difficult to isolate the source of his inconsistency, it seems to be at least in part due to Calvin's theological method. While he avows the greatest loyalty to scripture, he actually goes beyond scripture as a result of an almost irresistible tendency to rationalize on the basis of scriptural data. He affirms the sinfulness of human reason in no uncertain terms, but his own deductions reveal little doubt as to reason's full competence to theologize once the biblical premises are assumed. It was Calvin's intention to bring people into the living presence of the King of Glory; and his theology, as far as we can judge, was the context in which many did come into that presence. However, it must also be said that he sometimes substituted an abstract rationalization of an earthly king's glory for that living presence.

The answer to the third question, How do we glorify God? is manifold, as is the case with almost any personal response. In general, the only activity which glorifies God is that which arises from loving hearts.[38] God is glorified when we take refuge in him and ask forgiveness for the sins which we have committed.[39] Again,

> God has prescribed for us a way in which he will be glorified by us; namely, piety, which consists in the obedience of his Word. He that exceeds these bounds does not go about to honor God, but rather to dishonor him.[40]

Good works glorify God.[41] The glory of God is revealed when we know who he is.[42] God is glorified only when he receives that honor among human beings to which he is entitled. His glory is obscured when other "objects" are set over against him with antagonistic claims on human life.[43] He is glorified when people are grateful to him for his goodness[44] and when they deny themselves to love their enemies.[45]

These varied aspects of the glorification of God are well summarized in the Geneva Catechism:

---

[38]*CR* 33:186; 45:611.
[39]*CR* 26:166; 3.13.1ff.
[40]*CR* 49:51.
[41]*CR* 49:245.
[42]*CR* 47:377–378.
[43]*CR* 31:779.
[44]*CR* 24:157.
[45]*CR* 51:21.

Master: What is the chief end of human life?

Scholar: To know God by whom men were created.

M: What reason have you for saying so?

S: Because he created us and placed us in this world to be glorified in us. And it is indeed right that our life, of which himself is the beginning, should be devoted to his glory.

M: What is the highest good of man?

S: The very same thing.

M: Why do you hold that to be the highest good?

S: Because without it our condition is worse than that of the brutes.

M: Hence, then, we clearly see that nothing worse can happen to a man than not to live to God.

S: It is so.

M: What is the true and right knowledge of God?

S: When he is so known that due honor is paid to him.

M: What is the method of honoring him duly?

S: To place our whole confidence in him; to study to serve him during our whole life by obeying his will; to call upon him in all our necessities, seeking salvation and every good thing that can be desired in him; lastly, to acknowledge him both with heart and lips as the sole Author of all blessings.[46]

God is glorified not by the servile fear of human beings, but by their responsive love. God's glory is revealed in the total response of a person to the grace which created and redeems him or her. It includes, as the catechism indicates, the personal response of trust, service, obedience, dependence, and thanksgiving.

This personal response which the claim of God evokes in the life of the individual believer involves the total surrender of life. The principle of interpretation is found in the text of Romans 12:1. It is the duty of believers to present their bodies "a living sacrifice, holy, acceptable unto God."[47] Christians must not think, speak, meditate, or do anything except with a view to the glory of God. They must reflect that they have to do with God every moment of their lives.[48] Human beings live only to serve God.[49] It is not enough to pray with one's lips; the whole of life must be dedicated to God.[50] The most patent fact about Calvin's doctrine of the Christian life

---

[46]*CR* 6:9–10.

[47]3.7.1.

[48]3.7.2.

[49]*CR* 26:116, 224.

[50]*CR* 26:614.

is that it is a life lived under the exclusive and sovereign claim of God.[51]

> The first rule as to all our actions is to follow the call of God. Though one may excel in heroic virtues, yet all his virtues are mere fumes which shine before the eyes of men, unless the object be to obey God. The call of God then, as I have said, holds the first place as to the conduct of men; and unless we lay this foundation, we do like him who would build a house in the air. Disordered, then, will be the whole course of our life, unless God presides over and guides us, and raises up over us, as it were, his own banners.[52]

Calvin describes the true human relationship to God as that of slaves to their lord, of soldiers to their commander, and of children to their father.[53]

These affirmations of the thoroughgoing response which God's claim on human life evokes in the life of the believer call for intense living both in the personal and in the social spheres of life. This very intensity will serve to accentuate the cleavage which exists between the glory of God as revealed in the forgiving love manifest in Jesus Christ and the glory of God which is filtered through the analogy of some earthly potentate.

The obligation which rests on every human life to glorify God accentuates the human plight. Not only are fallen human beings blind to the true knowledge of God, but also their capacity to respond to God's claim on their lives has been dissipated by sin.[54] Briefly told, humankind's plight is this: Adam did not continue in the state wherein he was created, but rebelled against God.[55] His fall affected all posterity, and now the human condition must be read in the light of original sin, which is a "hereditary pravity and corruption of our nature, diffused through all the parts of the soul, rendering us obnoxious to the Divine wrath, and producing in us those works which the Scripture calls 'works of the flesh.' "[56]

In assessing the effects of the fall, it must be kept in mind that the image of God in which human beings were created involved two dimensions or relationships: the human and the divine.[57] Natural

---

[51]*CR* 23:59, 179; 24:213, 224, 418; 26:55, 67, 79, 136, 160, 225, 258, 302–303, 490–491, 608; 27:37, 158, 202, 221, 436; 28:708ff.; 29:117; 36:111, 150–151; 37:692; 45:446; 47:406; 49:42, 237, 259–260, 263; 51:42–43; 52:148, 268; 55:27.
[52]*CR* 43:208.
[53]*CR* 26:439–440, 650; 27:78–79; 28:210, 281; 37:104; 51:114; 52:361.
[54]2.2.1ff.
[55]Ibid.
[56]2.1.8.
[57]2.2.12ff.

human talents have been corrupted by sin, but the supernatural ones have been taken away.[58]

> Hence it follows, that he is exiled from the kingdom of God, in such a manner, that all the affections relating to the happy life of the soul, are also extinguished in him, till he recovers them by the grace of regeneration. Such are faith, love to God, charity towards our neighbours, and an attachment to holiness and righteousness. All these things, being restored by Christ, are esteemed adventitious and preternatural; and therefore we conclude that they had been lost.[59]

This means that there has been a rupture in the personal relationship of God to human beings.

On the human level, humankind remains *humanitas,* to borrow Brunner's phrase.[60] Reason is not destroyed but is debilitated and vitiated so that it exhibits nothing but deformity and ruin.[61] The will is not destroyed, but it becomes a slave of evil desires so that it cannot aspire after the good. Nevertheless, in political and civil order, in the arts and sciences, fallen human beings can achieve remarkable results. These results must not be despised, for the Spirit of God is the fountain of all truth.[62]

On the religious level, however, fallen human beings cannot know God, or his grace, or the method of regulating life according to the rule of the law.[63] While it is true that fallen human beings do have some knowledge of God, this knowledge is ineffectual for salvation.[64]

Furthermore, the wickedness of the human heart is such that the true knowledge of God is ineffective apart from inner cleansing. Therefore, before human beings can glorify God they must not only have a revelation of God's will for human life, but they must also have the regeneration of heart which will enable them to respond in faith and obedience to that claim.

B. Jesus Christ, the Law, the Bible

The human need for knowledge of the Christian life is met, according to Calvin, by the revelation of God in Jesus Christ, in the law, and in the Bible. Calvin variously appeals to all three as the norm of the Christian life, but he does not regard them as independent of

---

[58]2.2.12.
[59]Ibid.
[60]Emil Brunner, *Man in Revolt,* tr. Olive Wyon (New York: Charles Scribner's Sons, 1939), p. 96.
[61]2.2.12.
[62]2.2.14ff.
[63]2.2.18.
[64]2.2.18ff.

one another. Jesus Christ is the fulfillment of the law, and our knowledge of both Jesus Christ and the law comes to us from the Bible.

Calvin does recognize the validity of the law of nature, as his exposition of Romans 1:20 indicates.[65] This law stands in judgment on all secular society, but it is inadequate as a guide for the Christian life because of human sin.[66] As far as the Christian life is concerned, Calvin's consistent appeal is to the law as revealed in scripture, though he asserts that this law is not out of harmony with the law of nature.[67]

The full meaning of the Christian life has been revealed in Jesus Christ. In him the fullness of the Godhead dwelt bodily.[68] He is the living image of the eternal God.[69] The sovereign God rules humankind in Jesus Christ.[70] If we are to obey God and be his subjects, it is necessary that we embrace our Lord Jesus Christ, as he is our only master.[71] Furthermore, Jesus is the pattern, the example of the true life which we must strive to imitate.[72] He is the soul and the life of the law.[73] As will be seen later, Calvin repeatedly presents the cross of Christ as an example of the Christian life.[74] Jesus is also the

---

[65] J. T. McNeill, "Natural Law in the Teaching of the Reformers," *Journal of Religion* 26 (1946), 181: "[Calvin adopted the natural law tradition with modifications that do not denature it.] These modifications are such as to give increased emphasis to conscience and to reduce the medieval emphasis on reason. It is permissible to argue that natural law is, for Calvin, of secondary interest in relation to his main doctrines. This is the case only because the realm of mundane affairs is, for him, subordinate to the realm of the supernatural. Within the mundane society, natural law is not secondary but controlling—and this because it is not earthly but divine in origin, engraved by God on all men's hearts."

Cf. A. Lang, "The Reformation and Natural Law," *Princeton Theological Review* (1909), 177–218; G. Gloede, *Theologia naturalis bei Calvin;* Peter Barth, *Das Problem der natürlichen Theologie bei Calvin;* É. Doumergue, *Jean Calvin, les hommes et les choses de son temps,* 5, 465ff.; Emil Brunner, *Justice and the Social Order,* tr. Mary Hottinger (New York: Harper & Brothers, 1945); Emil Brunner, "Nature and Grace," *Natural Theology,* 39.

[66] 2.8.1: "But man, involved as he is in a cloud of errors, scarcely obtains from this law of nature the smallest idea of what worship is accepted by God; but is certainly at an immense distance from a right understanding of it. Besides, he is so elated with arrogance and ambition, and so blinded with self-love, that he cannot yet take a view of himself, and as it were retire within, that he may learn to submit and humble himself, and to confess his misery. Since it was necessary, therefore, both for our dulness and obstinacy, the Lord gave us a written law; to declare with greater certainty what in the law of nature was too obscure, and by arousing our indolence, to make a deeper impression on our understanding and memory."

[67] *CR* 24:723.
[68] *CR* 52:104.
[69] *CR* 26:128.
[70] *CR* 9:817; 31:43.
[71] *CR* 50:283.
[72] *CR* 52:24; 3.6.3.
[73] 2.7.2.
[74] E.g., *CR* 55:270.

King whose authority is absolute in his church and therefore in the Christian life. On the one hand, this means that Jesus Christ will protect his people,[75] but on the other it means that he alone is Lord.[76]

The Christian life also has as its norm the law of God. Calvin uses the term "law" in the broad sense which includes three parts: "first, the doctrine of life; second, threatenings and promises; third, the covenant of grace, which, being founded on Christ, contains within itself all the special promises."[77] At this point, however, we are concerned with the law in the more specific sense as the doctrine of life or as the *vraye reigle de bien vivre*. In this sense the law has found classic expression in the Ten Commandments, which play a prominent part in Calvin's exegetical and confessional writings.

In the law we find specific details of what God's claim means in everyday life. Yet if we concentrate on the specific requirements of the law, we will obscure an aspect of Calvin's interpretation of the law which is important, even though it is not consistently maintained. The law is the personal claim of God over against the personal existence of human beings. The content of the law is God himself.[78] The "true and pure religion was so revealed in the law, that God's face in a manner shone forth therein."[79] It is impossible to separate God from his justice, which he declares to us in the law.[80] The will of God is explained to us in the law, and insofar as we deviate from it, we deviate from our Lord.[81] The end of the law is that we should love God. True obedience arises when we hold God for our Father and live as his children.[82] This indicates that the law expresses the content of the personal response of sonship to the fatherly love of God on the part of his children. As will be seen, Calvin did not consistently maintain this point either in his teachings or in his ecclesiastical administration.

---

[75] 2.15.3.

[76] 4.10.1; 4.9.1.

[77] *CR* 36:19. Cf. *CR* 26:209; 42:198.

[78] Cf. Peter Barth, 'Was ist reformierte Ethik?" *Zwischen den Zeiten* 10 (1932), 428: "As the content of the Law, finally God himself always stands again before us. Not this and that is finally meant, but in all the One, that God as our Father and Lord may be glorified among us. And in this one has to remember that, for Calvin, God always is to be recognized by faith in his whole majesty, according to all sides of his revealedness. As our Father and Redeemer in Jesus Christ, and as our Lord and Master, as Creator of the world and as he who mysteriously reigns and guides the lives of peoples and of individuals, God wants to be glorified among us."

[79] *CR* 24:262.

[80] *CR* 27:559.

[81] *CR* 42:463.

[82] *CR* 27:558–559.

God's personal confrontation of human beings in the law does not obscure his moral transcendence. The righteousness of the law is not a full expression of the essential righteousness of God. God's righteousness is so high above all his creatures that it can be said that he finds no steadfastness even in the angels.[83] If we should keep the law perfectly, we would be reputed just before God; but we would have no merit or dignity in ourselves. It is purely of grace that God says whoever will do the things of the law shall live. God contents himself in his relation with humankind with the justice manifested in the law, but there is in God a justice which mounts far above the apprehension of his creatures.[84]

There is a moral transcendence in God which surpasses even his law, but for humankind that law is the expression of the perpetual claim which rests on every human life. In the law of God we have a perpetual rule of justice. It is certain that under the Ten Commandments God has given a rule of life which is eternal.[85] The law "is the eternal rule of a devout and holy life and must therefore be as unchangeable as the justice of God, which it embraced, is constant and uniform."[86] The law is not something which God has arbitrarily imposed on human existence. On the contrary, it is structural in the world. The law prescribes nothing which nature does not dictate to be most certain and most just and which experience itself does not show us to be profitable.[87]

Although the law is eternal in that it is the perpetual expression of God's claim on human life, in another sense it has been abrogated by Christ. We live under grace, not under the law. How can this abrogation of the law be harmonized with its eternal claim? The following statement from the tract against the Spiritual Libertines is a good summary of Calvin's viewpoint:

> There are two things to consider in the law: the first is to apprehend the doctrine which is the rule for a good life because our Lord shows to us that which is pleasing to him and that which he approves. Thus the doctrine of the law is to show us how our life should be conformed to the will of God. The second point is the rigor: inasmuch as it denounces to us that whoever is lacking in a single point will be cursed, and it does not promise salvation except to those who will have perfectly observed all his commandments. . . . Thus that is why the world despairs, if the law with its implications has authority

[83]*CR* 33:726. Cf. 3.12.1.
[84]*CR* 33:496.
[85]*CR* 26:287.
[86]*CR* 45:171.
[87]*CR* 24:723.

over us. Because it is not possible to satisfy its requirements. . . . We see clearly that this liberty is only in regard to the curse and to the rigor.[88]

The liberty of Christians lies in the fact that they do not have to earn salvation by obeying every jot and tittle of the law. In the chapter on Christian liberty, Calvin divides the doctrine into three parts. The first is justification by faith alone. In the fundamental matter of a person's relationship with God it is necessary to forget the righteousness of the law and to look to the grace of God.[89] In the second place the Christian yields voluntary obedience to the law. Obedience is the human response to paternal love.[90] Finally, in respect to external things which are indifferent in themselves, the Christian is free to accept or reject them.[91] The Christian is guided by love. Doumergue has observed, correctly I think, that this doctrine is essentially that of Luther.[92] It is significant that the chapter on Christian liberty in the 1559 *Institutes* is almost completely reproduced from the 1536 *Institutes,* in which Calvin depended heavily on Luther and Melanchthon.[93]

Christ brings us mercy, which liberates us from the obligation of obeying the law for salvation, and the spirit of regeneration, which enables us to obey it.[94] It is not the letter but the spirit which penetrates the heart and reforms us.[95] Christ is the soul of the law, and apart from him the law is dead.[96] Thus it is clear that Christ does not abrogate the relevance of the law to human life. The God who spoke in the law is also the God who speaks in the gospel.[97] It is Christ who makes the law a word of life rather than a word of death.

Calvin ascribes three main functions to the law. First, the law "warns every one of his own unrighteousness, places it beyond all doubt, convicts, and condemns him."[98] "Thus the law is like a mirror, in which we behold, first, our impotence; second, our iniquity, which proceeds from it; and last, the consequence of both, our ob-

---

[88]*CR* 7:206–207. Cf. *CR* 26:496; 2.7.14–15.
[89]3.19.2.
[90]3.19.4.
[91]3.19.7.
[92]Doumergue, *Jean Calvin, les hommes et les choses de son temps,* 4, 318ff.
[93]*OS* 4:282ff.
[94]*CR* 31:201.
[95]*CR* 38:690–691.
[96]2.7.2.
[97]*CR* 55:8.
[98]2.7.6.

noxiousness to the curse; just as a mirror represents to us the spots on our face."[99]

The second function of the law is that of preserving community by restraining people through fear of its penalties.[100] The type of obedience thus drawn forth is servile in contrast to the free and spontaneous obedience which is found in the regenerate.

The third function of the law is found in its relation to the faithful. To the regenerate the law provides both instruction as to what the good life is and exhortation to it.[101] It is an excellent instrument to give to the faithful a better understanding of the divine will. It places before their eyes the *vraye reigle de bien vivre.*[102] The purpose of the law is to reform people and subject them to God according to his will. As the true rule of the good life the law ever remains. Only the motive of obedience is changed. Human beings do not obey the law to gain salvation; obedience springs out of gratitude for redemption which has already been wrought in Christ.

> The law, so far as it is a rule of life, a bridle to keep us in the fear of the Lord, a spur to correct the sluggishness of our flesh—so far, in short, as it is "profitable for doctrine, for reproof, for correction, for instruction in righteousness"—. . . is as much in force as ever, and remains untouched.[103]

The third use of the law is the principal one, according to Calvin. On this point of emphasis he differs from Luther. Luther was well aware of this use of the law, but he does not say that the law is principally a guide and stimulant for the faithful. Luther, especially in the early 1520s, was willing to say that the believer did not really need the law at all.[104] Calvin would never go this far. This partially accounts for the fact that Lutheranism has had to guard against antinomian temptations while Reformed circles have been more likely to fall into legalism.

Calvin's use of the law has given rise to the serious charge of legalism.[105] Is this charge true? The evidence, which is not fully consistent, seems to preclude a categorical yes or no answer. A convenient approach to the problem is to be found in the rules which Calvin laid down for the interpretation of the law. "First, . . . the law

---

[99]2.7.7. Cf. *CR* 50:533–534; 33:495; 50:434.
[100]2.7.10–11.
[101]2.7.12; *CR* 24:726–727.
[102]*CR* 50:434.
[103]*CR* 50:221.
[104]*Works of Martin Luther* (Philadelphia: A. J. Holman Co., 1915), 1:190, 191, 199; 3:234–245.
[105]Cf. Choisy, *La théocratie à Genève au temps de Calvin,* p. 256.

inculcates a conformity of life, not only to external probity, but also to internal and spiritual righteousness."[106] God is a spiritual legislator and addresses himself to the soul as well as to the body. "Now, the murder of the soul is wrath and hatred; the theft of the soul is evil concupiscence and avarice; the adultery of the soul is lust."[107] In order to obey the law one must dedicate oneself *en tout et par tout* in the love and obedience of God.[108] God does not wish to be served by constraint but by a spontaneous love.[109]

The second rule is the observation that the commands and prohibitions always imply more than the words express.[110] This is to say that mere formal obedience to the law is not enough. The purpose or substance of the law must be considered above everything.[111]

> It is true that God has comprised in ten words all which he demands of us: but those ten words carry great weight. It is not a question of knowing the Ten Commandments as a magpie which speaks in a cage (as they say): but it is necessary that we consider well what they embrace and to what they lead. When our Lord has spoken a word to us, we must consider what he means, and then afterward, that which depends on it; and we shall see that we need to think on that, to occupy ourselves with it and to employ all our lifetime.[112]

These statements all point beyond any narrow legalism. In commenting on Matthew 5:21, Calvin makes clear that the law of God must never be turned into a political order or into the mere performance of outward duties.[113]

The law must be interpreted according to the intention of the lawgiver.[114] The best interpreter is Christ.[115] "We must listen to him as a faithful expounder, that we may know what is the nature of the law, what is its object, and what is its extent."[116] When Jesus has

---

[106]2.8.6.

[107]Ibid.

[108]*CR* 26:434.

[109]*CR* 26:439. Ernst Troeltsch has written: "The Bible itself lays stress on ethics as well as on doctrine. In the mind of Calvin this does not signify a reaction towards heteronomy or legalism . . . , since the value of moral achievement does not consist in particular actions, but in the spirit generated by faith in the whole personality, in the total change of heart effected by conversion." (*The Social Teaching of the Christian Churches,* tr. Olive Wyon [New York: Macmillan Co., 1931], 2:603.)

[110]2.8.8; *CR* 28:5.

[111]*CR* 27:327.

[112]*CR* 28:283.

[113]*CR* 45:175.

[114]*CR* 45:324; 2.8.8.

[115]2.8.7.

[116]*CR* 45:175.

interpreted a passage, we must not dispute any longer, but listen to him who is the true legislator of it.[117]

The third rule for interpreting the law is careful consideration of the reason for the twofold division in the law, that is, the distinction between the duties of religion and the duties of charity.[118] The point which Calvin is concerned to make is that religion is the foundation of righteousness.

> Nor is religion only the head of righteousness, but the very soul of it, constituting all its life and vigor; for without the fear of God, men preserve no equity and love among themselves. We therefore call the worship of God the principle and foundation of righteousness, because, if that be wanting, whatever equity, continence, and temperance men may practise among themselves, it is all vain and frivolous in the sight of God.[119]

Here again Calvin safeguards his use of law by rooting obedience to it in worship. Yet in his exhortations to righteousness as a proof of sincere religion he provides an occasion for legalism to develop.[120]

Furthermore, in Calvin's commentaries and sermons one does not find a legalistic system in the sense of laws which govern every area of life. Two cases will serve as good illustrations. One of the pressing problems which Calvin faced was that of usury. Here it would have been easy for him to have set a definite rate. Yet he insisted that no set rate could be a correct solution to the problem. The rate must be set according to the particular case.[121] Concerning the biblical injunctions with reference to usury, Calvin writes that we cannot truly interpret them by paying attention to the words alone, but rather we must consider their substance.[122] Another case which serves as an illustration is the use of luxuries. Calvin refused to set definite rules. "It is neither right nor possible to bind the conscience with the fixed and precise rules of law in this case; but since the scripture delivers general rules for the lawful use of earthly things, our practice ought certainly to be regulated by them."[123] Likewise, the amount of love we should exercise toward our neighbors in beneficence to them cannot be fixed by law.[124]

In theology Calvin's clear insistence on justification by faith alone stands in contradiction to the legalistic spirit. In church polity he

---

[117]*CR* 26:435.
[118]2.8.11.
[119]Ibid.
[120]*CR* 37:294.
[121]*CR* 28:114ff.
[122]*CR* 40:430.
[123]3.10.1.
[124]3.7.7.

asked for a consistory to guard against moral and religious aberrations; yet he refused to make discipline the decisive test of the
church's existence, as the tract against the Anabaptists indicates.[125]
Proper use of discipline is necessary for the perfection of the church
but not for the being of the church.[126]

Calvin's location of the exposition of the law in book II rather than
in book III as part of the section on repentance and the Christian life
must be significant. In the discussion of the Christian life the appeal
is more to the life and example of Jesus and to the corpus of Christian
theology as the source and guide for the Christian life.

All of this builds a strong case[127] against the charge of legalism,
But other evidence points in the opposite direction. Even though
Calvin has great sections on the spontaneity of love, it is possible that
he understood the "oughtness" of love better than its spontaneity.[128]
His discussion of the story of the woman taken in adultery reveals
a failure to rise above the bounds of legalism.[129] The same is true of
his justification of the punishment of heretics.[130] The Geneva *ordonnances,* which set up a consistory to regulate the conduct of the
Christian community and which required a public confession of
faith, laid the basis for a legalistic development. The officials of
Calvin's Geneva did not hesitate to force people to go to church.[131]
They also investigated and regulated many details of daily life. Par-
ents were prohibited from naming their children for the saints.[132] A
man was denied the Lord's Supper for accepting a charm to cure a

---

[125]*CR* 7:65ff.

[126]Ibid.

[127]Fröhlich, *Gottesreich, Welt und Kirche bei Calvin,* p. 39: "For Calvin, the law is a thoroughly
living reality. By no means does he legalize piety as a whole. The Bible, the Word of God,
in spite of his strict biblicism, is for him no rigid statutory 'Book of Law': his sharp polemic
against the legalistic use of scripture by the Anabaptists already witnesses to this. No, the law
of God that majestically faces him in the Decalogue is only one of the great symbols of the
'living will of God' which let the glory of God become great."

P. Barth, "Calvin," *RGG* 1:1431: "Therefore to raise the reproach of legalism against Calvin
is wrong. Calvin did not recoil even from making fruitful the biblical idea of reward given to
obedience; therefore the reproach of eudaemonism has been made against him unjustly.
Calvin's whole theology stands under the sign of eschatological promise. This includes both
Testaments. The law and grace point toward the yet awaited, otherworldly fulfillment. Christ's
earthly appearance is the pledge for the fulfillment of that which is promised."

[128]Cf. Paul Wernle, *Calvin,* vol. 3, *Der evangelische Glaube nach den Hauptschriften der
Reformatoren* (Tübingen: J. C. B. Mohr [Paul Siebeck], 1919), pp. 322ff. He thinks it significant that Calvin discusses neighborly love under self-denial.

[129]*CR* 24:649.

[130]*CR* 27:244, 247, 436ff.

[131]*CR* 21:303, 305, 306, 653. Cf. Amédée Roget, *Histoire du peuple de Genève* (Geneva: John
Jullien, 1870), 1:4.

[132]*CR* 21:386.

fever.[133] A woman was reproved for saying *"Requiescat in pace"* at the grave of her husband.[134] Dancing was frowned on,[135] and gamblers were called to task.[136] Such examples of the work of the Geneva Consistory are indications of a legalistic approach to the problems of the Christian life.

A possible source of Calvin's legalism was his study of law at Bourges and Orleans. The trained jurist cannot be separated from the theologian and churchman. His first task on returning to Geneva in 1541 was to codify the laws of Geneva. Another fact which probably led to legalism was his intense desire for the church to be coextensive with the community. At least insofar as Geneva was concerned, Calvin never gave up the medieval ideal of the *corpus Christianum;* but he sought to make the Genevan community the true body of Christ. Banishment, which eliminated the more recalcitrant members of the community, helped in the achievement of this ideal; but those who remained continually fell short of Calvin's standards. The pressure of achieving the ideal community may have caused the Reformer to resort to legalistic methods.

In sum, Calvin was not by intention a legalist. As has been seen, he avowed the opposite. Yet his writings and especially his practice reveal an unmistakable legalistic tendency. Thus no easy yes or no answer can be given to the question, Was Calvin a legalist? He gave a persuasive and powerful statement of the personal claim of the living God on every human life; yet his efforts to compel people to submit to this claim tended to substitute precisely formulated rules for the personal reign of God. In theory at least, Calvin well understood that the rules at best are only the context in which the claim of God is heard and obeyed; but in actual practice he sometimes substituted rules for the personal claim of God. This very fact makes it all the more necessary for those who would learn from Calvin today to be aware of his inconsistency.

The third norm of the Christian life, which is also the source of our knowledge of Jesus Christ and the law, is the Bible. The first article of the confession to which all the citizens of Geneva were asked to assent left no doubt about its place in the life of the Christian.

> First we protest that for the rule of our faith and religion we wish to follow the only scripture, without mixing with it anything which has been forged from the minds of men without the Word of God: and we

---

[133]*CR* 21:653.
[134]*CR* 21:422.
[135]*CR* 21:377.
[136]*CR* 21:327.

do not pretend for our spiritual government to receive any doctrine other than that which we have been taught through this word, without its being added to or subtracted from, as our Lord commands it.[137]

"God has placed on one side his Word and on the other side our life. This is the true balance to which we must come."[138] It does not matter what the multitude says. The true balance of life always has God's Word as its counterpoise.[139] The standard of godliness must be taken from the Word of God.[140] The true religion differs from all others in that the Word of God is the only rule of it.[141] Muhammad and the pope agree in holding as a principle of their religion that the scripture does not contain a perfection of doctrine.[142] It is from God, not from human beings, that we have the rule of good service, which is the foundation of our religion.[143] Calvin makes as emphatic as possible the conviction that the whole rule of faith and life is to be found in the scripture. This is a basic principle of his theology.[144]

This word of God is sufficient for the good regulation of life.[145]

If it be objected that the scriptures do not contain everything, and that they do not give special answers on those points of which we are in doubt, I reply that everything that relates to the guidance of our life is contained in them abundantly. If, therefore, we have resolved to allow ourselves to be directed by the word of God and always seek in it the rule of life, God will never suffer us to remain in doubt, but in all transactions and difficulties will point out to us the conclusions. Sometimes, perhaps, we shall have to wait long, but at length the Lord will rescue and deliver us, if we are ready to obey him.[146]

Furthermore, "there is nothing revealed in scripture that is not profitable to be known."[147] There is nothing human mixed with the

---

[137]*CR* 9:693.
[138]*CR* 51:76.
[139]Ibid.
[140]*CR* 21:37–38.
[141]*CR* 48:569.
[142]*CR* 47:335.
[143]*CR* 26:667–668. Cf. *CR* 26:101–102, 115–116, 496, 514, 696; 27:228, 494; 33:204; 47:384–385.
[144]Peter Barth, "Die biblische Grundlage der Prädestinationslehre bei Calvin," in Nijhoff, ed., *De l'élection éternelle de Dieu*, p. 21: "Over the whole theology of Calvin, over his fight for the right formation of the church and of the order of the state, there stands the guiding principle that God, as he reveals himself to us in the Holy Scriptures, must be heard by us, that we must be open and willing to give ear to how God here, in the witness of scripture, reveals himself to us."
[145]*CR* 27:616.
[146]*CR* 36:507–508.
[147]*CR* 49:460–461.

Bible.[148] In general, scripture is very clear and simple so that every Christian can profit therein.[149] God will not leave the person in doubt who resolves to direct his or her life by the Bible.[150] Yet Calvin admitted that some portions are abstruse.[151] Consequently, commentaries and other helps must not be despised; interpreters and teachers are given to us as well as scripture.[152] In sum, (1) "everything that relates to the guidance of our lives is contained in [the scriptures] abundantly";[153] (2) "there is nothing revealed in the scriptures that is not profitable to be known";[154] (3) the essence of scripture is very clear so that every Christian can profit therein.[155] These three assertions concerning the scripture were important in determining Calvin's methodology as an interpreter of scripture and as a theologian.

The wholesome effect of this word of God is the conversion of people, which is not only the beginning of health but also a certain resurrection from death to life.[156] It is the means by which God pierces our hearts.[157] God personally confronts us in the Bible, where his living image is revealed.[158]

> It is the mirror in which we contemplate the face of God in order to be transfigured in his glory. It is the royal scepter with which he governs us as his people, and the staff which he gives us to teach us that he wishes to be our Shepherd. It is the instrument of his alliance which he has made with us . . . in order to be joined with us in a perpetual bond. It is the witness of his good will through which we have repose in our consciences, knowing where our salvation lies. It is the only pasture of our souls, to nourish them into eternal life.[159]

For these reasons Calvin recommended daily Bible reading as an indispensable spiritual exercise for the Christian.[160] "If the body is badly disposed when it is denied meat, then it is certain that the soul is in still worse shape when it has lost the taste and desire of the Word

---

[148]*CR* 52:383.
[149]*CR* 48:439; 28:547, 571–572.
[150]*CR* 36:507.
[151]*CR* 48:193–194.
[152]*CR* 48:192.
[153]*CR* 36:507; 3.21.3: "The scripture is the school of the Holy Spirit, in which, as nothing necessary and useful to be known is omitted, so nothing is taught which it is not beneficial to know."
[154]*CR* 49:460–461.
[155]*CR* 48:439.
[156]*CR* 48:572.
[157]*CR* 48:65.
[158]*CR* 8:395; 28:303, 547.
[159]*CR* 9:823.
[160]*CR* 11:735–736; 18:313.

of God."[161] As long as we are in this world we must profit in God's Word because our spiritual life lies there.[162]

The important place which Calvin gave to the Bible as a source of knowledge and piety accentuates the significance of his methodological use of the Bible. Here we are confronted with one of the most confused areas of Calvin study. Competent scholars are divided in their opinions. The historian of Christian dogma Reinhold Seeberg has written:

> Thus Calvin establishes the authority of the scriptures partly upon their divine dictation, and partly upon the testimony of the Holy Spirit working through them. Historically considered, he thereby combines the later medieval conception of inspiration with the theory of Luther. Calvin is therefore the author of the so-called inspiration theory of the older dogmaticians.[163]

Georgia Harkness, an American liberal, has called Calvin "a thoroughgoing fundamentalist."[164] B. B. Warfield, a traditional Calvinist, has vigorously affirmed that Calvin taught that the scriptures were free from all error.[165] E. Choisy writes that Calvin used the Bible as a code of moral prescriptions, or a code for an ecclesiastical police, and as a catechism of doctrines.[166] On the other hand, such competent scholars as the Barthians hold a diametrically opposite position. They vigorously deny that Calvin taught a doctrine of verbal inspiration or that he was guilty of a biblical literalism.[167] In seeking to discover the source and reason for these diverse interpretations, it seems to me that Calvin's beliefs about inspiration, the unity of the Bible, and the authority of the Bible are of especial importance. The crux of the controversy roots in what he had to say on these three subjects.

Calvin was fully convinced that the Bible was the word of God. He used the strongest language to give expression to this conviction. The Bible is the authentic record of God's truth.[168] "The apostles

---

[161]*CR* 19:611. Cf. *CR* 15:223.

[162]*CR* 50:647.

[163]Reinhold Seeberg, *Textbook of the History of Doctrines,* tr. Charles E. Hay (Philadelphia: Lutheran Publication Society, 1905), 2:395–396.

[164]Georgia Harkness, *John Calvin, the Man and His Ethics* (New York: Henry Holt & Co., 1931), p. 66.

[165]B. B. Warfield, *Calvin and Calvinism,* pp. 60ff.

[166]*La théocratie à Genève au temps de Calvin,* p. 256.

[167]Cf. P. Barth, "Calvin," *RGG;* Quervain, *Calvin, sein Lehren und Kämpfen;* Niesel, *Die Theologie Calvins,* pp. 19ff.

[168]*CR* 3:86 (French edition, 1560): "It was necessary that God had his authentic register in order to lay down there his truth, that it not perish by forgetfulness or fade away by error,

were the certain and authentic amanuenses of the Holy Spirit, and therefore their writings are to be received as the oracles of God."[169] "We owe to the scripture the same reverence which we owe to God, because it has proceeded from him alone and has nothing belonging to man mixed with it."[170] Calvin nowhere specifically elaborates a doctrine of inspiration, but he frequently uses the phrase "dictated by God" as descriptive of the scriptures.[171] It would seem from these statements that Calvin completely identified the word of God and the Bible.[172] A critical question is Calvin's understanding of dictation and the relation of sixteenth-century usage to our usage today.

Nevertheless, other evidence points to a less strict identification of the word of God and the Bible. In the Geneva Catechism of 1545, in response to the question as to where the word of God may be found, Calvin does not say that the Bible is the word of God. Rather, he says that the word of God can be found in the Holy Scriptures, which contain it.[173]

In his commentaries on the Bible Calvin exhibits real concern for the historical setting of the writings and seeks to arrive at the histori-

---

or be corrupted by man's impudence." Cf. John Calvin, *Institution de la religion Chrétienne*, ed. J. Pannier (Paris, 1936–39), 1:63. Also cf. Latin edition (1559), *OS* 3:63.

[169]4.8.9.

[170]*CR* 52:383.

[171]*CR* 25:356: "Adde quod non iam ex coniecturis iudicat quid facturi sint, sed diserte exprimit se certo scire: haud dubie quia spiritus, canticum dictando, simul etiam quid facturi essent docuit."

CR 40:530: "Primo res ipsa ostendit, Danielem non loquutum esse ex proprio sensu, sed dictatum fuisse a spiritu sancto quidquid protulit."

CR 40:531: "Hoc igitur iam magnum est, et non poenitendi fructus, ubi certo cognoscimus Danielem fuisse duntaxat organum spiritus sancti, neque proprio instinctu quidquam in medium protulisse."

CR 28:647: "Now as for the first, note that this word of scripture means that Moses was not the author of the Law or of the Canticle, but that he was only the writer or scribe under the mouth of God; just as a secretary will write what he has been told to write: thus notably it is here made clear that Moses wrote what he received from God, and not what was forged in his own mind."

CR 33:25: "But let's take something about which there can be no doubt, and that is to know that the Holy Spirit dictated this book for this usage."

CR 47:8: "Sic ergo quatuor evangelistis dictavit quod scriberent, ut distributis inter ipsos partibus corpus unum integrum absolveret." Also cf. *CR* 52:383.

1.18.3: "Antequam tamen respondeam, monitos iterum volo lectores, cavillum hoc non in me sed in spiritum sanctum torqueri, qui certe hanc sancto viro Iob confessionem dictavit."

4.8.6: "His simul accesserunt historiae, quae et ipsae prophetarum sunt lucubrationes, sed dictante spiritu sancto compositae."

[172]Cf. Warfield, *Calvin and Calvinism*, pp. 60ff. Doumergue holds that such words as "scribe," "amanuensis," and "mouth of God" are picture words and not scientific theological formulas in the seventeenth-century sense. (*Jean Calvin, les hommes et les choses de son temps*, 4:73.)

[173]*CR* 6:109, 110: "As it is contained for us in the Holy Scriptures" (In scripturis sanctis, quibus continetur).

cal sense. This factor has been recognized by biblical scholars.[174] He generally refuses to push the meaning of the text to make it fit some particular theory of his own.[175] He examines with objectivity the problems of authorship.[176]

In his exposition of the biblical material Calvin contends that he is concerned with the meaning and not with the words.[177] He exhibits a freedom in dealing with the material which points away from any rigid theory of dictation. Here are a few examples.[178] In commenting on Matthew 27:9 he notes that the writer uses Jeremiah where he should have put the name Zechariah.[179] Calvin admits that he does not know how this came about and adds, "I do not trouble myself to inquire." On Mark 1:2 Calvin sees no objection to changing the words of Malachi to make the meaning clearer.[180] On Matthew 27:51 he admits that Luke inverts the order: "The evangelists as we have seen are not careful to mark every hour with exactness."[181] There is a similar statement on Luke 24:12.[182] On Ezekiel 12:4–6 he ventures to criticize Ezekiel's style.[183] In his commentary on Romans there are several statements which are contrary to any theory of literal dictation.[184]

In principle at least, Calvin condemned the use of the Bible as a scientific textbook. In commenting on Genesis 1:16 he stated that Moses did not write either as a philosopher or as a scientist.

> Moses makes two great luminaries, but astronomers prove by conclusive reasons that the star of Saturn, which on account of its great distance appears least of all, is greater than the moon. Here lies the difference; Moses wrote in a popular style things which, without instruction, all ordinary persons endued with common sense are able to understand; but astronomers investigate with great labor whatever the sagacity of the human mind can comprehend. Nevertheless, this study

---

[174]Cf. A. J. Baumgartner, *Calvin hébraïsant et interprète de l'Ancien Testament* (Paris: Fischbacher, 1889), pp. 39ff.

[175]E.g., *CR* 23:15. Cf. Baumgartner, op. cit., p. 37.

[176]*CR* 25:421ff., Argument to the Book of Joshua; 55:5ff., Argument to the Book of Hebrews; 55:441ff., Argument to the Book of 2 Peter.

[177]*CR* 55:40; 45:84.

[178]For supplementary treatment cf. Gauteron, *L'autorité de la Bible d'après Calvin*, pp. 68ff.; Doumergue, *Jean Calvin, les hommes et les choses de son temps*, 4:76ff.

[179]*CR* 45:749.

[180]*CR* 45:108.

[181]*CR* 45:782.

[182]*CR* 45:800.

[183]*CR* 40:256.

[184]*CR* 49:65, "Legis quidem nomen improprie fidei tribuitur: sed hoc *apostoli* sensum minime obscurat"; *CR* 49:137: "Legem spiritus improprie vocat Dei spiritum, qui animas nostras Christi sanguine adspergit, non tantum ut a peccati labe amundet, 'quoad reatum: sed in veram puritatem sanctificet.' "

is not to be reprobated, nor this science to be condemned, because some fanatic persons are wont boldly to reject whatever is unknown to them. For astronomy is not only pleasant, but also very useful to be known; it cannot be denied that this art unfolds the admirable wisdom of God.[185]

He appreciated the work of the scientist; and so far as I know, he did not condemn scientists such as Copernicus. His own knowledge of current scientific investigations appears to have been scant, and in general he seems to have accepted the popular views of the day.[186]

In sum, the evidence concerning Calvin's doctrine of inspiration is not clear-cut. He was certainly convinced that the Bible is the word of God. The discrepancies which he notes appear to be rather incidental and limited to matters of history, chronology, and style. So far as I know, Calvin never wavered from the conviction that all passages involving ethical and religious teachings were the word of God. He never, to my knowledge, sought to avoid the difficulties which some passages raised on the basis of their lack of inspiration. Yet Warfield seems to go too far in his assertions that Calvin admitted no errors in the scriptures. He is well aware of instances in which Calvin points out chronological discrepancies in the Gospels, but he adds that this is no error, since Calvin knew that the writer never intended to give the chronological facts anyway.[187] It seems to me that there is more freedom in his use of scripture than either Warfield or Seeberg admits. On the other hand, P. Barth and others of his school of thought have placed too much emphasis on the instances in which Calvin points out some discrepancy and have overlooked the fact that in actual practice Calvin used the Bible as though it were verbally inspired.[188]

In assessing Calvin's doctrine of scripture, especially the doctrine

---

[185]*CR* 23:22. Cf. *CR* 31:806; 45:82; 49:429.

[186]A. Lecerf maintains that Calvin's teaching has promoted scientific research. ("De l'impulsion donnée par le Calvinisme à l'étude des sciences physiques et naturelles," *Bulletin de la Société de l'Histoire du Protestantisme français* 84 (1935), 192–201. Cf. P. Imbart de la Tour, *Calvin et l'Institution Chrétienne,* vol. 4 of *Les origines de la Réforme* (Paris: Firmin-Didot & Cie., n.d.), p. 177. He claims that Calvin had little appreciation for science.

[187]Warfield, *Calvin and Calvinism,* p. 65.

[188]The consensus of Calvin scholars favors a freer interpretation of Calvin's doctrine of inspiration than Warfield or Seeberg admits. Cf. Doumergue, *Jean Calvin, les hommes et les choses de son temps,* 4:76ff.; Gauteron, op. cit., pp. 68ff.; Peter Barth, "Calvin," *RGG* 1:1430.

Jacques Pannier, "L'autorité de l'Écriture sainte d'après Calvin," *Revue de Théologie et des Questions Religieuses* (1906), p. 377: "It isn't that Calvin had accepted the form of the 'Consensus Helveticus' of 1656, or the theopneusty of the nineteenth century; he knew very well that there could be textual errors but only in unimportant details, and never in regard to questions of faith. As for religious foundation, we can trust unreservedly in the Holy Scripture."

of inspiration, it is critically important to accept Calvin as a six-teenth-century theologian for whom today's questions had not been raised and hence are not answered in his theology.

Another important factor in Calvin's use of the Bible was his understanding of its unity. It is clear that he was convinced of the substantial unity of the Bible. "The covenant of all the fathers is so far from differing substantially from ours that it is the very same; it only varies in the administration."[189] Again he stated in a sermon:

> It is true that all that which was written by the Spirit through Moses belongs to the law, and what the prophets have left to us and what has been finally completed in the gospel contains only one substance: and the Bible is large enough: but with so much there God has given one certain purpose, in order that we be not distracted or lost, and that we not inquire after much where it is necessary to strain ourselves.[190]

In establishing the unity of the Old and New Testaments, Calvin was concerned to point out that they were the same in the hope of immortality, salvation by the grace of God, and the mediatorship of Jesus Christ.[191]

Yet he also found a progressive movement in the Bible. In the New Testament earthly blessings do not have the same place as they do in the Old Testament; reality replaces the figures; spiritual doctrine replaces literalism; love takes the place of fear; and universalism is taught instead of particularism.[192]

The fullness of God's revelation is not equally present in all portions of the Bible. God "descends to us by his word. This, at length, was fully accomplished in the person of Christ."[193] Again Calvin writes:

> Therefore, in the beginning, when the first promise was given to Adam, it was like the kindling of some feeble sparks. Subsequent accessions caused a considerable enlargement of the light, which continued to increase more and more, and diffused its splendour through a wide extent, till at length, every cloud being dissipated, Christ, the Sun of Righteousness, completely illuminated the whole world.[194]

As noted earlier, he regarded Jesus Christ as the true interpreter of the law. All of this indicates a belief in a progressive revelation.

Furthermore, the fact that Calvin did not comment on some of the books of the Bible has surely some significance. It is very difficult to

---

[189] 2.10.2. Cf. *CR* 10:154.
[190] *CR* 26:386.
[191] 2.10.2ff.
[192] 2.11.1ff.
[193] *CR* 23:471.
[194] 2.10.20. Cf. *CR* 33:720; 50:219–220.

explain his failure to comment on such books as Chronicles, Song of Solomon, Proverbs, Ecclesiastes, and Revelation as accidental or due to the brevity of his life. Unquestionably in practice he regarded some portions of the Bible as being of far greater importance than other portions.[195]

Calvin also insisted that the Bible should be interpreted according to the analogy of faith.[196] This is another way of saying that biblical interpretation must take place within the environment of the responsible Christian community. Calvin designed his own *Institutes* as a handbook for biblical study,[197] but he interpreted the Bible in the light of the Apostles' Creed.

Yet it must also be stated that he sometimes used the Bible as though it were all of one cloth. He did not always observe his own distinctions between the Old and New Testaments or his assertion that the fullness of God's revelation was to be found in Jesus Christ. For example, he did not really face the problem raised by the incompatibility of the rules of war as listed in the Old Testament with the revelation of God in Jesus Christ.[198] Calvin's conviction that Jesus Christ is the author of all of scripture precluded an adequate recognition of the disparity between portions of the Old Testament and the Gospels.[199] This fact, it seems to me, is of considerable importance, for Calvin attempted to apply the Bible in its totality to the Genevan

---

[195]In the *Institutes*—according to Henri Clavier in *Études sur le Calvinisme* (Paris: Fischbacher, 1936), Appendix 4—Calvin quoted the New Testament 3,098 times and the Old Testament 1,755 times. He quoted most frequently from the following: Psalms 457, Romans 396, Matthew 352, John 340, 1 Corinthians 286, Acts 233, and Genesis 190 times (pp. 86–87). [These figures should be checked in the light of the Library of Christian Classics edition (1960). See John H. Leith, "John Calvin—Theologian of the Bible," *Interpretation,* July 1971.]

[196]Jean Calvin, *Épitre au roi,* ed. Jacques Pannier (Paris: Fischbacher, 1927), p. 7.

[197]*OS* 3:5–6.

[198]*CR* 24:353–354; 25:317. Cf. *CR* 27:616ff.

[199]*CR* 10:154: "When we speak of the scriptures, it is fitting to distinguish between the Old and New Testaments, between the Law and the Prophets. For although the whole comes from Jesus Christ, inasmuch as he has always been the sovereign angel and the principal ambassador by whom God has communicated with man, common usage does not say that Christ said this through Moses, or that through David, but rather simply [that] God [spoke these things]. The reason is that Christ was not yet made manifest at that time. For that reason we must believe, according to the doctrine of St. Paul, that all the holy prophets have spoken through the spirit of Jesus Christ; and, according to the doctrine of St. Paul, that he was the leader of the people of Israel and even that the Law was given by his hands. Still, following the general style of scripture by citing something from the Old Testament we will not say that Jesus Christ said this through the mouth of Isaiah or Moses, but we will say that God said it, or rather, the Spirit of God. In the New Testament there is another reason. For Jesus Christ, coming into the world, has been commanded by the Father and Master to announce all the truth to us. Thus, he must be followed and called by us the author of all the doctrine of the apostles, as St. Paul said that he speaks in him."

community. Although it is possible to minimize unduly the distinctions which Calvin did make in regard to the scriptures, it is clear that his theological method is sometimes guided by premises which ignored even his own distinctions.

Let us now turn to the question of biblical authority. In theory at least, Calvin denied that the Bible is authoritative simply because some person or some institution says it is. Nor is it authoritative because it is possible to establish its authority by rational argument. It becomes authoritative only when the individual is persuaded that God is the author of it, and this persuasion must be the result of the *testimonium Spiritus Sancti.* [200] "The external word is of no avail by itself unless animated by the power of the Spirit. . . . All power of action, then, resides in the Spirit himself, and thus all praise ought to be entirely referred to God alone."[201] It is preposterous to try to produce sound faith in the scripture by disputation, for the Word never gains credit in the hearts of human beings until it is confirmed by the internal testimony of the Holy Spirit.[202] Consequently, biblical authority is not located in any external book but in a personal experience in which the Book and the Holy Spirit concur.

Yet Calvin's doctrine must not be confused with any autonomous subjectivism. He vigorously refutes any notion which suggests that the Christian ever receives a revelation by the Spirit which is beyond or contradictory to the Bible. There is an "inviolable union," a "mutual connection" which God has established between his word and his Spirit.[203] The testimony of the Holy Spirit does not give new knowledge but, rather, the conviction that God is personally addressing the Christian in his word. This experience is the existential moment for the one who stands in the presence of God's word.[204] Cramer has written:

> Calvin does not, it is true, tell us in so many words precisely what this *testimonium Spiritus Sancti* is, but it is easy to gather it from the whole

---

[200]Quervain, *Calvin, sein Lehren und Kämpfen,* p. 25: "Only in faith can the divinity of scripture be spoken. Only to him who believes, it testifies itself to be God's Word. And therefore an apologetic certain of victory would be far worse even than the dispute of the scholastics—which Calvin fights—because it would testify of a far narrower vision. . . . Not speculation but faith, not demonstration of God but recognition of God in Christ Jesus, that is the result."

[201]*CR* 40:61–62.

[202]1.7.4.

[203]1.9.1–3; *CR* 33:720.

[204]Warfield's very careful study of this subject indicates that the testimony of the Holy Spirit is part of Calvin's general doctrine of the function of the Holy Spirit in eliciting faith (*Calvin and Calvinism,* pp. 70ff.). This is a very able study of the subject.

discussion. He is thinking of the Holy Spirit, who, as the Spirit of our adoption as children, leads us to say Amen to the Word which the Father speaks in the Holy Scriptures to his children.[205]

This doctrine does not supplant the function of reason. It does not, for example, decide the matter of the canon.[206] Calvin himself makes use of rational proofs to aid in establishing belief in the scriptures. He only insists that reason is insufficient to convince one that the scripture is the word of God. However, once the conviction has been established, "we shall then derive great assistance from things which before were not sufficient to establish the certainty of it in our minds."[207]

In the preface to the Geneva Bible Calvin attempted to put together the living Lordship of Jesus Christ and the authority of the Bible. This double sovereignty is one because the one thing to search for in the Bible is Jesus Christ,[208] who is the living Lord of all of life.[209] Yet Calvin himself was not always successful in putting together the living Lordship of Jesus Christ and the sovereignty of his revelation in the Bible.

The formal allegiance which the citizens of Geneva were asked to swear to the Bible almost inevitably led to some sort of legalism.[210] While it would have been difficult to assert in more vigorous fashion than Calvin did the personal authority of the Bible, the principles which sometimes governed his theological method[211] and his tendency toward legalism continually obscured this basic truth.

This survey of the norms of the Christian life has not enabled us to pigeonhole Calvin's views. The evidence is varied. Yet it is clear that he was convinced that the living God personally confronts us in Jesus Christ, in the law, and in the Bible. This was the insight which gave power to his teaching. On the other hand, it is also clear

---

[205]J. Cramer, *Nieuwe Bijdragen op het gebied van Godgeleerdheid en Wijsbegeerte,* pp. 122–123, as quoted by Warfield, op. cit., p. 77, note 55.

[206]Warfield, op. cit., pp. 90ff.; Doumergue, *Jean Calvin, les hommes et les choses de son temps,* 4:67ff.

[207]1.8.1.

[208]*CR* 9:815: "Here, in sum, is what we must look for in the scriptures. It is to recognize Jesus Christ and the infinite riches which are contained in him and which are offered to us from God the Father through him. For when we examine the Law and the Prophets closely, we will not find a single word which doesn't transform us and lead there. Indeed, all the treasures of wisdom and intelligence are hidden in him. There can be no question of another goal or direction, unless we want, by deliberate design, to turn away from the light of truth to lose our way in the darkness of lies."

[209]*CR* 9:807.

[210]Cf. *CR* 22:85.

[211]Cf. p. 56 in this chapter.

that the law and the Bible sometimes became, in Calvin's hands, a substitute for the living Lordship of Jesus Christ and the personal confrontation of God instead of the context in which this living relationship takes place.

C. Repentance

Our inability to glorify God stems from our bondage to sin, which has not only distorted our knowledge of God but also crippled and imprisoned our total personality. Deliverance from the shackles of sin is a prerequisite of the Christian life. This deliverance, according to Calvin, has been accomplished by Jesus Christ, who

> has been sent to us to the end that we be restored to the image of God. Truly through his death and passion he has reconciled us to God his Father; he has poured out his blood to the end that we be washed of all our sins and that we be freed from condemnation to eternal death. He has made satisfaction for us, offering himself in sacrifice, so that when we come to Jesus Christ to obtain remission from our sins, we are esteemed righteous before God through his gratuitous goodness, so much that he does not regard us for what we are, but removes all our faults; and does not forbid us from having agreeable things as his children, although we be poor sinners: we obtain that benefit through Jesus Christ. But there is a second benefit: it is that we are to be sanctified through his Holy Spirit. If, therefore, we desire to be received into the mercy of God through the death and passion of his only Son, and if our sins are not to be imputed to us as much as he has made acquittal and payment for them, and if we know he is given to us for sanctification to the end that we be governed through his Holy Spirit, therefore, when we wish to begin to rule our lives well, it is necessary for us to renounce ourselves and to fight against that which is in our nature.[212]

Salvation, therefore, consists of pardon and sanctification, and it is available to all those who are united with Jesus Christ by faith through the work of the Holy Spirit.[213] Our chief concern in this study is with the gift of sanctification, by which the image of God is gradually restored and which manifests itself in daily life in the exercises of self-denial, cross bearing, and meditation on the future life. Yet it must be constantly borne in mind that the pardon of sins is the prerequisite and milieu in which sanctification takes place.

Calvin usually called this process by which the image of God is restored "repentance," though he sometimes used the term "sanc-

---

[212]*CR* 51:612–613.

[213]3.1.2.

tification," as in the above definition. Repentance is a far more inclusive term for Calvin than for later Reformed theology. The Westminster Assembly, for example, sharply distinguished repentance and sanctification.[214] Calvin included under repentance the whole process by which a sinner turns to God and progresses in holiness.

In the *Institutes* of 1536 Calvin deals with repentance in the section on the False Sacraments of Rome. His own treatment of the subject is not so extensive as in later editions, and he draws heavily on Lutheran thought. He notes that some learned men have simply divided repentance into two parts: mortification and vivification.[215] Others have distinguished two kinds of repentance in the scriptures.[216] The one is legal repentance, which is produced by fear of the divine wrath, as was the case with Cain, Saul, and Judas; but this is only the antechamber to hell. Evangelical repentance is seen in those who have been not only distressed by their sins but also raised from their depression, reinvigorated by a confidence in the divine mercy, and converted to the Lord. In all of these observations Calvin recognizes some truth, but none of them fully satisfied him. For one thing, this definition tends to mingle faith and repentance. Calvin insisted that these two doctrines must be kept wholly distinct but never separated. They are perpetually and indissolubly united, but never confounded.[217] Positively, Calvin defines repentance in the following way: "Repentance is the mortification of our flesh and the old man which a true and sincere fear of God works in us."[218]

In the Catechism of 1537 there is a much more positive formulation of doctrine. Here again he notes that repentance is always joined with faith, and he goes on to develop the doctrine as follows:

> For penitence signifies conversion through which, the perversity of the world left behind, we turn again to the way of the Lord. . . .
>   The effect of this penitence depends on our regeneration, which consists of two parts, in the mortification of our flesh, which means the corruption engendered in us, and in the spiritual vivification through which the nature of man is restored to integrity. Therefore it is necessary for us to keep before us all our lives that, being dead to

---

[214]Westminster Shorter Catechism (Questions 35 and 87) and Westminster Confession of Faith (Sections 11, "Of Justification," and 13, "Of Sanctification") [*The Constitution of the Presbyterian Church (U.S.A.)*, Part I, *Book of Confessions* (New York and Atlanta: Office of the General Assembly, 1983)].

[215]*OS* 1:170. Here the reference is to Melanchthon's *Loci Communes* of 1521.

[216]*OS* 1:170–171.

[217]*OS* 1:171.

[218]Ibid. (*Institutes*, 1536).

sin and to ourselves, we live in Christ and his righteousness. And since this regeneration is never accomplished as long as we remain in the prison of this mortal body, it is necessary that the longing for penitence be perpetual with us even unto death.[219]

The Catechism of 1545 puts it more briefly. Repentance is "dissatisfaction with and a hatred of sin and a love of righteousness, proceeding from the fear of God, which things lead to self-denial and mortification of the flesh, so that we give ourselves up to the guidance of the Spirit of God and frame all the actions of our life to the obedience of the Divine will."[220]

The definition we may take as basic is that which is found in the *Institutes* of 1559. It was first written in the *Institutes* of 1539 and is apparently a rewriting of the definition which had appeared in 1536. It is as follows: "Wherefore I conceive it may be justly defined to be 'a true conversion of our life to God, proceeding from a sincere and serious fear of God, and consisting in the mortification of our flesh and of the old man, and in the vivification of the Spirit.' "[221]

Calvin's exegetical and polemical writings abound in statements on repentance. We shall confine ourselves to three statements which will help to interpret the definitions given earlier. In his commentary on Isaiah 55:7 Calvin wrote:

By three forms of expression he describes the nature of repentance, first, "Let the wicked man forsake his way"; secondly, "The unrighteous man his thoughts"; thirdly, "Let him return to the Lord." Under the word "way" he includes the whole course of life, and accordingly demands that they bring forth the fruits of righteousness as witnesses of their newness of life. By adding the word "thoughts" he intimates that we must not only correct outward actions but must begin with the heart; for although in the opinion of men we appear to change our manner of life for the better, yet we shall have made little proficiency if the heart be not changed. This repentance embraces a change of the whole man; for in man we view inclinations, purposes, and then works. The works of men are visible, but the root within is concealed. This must first be changed, that it may afterward yield fruitful works. We must first wash away from the mind all uncleanness and conquer wicked inclinations, that outward testimonies may afterward be added. And if any man boast that he has been changed and yet live as he was wont to do, it will be vain boasting; for both are requisite, conversion of the heart and change of life.[222]

---

[219]*OS* 1:394–395.
[220]*CR* 6:49–50.
[221]3.3.5.
[222]*CR* 37:288–289.

In his *Antidote to the Articles of Paris,* Calvin wrote:

> The Spirit of God calls us to repentance everywhere, in the law, the prophets, and the gospel; at the same time he also defines what he understands by the terms when he orders us to be renewed in our hearts, to be circumcised to the Lord, to be washed, and to cease from wicked pursuits, to loose the bond of iniquity bound within us, to rend our hearts and not our garments, to put off the old man, to renounce our own desires, and to be renewed in the image of God; besides enumerating, as the fruits of repentance, acts of charity and the exercises of a pious and holy life.[223]

Commenting on Acts 20:21, Calvin makes repentance coextensive with his treatment of the Christian life in the *Institutes:* "Therefore, the doctrine of repentance contains a rule of good life; it requires the denial of ourselves, the mortifying of our flesh, and meditating on the heavenly life."[224]

On the basis of those statements it is clear that Calvin did not limit repentance to the experience of terror which one feels in the presence of the wrath of God. In a general sense he defined repentance as conversion to God which is coextensive with the whole of life, that is, penetrating into every area of human existence and extending through all of life.

He observes that the Hebrew for "repentance" denotes conversion or return, whereas the Greek means conversion or change of mind. Repentance, he feels, comprehends both ideas: "That, forsaking ourselves, we should turn to God, and laying aside our old mind, should assume a new one."[225] By using the term "conversion," Calvin requires a transformation of life in its totality.[226] This transformation of life is essential for fellowship with God. God seeks us to associate himself with us, but holiness must be the bond of this union.[227]

Repentance is essentially a matter of the heart. It involves a conversion in the inmost being of a person. "Repentance is an inward matter that has its seat in the heart and soul, but afterward yields its fruits in a change of life."[228] Fasting and other exercises, Calvin admitted, may at times be useful, but they are always aids and never the thing itself.[229]

As repentance extends inwardly to one's inmost soul, so it extends

---

[223]*CR* 7:10–11.
[224]*CR* 48:462.
[225]3.3.5.
[226]3.3.6.
[227]3.6.2.
[228]*CR* 45:118. Cf. *CR* 26:375; 37:586; 43:254; 48:51, 52; 49:31; 3.3.6.
[229]*CR* 26:672.

chronologically throughout one's life. The Anabaptists and Jesuits were singled out for condemnation because they limited repentance to certain exercises, whereas it should be coextensive with life.[230] "This work of God is not perfected the same day it is begun in us, but it increases by little and little, and by daily increments as by degrees is brought to perfection."[231] "There still remains in a regenerate man a fountain of evil, continually producing irregular desires which allure and stimulate him to the commission of sin."[232] On this point Calvin stands in opposition both to the Roman Catholic doctrine and to the Anabaptists. Even Augustine does not give the same emphatic sound on this point.

> Between him [Augustine] and us, this difference may be discovered— that while he concedes that believers, as long as they inhabit a mortal body, are so bound by concupiscence that they cannot but feel irregular desires, yet he ventures not to call this disease by the name of "sin," but, content with designating it by the appellation of infirmity, teaches that it only becomes sin in cases where either action or consent is added to the conception or apprehension of the mind, that is, where the will yields to the first impulse of appetite.[233]

Calvin, on the contrary, maintains that all desires opposed to the divine law are sin. In the 1559 edition Calvin adds a citation from Augustine which gives support to this viewpoint.

The matter points up one of the most profound insights of Luther and Calvin: the heinousness of sin. They understood, as few have, the absolute character of the divine claim on human life. "Since all the powers of our soul ought to be thus occupied by the love of God, it is evident that the precept is not fulfilled by those who receive into their hearts the least desire, or admit into their minds any thought, which may draw them aside from the love of God into vanity."[234] It is one of the great achievements of Calvin and Luther that they neither scaled down the absoluteness of the divine claim on human life to meet human ability, nor minimized the incapacity of fallen human beings. This fact produced the distinctive theology of the Reformation.

The regenerate person is constantly at war against the forces and personages of sin, and the struggle continues until death.[235] Because we do not arrive at perfection in this life, "it behoves us to make

---

[230] 3.3.2.
[231] *CR* 49:108. Cf. *CR* 47:308; 49:312; 50:493; 55:393; 3.3.10–14.
[232] 3.3.10. Also, *CR* 55:393.
[233] 3.3.10.
[234] 3.3.11. Cf. 3.12.1.
[235] 3.3.20.

continual advances; and being entangled in vices, we have need to strive against them every day."[236]

It is difficult to determine the exact relationship of death to the struggles of the regenerate person. It is clear that death marks the end of the struggle.[237] Beyond this fact, however, the details of the relationship are somewhat obscure. A passage in *Psychopannychia* describes this relationship in language which has a Platonic overtone.[238] Death is here described as deliverance from the body, which at best served a utilitarian purpose for the self and at worst was a restriction of the self and a temptation of the self away from its true destiny. There is a basis in Calvin's own writings for the opinion of later Calvinists who regard bodily functions, instincts, impulses, and desires as evil and a hindrance to, not an integral dimension of, the goodness of the person. Nevertheless, such statements must be read in the light of the Hebraic elements in Calvin's thought.[239] On this basis of the total picture it seems best to conclude that while death marks the end of corruption of sin in the regenerate person, it does not mark the end of progress in the Christian life. The advancement in the grace of Christ extends at least to the resurrection of the flesh.[240]

Thus far we have dealt with repentance as "conversion to God" which extends to the inmost being of a person and throughout all of life. More specifically, Calvin defined repentance in terms of the reconstruction of the image of God: "In one word I apprehend repentance to be regeneration, the end of which is the restoration of the Divine image within us; which was defaced, and almost obliterated, by the transgression of Adam."[241] The reconstruction of the image of God is the achievement of the process we call Christian life and is one of the most frequent notes in Calvin's theology. The

---

[236] 3.3.14.

[237] 3.3.9.

[238] *CR* 5:196: "We are better taught by the Sacred Writings. The body, which decays, weighs down the soul and, confining it within an earthly habitation, greatly limits its perceptions. If the body is the prison of the soul, if the earthly habitation is a kind of fetters, what is the state of the soul when set free from this prison, when loosed from these fetters? Is it not restored to itself, and, as it were, made complete, so that we may truly say that all which it gains is so much lost to the body? Whether they will or not, they must be forced to confess that when we put off the load of the body, the war between the spirit and the flesh ceases. In short, the mortification of the flesh is the quickening of the spirit." (This was written in 1534. In general, this Platonic note is more pronounced in the early Calvin.) It is appropriate to relate this passage to Calvin's facing of his own death. The separation of soul and body was not for him the wrenching experience which many Christians have believed.

[239] "The image of God extends to the body" (1.15.3; *CR* 23:26–27); "The body must be saved" (*CR* 49:560; 3.6.3); "Resurrection of the body" (3.25.1ff.).

[240] *CR* 52:9–10.

[241] 3.3.9. Cf. 1.15.4; *CR* 51:208–209.

renewal of life or regeneration of the spirit is nothing else than the restoration of the divine image.[242]

The words Calvin used to describe the Christian life point back to some previous state. *Reparatio, regeneratio, instauratio, reformatio, renovatio,* and *restitutio* all indicate that the Christian life is a redoing of something that has been done. On occasions, this work of repairing, renewal, restoration is spoken of as creation. At first sight this is something of a contradiction, but on closer examination the word "creation" does not indicate a complete break in the continuity of the old person and the new person. Redemption is renewal, not the substitution of one person for another. The word "creation" underscores the fact that this work is of God and not of humans. Because repentance is a kind of second creation, it follows that it is not in human power.[243] The point is that the grace of repentance does not create a new person but renews a person who has been broken by sin.

Calvin defines the image of God in terms of the perfection of human beings:

> The image of God includes all the excellence in which the nature of man surpasses all the other species of animals. This term, therefore, denotes the integrity which Adam possessed, when he was endued with a right understanding, when he had affections regulated by reason, and all his senses governed in proper order, and when, in the excellency of his nature, he truly resembled the excellence of his Creator.[244]

This original perfection embraced two dimensions or relationships. The one was human and the other divine. Human beings "possessed reason, understanding, prudence, and judgment, not only for the government of [their] life on earth but to enable [them] to ascend even to God and eternal felicity."[245]

We cannot get a complete definition of this image by looking at ourselves, for it has been defaced, and an unbridgeable gulf separates us from the original state of Adam.[246] "Since the image of God has been destroyed in us by the fall, we may judge from its restoration what it originally had been."[247] Thus Calvin bases his definition of the content of image principally on those passages in which Paul

---

[242]*CR* 7:470; 28:673; 33:491; 48:111, 466, 568–569; 49:128, 560; 52:121; 55:71–72, 219, 221, 331, 352.

[243]*CR* 40:246, 446; 48:111.

[244]1.15.3.

[245]1.15.8.

[246]1.15.4.

[247]*CR* 23:26.

describes the regeneration of the Christian. It is axiomatic with him that those things which hold the principal place in the reconstruction of the image held the same place in the creation of it in the beginning. On the basis of what Paul has to say chiefly in Colossians 3:10 and Ephesians 4:24, Calvin summarizes the material in this way:

> Now, we may see what Paul comprehends in this renovation. In the first place, he mentions knowledge, and in the next place, sincere righteousness and holiness; whence we infer, that in the beginning the image of God was conspicuous in the light of the mind, in the rectitude of the heart, and in the soundness of all the parts of our nature.[248]

The image is partly visible in the regenerate, but it will only obtain its full glory in heaven.[249]

More specifically, we can see what the image of God means in Christ, who is the most perfect image of God.[250] Our Lord Jesus Christ is the living image of God[251] and we must be transfigured into that image.[252]

The principal seat of the image is the heart and mind or the soul and its faculties, but it extends over the whole person.[253]

> Thus the chief seat of the image was in the mind and heart, where it was eminent; yet there was no part of him [Adam] in which some scintillation of it did not shine forth. . . . In the mind perfect intelligence flourished and reigned, uprightness attended as its companion, and all the senses were prepared and molded for due obedience to reason; and in the body there was a suitable correspondence with this internal order.[254]

The extension of the image to the body is made emphatic in the exposition of 1 Corinthians 15:50:

> What I have said as to bearing the image of the heavenly Adam means this—that we must be renewed in respect of our bodies, inasmuch as our bodies, being liable to corruption, cannot inherit God's incorruptible kingdom. Hence there will be no admission for us into the kingdom of Christ otherwise than by Christ's renewing us after his own image. Flesh and blood, however, we must understand according to the condition in which they at present are, for our flesh will be a

---

[248]1.15.4. For similar passages cf. *CR* 23:26; 51:208–209; 52:121.

[249]1.15.4.

[250]Ibid. Cf. Peter Barth, *Das Problem der natürlichen Theologie bei Calvin,* p. 32. He writes: "The true image of God faces us only in Christ."

[251]*CR* 26:128; 48:464.

[252]*CR* 58:181.

[253]1.15.3.

[254]*CR* 23:26–27.

participant in the glory of God, but it will be as renewed and quickened by the Spirit of Christ.[255]

This point is important in the light of charges that Calvin held to a Platonic doctrine of soul and body.[256] Some of his early writings do contain passages which are unquestionably Platonic in content.[257] He speaks repeatedly of the prison of the body, but in general this emphasis is more apparent in his early writings than in his later works.[258] The charge of Platonism must be balanced by statements extending the image to the body, which assert not only the resurrection of the body but also the salvation of the body as well as the soul.[259]

The image of God means that God and human beings stand over against each other. They correspond to each other, but they are not the same. This is to say that human beings are made for fellowship with God but that they are not God. The image of God in human beings is God's creation, that is, origination out of nothing. Calvin fiercely opposed the notion that this image was any sort of transfusion of the divine essence. He felt that he saw this very heresy in both Servetus and Osiander.[260]

The image of God, when understood in a structural sense, is not an end in itself. It is rather a means to fellowship with God. When humankind alienated itself from God, the image of God within it was destroyed.[261] The restoration of the image is the renewal of fellowship with God. Insofar as the image is renewed within us, we have eyes prepared to see God.[262] We have been created in the image of God so that we can know God and give ourselves fully to him. "For we are created in the image of God so that we may have reason and intelligence: and to what should we apply such a gift, if it is not to know God and to give ourselves fully to him?"[263]

The question can be legitimately asked whether this restoration of the image of God by Christ is mere restoration. At its completion, is the redeemed person further along than Adam was at the begin-

---

[255]*CR* 49:560.

[256]E.g., Schulze, *Meditatio futurae vitae.*

[257]Especially *Psychopannychia.*

[258]Cf. Gloede, *Theologia naturalis bei Calvin,* p. 28.

[259]3.6.3.

[260]1.15.5. Professor R. H. Bainton concludes that the doctrine of man was the focus of Calvin's opposition to Servetus. [See Roland H. Bainton, *Hunted Heretic: The Life and Death of Michael Servetus, 1511–1553* (Boston: Beacon Press, 1953).]

[261]*CR* 28:488; 2.1.5.

[262]*CR* 55:331.

[263]*CR* 26:176.

ning? The answer is yes, for Calvin did regard the condition of the
regenerate person as superior to that of Adam. There is a far richer
and more powerful manifestation of divine grace in redemption than
in the first creation.[264] We are not only born sons of Adam, but we
are also the brothers of angels and members of Christ.[265] Again
Calvin writes: "The condition that we obtain through Christ is
greatly superior to the lot of the first human being, because a living
soul was conferred on Adam in his own name and in that of his
posterity, but Christ has procured for us the Spirit, who is life."[266]
Göhler contends that this superiority of the second creation consists
in the formal advantage that the regenerate person is confirmed in
this state, whereas Adam was on probation.[267] This, however, seems
to be inadequate in the light of the above statements, which certainly
have a qualitative sound.

D. Mortification—Vivification: Self-Denial, Cross Bearing, Meditation on the Future Life

Repentance consists of two parts: mortification and vivification.[268]
The image of God is restored by the death of the old nature and the
vivification of the Spirit.[269] This division of repentance into two parts
was in Calvin's earliest edition of the *Institutes*, but it received more
amplification in later editions.[270] The doctrine becomes more positive
in the edition of 1559, where he makes clear that he does not agree
with those who define vivification chiefly in terms of contrition. He
added the following lines to the treatment of the subject which had
been carried over from the edition of 1536:

> These terms [mortification and vivification], provided they be rightly
> understood, are sufficiently adapted to express the nature of repent-
> ance; but when they explain vivification of that joy which the mind
> experiences after its perturbations and fears are allayed, I cannot

---

[264]*CR* 51:209. Also, *CR* 40:456; 49:558–559.

[265]*CR* 40:456.

[266]*CR* 49:558.

[267]Göhler, *Calvins Lehre von der Heiligung,* p. 32.

[268]3.3.3; *OS* 1:170. Calvin is probably indebted to Melanchthon's *Loci Communes* of 1521.

[269]*CR* 48:258, 307; 50:119; 51:29, 207, 612.

[270]Ritschl has made the charge that Calvin's doctrine of repentance in the 1536 *Institutes* is
essentially negative. This is true only in emphasis. Strathmann has shown that in outline the
later doctrine is present in the *Institutes* of 1536. Certainly the doctrine appears fully developed
in the Catechism of 1537. (A. Ritschl, *A Critical History of the Christian Doctrine of Justification and Reconciliation,* ed. and tr. H. R. Mackintosh and G. B. Macaulay [New York: Charles
Scribner's Sons, 1900], p. 192; H. Strathmann, "Die Entstehung der Lehre Calvins von der
Busse," in J. Bohatec, *Calvinstudien,* pp. 188ff.)

coincide with them; since it should rather signify an ardent desire and endeavour to live a holy and pious life, as though it were said, that a man dies to himself, that he may begin to live to God.[271]

Calvin devoted more space to mortification than to vivification, if an attempt is made to separate the two factors, but this does not mean that his doctrine is negative.

> Both these branches of repentance are effects of our participation of Christ. For if we truly partake of his death, our old man is crucified by its power, and the body of sin expires, so that the corruption of our former nature loses all its vigour. If we are partakers of his resurrection, we are raised by it to a newness of life, which corresponds with the righteousness of God.[272]

Mortification is not an end in itself. It is a means to vivification.

Mortification is essentially the destruction of the sinful corruption which has entered into humanity since the fall. It is not a curtailment of true humanity. Yet it is not enough simply to be displeased with oneself. There must be the positive vivification. By vivification Calvin means fundamentally a life in which the Spirit of God lives and rules. "The death of the flesh is the life of the Spirit. If the Spirit of God lives in us, let him govern our actions."[273] The life which the Spirit governs conforms to the will of God.

The example we are to follow in this process of mortification-vivification can be seen in Jesus Christ.

> The scripture recommends to us a twofold likeness to the death of Christ, that we are to be conformed to him in reproaches and troubles, and also that the old man being dead and extinct in us, we are to be renewed to a spiritual life (Phil. 3:10; Rom. 6:4). Yet Christ is not simply to be viewed as our example, when we speak of the mortification of the flesh; but it is by his Spirit that we are really made conformable to his death, so that it becomes effectual to the crucifying of our flesh.[274]

As Christ was raised to an incorruptible life, so must we be regenerated by the grace of God.[275] The process of repentance, therefore, must take place in communion with the example and life-giving Spirit of Jesus Christ.

---

[271] 3.3.3. Cf. *OS* 4:58, note 1. The editors of the *Opera Selecta* feel that this passage reveals the influence of Bucer, whereas the former treatment was Lutheran. This positive note, however, was present as early as the 1537 Catechism.
[272] 3.3.9.
[273] *CR* 50:256. Cf. *CR* 51:612, 616; 55:345.
[274] *CR* 55:270.
[275] *CR* 49:10.

In his exposition of the Christian life, Calvin lists self-denial, cross bearing, and meditation on the future life as specific aspects of the process we have defined as repentance. The emphasis here would appear to be weighted on the side of mortification, but on close examination it will appear that vivification is involved not only in meditation on the future life but also in cross bearing and self-denial. In order to interpret these concepts truly, we must keep in mind that vivification and mortification are dimensions of the same experience.

Mortification is used in two senses. It means self-denial, by which we renounce the lusts of the flesh and are renewed to obedience to God. It also means the afflictions by which we are stirred up to meditate on the termination of the present life. Calvin designates the first as inward mortification and the second as outward mortification. Both make us conform to Christ, the one directly and the other indirectly, so to speak.[276]

The first step in the Christian life is to depart from ourselves that we may apply all the vigor of our faculties to the service of the Lord.[277] Calvin was strongly convinced that this denial of self is absolutely essential for the Christian life. Even the philosophers who advocate virtue for its own sake display a marked arrogance. Christians have to do with God every moment of their lives. Consequently the whole orientation of personality must be toward God, not toward self. Where this self-denial takes place, Christ reigns. Where it does not take place, vices of all kinds creep in.[278]

Self-denial is the basis of true love of neighbor. It is the only possible basis for this love. "Unless you quit all selfish considerations, and, as it were, lay aside yourself, you will effect nothing in this duty."[279] The basis for this love of neighbor rests in two facts. First, we are not owners, fee simple, of the goods God has placed at our disposal. Rather, we are stewards of these goods; and we are members of a community which is like the human body; that is, every member must help every other member. In the second place human beings should be the objects of love, not because of any intrinsic human merit, but because of the image of God which is in them. "Say that he [a person in need] is unworthy of your making the smallest exertion on his account; but the image of God, by which he is recommended to you, deserves your surrender of yourself and all that you possess."[280] It is unmistakably clear that self-denial involves

---

[276]*CR* 50:55.
[277]3.7.1.
[278]3.7.2.
[279]3.7.5.
[280]3.7.6.

the positive function of love of neighbor, and it is on this positive function that Calvin's emphasis rests.[281] Christians must positively imagine themselves in the position of those who are in need and thus frame their actions.[282]

Self-denial, however, is principally related to God. Here it means full commitment to God. It means full dependence on God and confidence that God sustains and governs the destiny of human life. The consequence of such self-denial is that human beings will not feverishly attempt to find life's security and meaning in wealth, success, and other forms of human achievement. Calvin believed that life was possible only on this basis. When one calls to mind his experiences at Strasbourg in 1539, the following passage becomes strikingly autobiographical:

> The great necessity of this disposition will appear, if we consider the numerous accidents to which we are subject. Diseases of various kinds frequently attack us: at one time, the pestilence is raging; at another, we are cruelly harassed with the calamities of war; at another time, frost or hail, devouring the hopes of the year, produces sterility, which brings us to penury; a wife, parents, children, or other relatives, are snatched away by death; our dwelling is consumed by a fire; these are the events, on the occurrence of which, men curse this life . . . , reproach God. . . . But it behoves a believer, even in these events, to contemplate the clemency and truly paternal goodness of God.[283]

Self-denial, therefore, is more than a negative concept. It includes vivification as well as mortification. On the one side, there is the death of self-centeredness. On the other, there is the positive love of neighbor and full commitment of self to God.

A second branch of the Christian life is cross bearing, which is an essential part of the Christian warfare.[284] It has its divine sanction not only in the words of Jesus but also in his life, which was "nothing but a kind of perpetual cross."[285] We are partakers of the sufferings of Christ when we bear the cross.[286]

The cross is not a burden which is unjustly imposed on the Christian. God does not treat us rudely without cause, or because our enemies want us so afflicted, but because he knows that it is good for

---

[281]This is one of the points at which Schulze misunderstood Calvin in his work *Meditatio futurae vitae*, p. 12.

[282]3.7.6.

[283]3.7.10.

[284]*CR* 26:709; 44:483; 45:295, 411; 48:10; 49:160–161; 50:59; 52:211; 55:278.

[285]3.8.1.

[286]Ibid.

us.[287] Afflictions are not always signs of God's displeasure. He afflicts us on one side, but he helps us on the other.[288] We must always be persuaded that God does not send affliction on us unjustly.[289]

The cross is a means in the hands of God by which he purges his children from sin and defilement.

> It is indeed a singular consolation, calculated to mitigate the bitterness of the cross, when the faithful hear that by sorrows and tribulations they are sanctified for glory as Christ himself was; and hence they see a sufficient reason why they should lovingly kiss the cross rather than dread it.[290]

By afflictions God destroys the vices which are in fallen human beings.[291]

Calvin speaks of the cross in terms of discipline, chastisement, and persecution. As discipline the cross destroys pride. It reveals to us our extreme frailty.[292] God humbles us by affliction so that we will not put our trust in the world and thus be tied to things of earth.[293] The discipline of the cross also teaches us to rely on God alone. Realizing the insufficiency of our own lives, we transfer our confidence to God.[294] Finally, the cross teaches obedience and patience. Affliction brings forth the gift of patience and exercises it.[295] "By the cross they are also, I say, instructed to obedience; because they are thus taught to live, not according to their own inclination, but according to the will of God."[296]

The cross is likewise a means of chastisement. In every affliction we ought immediately to recollect the course of our past life.[297] God chastises us to warn us to repent.[298] Thus even the most bitter tribulation is an evidence of God's mercy and his continual effort to promote our salvation.[299] Unbelievers are only rendered more obstinate by God's chastisements; but believers, like ingenuous children, are led to repentance.[300]

---

[287]*CR* 33:74.
[288]*CR* 33:86.
[289]*CR* 35:147–148.
[290]*CR* 55:27.
[291]*CR* 33:69–70.
[292]3.8.2.
[293]*CR* 26:629–630. Cf. *CR* 33:68, 260, 380, 557.
[294]3.8.6.
[295]3.8.4. Cf. *CR* 49:271, 544; 55:212.
[296]3.8.4. Cf. *CR* 26:629–630; 34:366; 49:544.
[297]3.8.6.
[298]*CR* 35:146–147.
[299]3.8.6.
[300]Ibid.

The third type of cross is persecution, which Calvin interpreted in a very broad sense. It is "persecution for righteousness' sake, not only when we suffer in defence of the gospel, but also when we are molested in the vindication of any just cause."[301] Opposition to the falsehood of Satan and the protection of innocent people against the injuries of the wicked both constitute a cross. Yet these persecutions are very useful to the Christian, for they are exercises in piety and enable them to make progress in the Christian life.[302]

The cross must be borne willingly, or else it is not a cross. Our Lord was under no necessity of bearing a cross.[303] A burden becomes a cross only when we willingly accept it and use it in the light of God's revelation of his will in the scripture and in experience.

> Though God lays both on good and bad men the burden of the cross, yet unless they willingly bend their shoulders to it they are not said to bear the cross; for a wild and refractory horse cannot be said to admit his rider, though he carries him. The patience of the saints, therefore, consists in bearing willingly the cross which has been laid on them.[304]

Is Calvin's doctrine of cross bearing a form of stoic adjustment to the necessities of life? Calvin did not think so. For one thing he deduces the principal reason for bearing the cross from a consideration of the divine will.[305] The cross is one of the means God uses to prepare us for the life of fellowship with him for which we were created. Furthermore, cross bearing is not a blind hardness which runs roughshod over the tender emotions and sentiments of human life. Calvin condemned the "modern" Stoics who think it sinful not only to groan but even to experience sadness and solicitude.[306] Even Jesus experienced sorrow. Christians have nothing to do with an "iron-hearted philosophy." Only afflictions must not triumph over faith. In the midst of tears, faith must reign with confidence in God's goodness and with the sure hope that the salvation which is begun shall be carried to its conclusion.[307]

A third exercise of the Christian life is meditation on the future life.[308] Christians must habituate themselves to a contempt of the

---

[301] 3.8.7.
[302] *CR* 52:21; 55:172–173.
[303] 3.8.2.
[304] *CR* 45:481–482.
[305] 3.8.11.
[306] 3.8.9. Cf. *CR* 48:175; 50:28.
[307] In Calvin's letters many illustrations may be found of a triumphant faith in the midst of genuine sorrow, in particular, the letter which he wrote to the father of the boy who died in his home. *CR* 11:188ff.
[308] For supplementary treatment, see Chapter 4.

present life that they may thereby be excited to meditation on that which is to come.[309] Calvin felt that Christians were too much tied down to things of earth, and he sought to break this fascination by the use of the strongest language. "There is no medium between these two extremes; either the earth must become vile in our estimation, or it must retain our immoderate love."[310] Such statements, which may be found with some frequency in Calvin, must, however, be interpreted in the light of the following sentence: "But believers should accustom themselves to such a contempt of the present life, as may not generate either hatred of life, or ingratitude towards God."[311]

Is the meditation on the future life merely world-denying other-worldliness? It has been so interpreted.[312] Such an answer, while having a basis in some texts, fails to take account of a much larger body of material which supports a Johannine view of meditation, and it also fails to give a sufficient rationale of the actual historical development of Calvinism.

There is a firm basis in Calvin's writings for interpreting meditation on the future life in the Johannine sense of present participation in eternal life here on earth. Christ has brought us a life-giving spirit that he might regenerate us to a better life which is elevated above the earth.[313] Meditation on the future life stirs up our affections both to worship of God and to exercises of love.[314] "It is truly base and shameful that men who were created for a heavenly life should be under the influence of such brutish stupidity as to be entirely carried away after transitory things."[315] Communion with God in the hope of a blessed immortality distinguishes a human being from a beast.[316] Calvin took exception to Plato's meditation on death and insisted that life should rather be a meditation on repentance.[317] Even now we begin to bear the image of Christ.[318] As a commentary on Galatians 2:20 Calvin wrote:

> The life, therefore, which we attain by faith is not visible to the bodily eye, but is inwardly perceived in the conscience by the power of the Spirit, so that the bodily life does not prevent us from enjoying, by

[309] 3.9.1.
[310] 3.9.2.
[311] 3.9.3.
[312] Schulze, op. cit., p. 1.
[313] *CR* 49:559.
[314] *CR* 52:79.
[315] *CR* 45:399.
[316] *OS* 1:464.
[317] 3.3.20.
[318] *CR* 49:560.

faith, a heavenly life. "He hath made us to sit together in heavenly places in Christ Jesus" (Eph. 2:6). Again, "Ye are fellow-citizens with the saints and of the household of God" (Eph. 2:19). And again, "Our conversation [commonwealth] is in heaven" (Phil. 3:20). Paul's writings are full of similar assertions 'that while we live in the world, we at the same time live in heaven, not only because our Head is there, but because, in virtue of union, we enjoy a life in communion with him (John 14:23).[319]

The language Calvin uses with reference to meditation is strikingly similar to the language he uses to describe faith.

> Now it remains for us to know what is the nature of faith; it is to contemplate the things incomprehensible to our senses; it is to forsake the world and to look for the kingdom of God; it is to cling to the pure and simple word proceeding from the mouth of God, and not to regard that which we are able to perceive here.[320]

The meditation on the future life is an aspect of faith.[321] It is an experience here and now of what shall be brought to completion beyond death.[322] By our union with Christ we are made participants in the celestial life.[323]

These statements, which indicate that meditation on the future life is essentially the participation in that life here and now, become convincing when placed in the context of countless passages which affirm the value of the life on earth.[324] Undoubtedly Calvin was influenced by Platonism, but it is fundamentally wrong to call his

---

[319]*CR* 50:199. Cf. 3.18.1: "But as soon as they are introduced, by the knowledge of the gospel and the illumination of the Holy Spirit, into communion with Christ, eternal life is begun in them." Also cf. *CR* 5:194: "I wish we could with true faith perceive of what nature the kingdom of God is which exists in believers, even while they are in this life. For it would at the same time be easy to understand that eternal life is begun. He who cannot deceive promised thus: 'Whoever hears my words has eternal life, and does not come into condemnation, but has passed from death unto life' (John 5:24). If an entrance has been given into eternal life, why do they interrupt it by death?"

[320]*CR* 50:444–445. Cf. *CR* 27:495–496; 37:14; 47:445.

[321]Peter Brunner writes: "Faith and trust are not thinkable without eschatology. . . . Expectation of eternal life (*vitae futurae exspectatio*) is very closely connected with faith (3.2.28). It is in this being-anxious of something future, eternal, otherworldly, which encloses this expectation in itself, that the eschatological element in the faith is most clearly recognized." (*Vom Glauben bei Calvin* [Tübingen: J. C. B. Mohr (Paul Siebeck), 1925], p. 147.)

[322]Peter Barth, *Das Problem der natürlichen Theologie bei Calvin* (*Theologische Existenz heute*, no. 18; Munich: Chr. Kaiser, 1935), p. 32: "Thus we have, in faith in Christ, the promise even of our restoration to the image of God. In this Calvin understands the renewal through Christ and the restoration of the image of God within us—under a most sober preservation of the eschatological perspective, which thereby dominates the Christian life—as a process beginning here and progressing."

[323]*CR* 50:443.

[324]Cf. Chapter 4.

doctrine of the meditation on the future life Platonic in contrast to the Hebrew teaching. The point Calvin is endeavoring to make is that the Christian life is life in fellowship with God, not life in the things of earth. This is not world-denying, as subsequent Calvinism proved.

E. The Ethos of the Christian Life

Calvin's interpretation of the Christian life inspired a vigorous and aggressive spirit. On the human level it involved a real conquest of evil. In its relation to God it had no less incentive than his glory. It followed naturally for the Calvinist to exhibit an unusual aggressiveness in history. Calvin himself described the Christian life in terms of progress, conquest, and heroism.

Christians are like young people growing toward adulthood. They are marked by a constant desire and progress toward those attainments which they will ultimately reach.[325] They are not merely taught patience, godliness, temperance, and love, but they continually make progress in those endowments.[326] Every believer ought to make daily progress in good works.[327] The end of the gospel is that "God may reign in us. Regeneration is the beginning of this kingdom, and the end thereof is blessed immortality; the middle proceedings are in a more ample going forward and increase of regeneration."[328] "None are qualified for receiving the grace of the gospel but those who disregard all other desires and devote all their exertions and all their faculties to obtain it."[329] It is impossible to obtain eternal life without great and appalling difficulties.[330] Thus it is clear that for Calvin there is no Christian life without growth in regeneration.

What is true of the individual life can also be projected to the life of the group. Karlfried Fröhlich is essentially correct when he writes that it is possible to talk with all prudence of a history of the kingdom of God in the light of Calvin's theology.[331] This kingdom of God plays in and behind all history, but it is only visible to eyes of faith.

---

[325]*CR* 51:201.
[326]*CR* 55:447–448.
[327]*CR* 7:458.
[328]*CR* 48:4. Cf. *CR* 49:21; 52:51, 178.
[329]*CR* 45:375.
[330]*CR* 45:222.
[331]Fröhlich, *Gottesreich, Welt und Kirche bei Calvin*, p. 5. Peter Barth has criticized Fröhlich's book because it interprets the kingdom of God in Calvin's theology in terms of an evolutionary optimism. ("Funfundzwanzig Jahre Calvinforschung 1909–1934," *Theologische Rundschau* [1934], p. 250.)

The kingdom of Christ is on such a footing that it is daily growing and making improvement, while at the same time perfection is not yet attained, nor will be until the final day of reckoning. Thus both things hold true—that all things are now subject to Christ and that this subjection will, nevertheless, not be complete until the day of resurrection.[332]

The dynamic, active character of Calvin's doctrine of the Christian life is made clear in the metaphors he uses to describe it. Repentance is a race which God assigns Christians to run during their entire lives.[333] In athletics only one wins the prize, but the Christian's condition is superior in that there may be many winners.

For God requires of us nothing more than that we press on vigorously until we reach the goal. Thus one does not hinder another. . . . Those who run the Christian race are mutually helpful to each other. . . .
It is not enough to have set out, if we do not continue to run during our whole life. For our life is like a racecourse. We must not, therefore, become wearied after a short time, like one who stops short in the middle of the racecourse, but instead of this, death alone must put a period to our running.[334]

Christians must always be scholars.[335] They must always be students in the Lord's school, learning to maintain composure of mind and a posture of patience, expectation, and trust under the pressure of distress.[336] Christian scholarship involves the study of God's word, attention to preaching for the purpose of edification, and a study of God's activities in history. It also involves a study of one's personal life and the afflictions God sends to chastise his people. In Geneva, Calvin took concrete measures to be sure that the people were progressing in a knowledge of God. These measures took the form of preaching, catechetical instruction, public confession of faith, and schools. It is easy to criticize this aspect of Calvin's work as a sort of intellectualism. Nevertheless, Karl Holl has observed, correctly it seems to me, that in large measure the strength of Calvinism stems from this "intellectualism." Primitive Calvinists knew what they believed and why.[337] The problem is not that Christian scholarship, as Calvin conceived it, is wrong, but how to keep it from becoming a mere intellectualism.

The Christian is also a wrestler. The design of the vision of Jacob's

---

[332]*CR* 52:29.
[333]3.3.9.
[334]*CR* 49:449.
[335]*CR* 23:734; 28:283, 404, 425, 536, 573; 32:595; 33:202, 241; 46:11; 51:75.
[336]*CR* 32:23–25.
[337]Karl Holl, "Johannes Calvin," *Calvinreden,* p. 15.

wrestling "is to present all the servants of God in this world as wrestlers, because the Lord exercises them with various kinds of conflicts."[338] Those who serve God are athletes whom he exercises in piety.[339] Again, Calvin changes the metaphor when he exhorts, "Let us every one proceed according to our small ability, and prosecute the journey we have begun."[340]

All of these metaphors come to focus in the use of military terms. The Christian soldier is the most important and dominant designation Calvin gives to the Christian life.[341] The Christian life is a warfare against a real and deadly enemy. "Now we have a more general doctrine, that we are all soldiers of our Lord Jesus Christ and that our condition is such that it is necessary for us to fight, not only for a day, but for all our lifetime."[342] In his reply to Sadolet, Calvin wrote:

> Give me, I say, not some unlearned man from among the people, but the rudest clown, and if he is to belong to the flock of God, he must be prepared for that warfare which he has ordained for all the godly. An armed enemy is at hand, on the alert to engage—an enemy most skillful and unassailable by mortal strength. . . . The only sword with which he [the Christian] can fight is the word of the Lord. A soul, therefore, when deprived of the word of God is given up unarmed to the devil for destruction.[343]

The warfare in which Christians are engaged is not indiscriminate. They must fight their battles under the insignia of their captain, Jesus Christ.[344] Neither is this warfare intermittent. They must fight all their days.[345] The costs and preparation which war demands are also true of the Christian life.

> The condition of military discipline is such that as soon as a soldier has enrolled himself under a general, he leaves his house and all his affairs and thinks of nothing but war; and in like manner, in order that we may be wholly devoted to Christ, we must be free from all the entanglements of this world. . . .
> Everyone who wishes to fight under Christ must relinquish all the hindrances and employments of the world and devote himself unreservedly to the warfare.[346]

[338]*CR* 23:442.
[339]Ibid.
[340]3.6.5.
[341]Cf. Fröhlich, op. cit., p. 19.
[342]*CR* 27:612.
[343]*OS* 1:477–478. Cf. *CR* 26:573; 32:23; 49:130; 50:114.
[344]*CR* 51:5; 26:650.
[345]*CR* 55:363.
[346]*CR* 52:361.

The Christian warfare is not carried on by the strength of Christians alone. They are armed by the Holy Spirit, and they are already partakers of victory as though they had already conquered.[347] God battles for them.[348] To the Duchess of Ferrara Calvin wrote that God was sufficient to strengthen her for victory in the combat.[349]

The Christian combat is not merely that of the individual. Calvin speaks of the warfare of the church.[350] Christ subdues the world to himself and at the simple hearing of his name makes those obedient to him who had been rebels against him. He will make a conquest of the Gentiles by the preaching of his gospel and bring them to voluntary submission to his dominion.[351]

The chief combat we have is against spiritual enemies.[352] The devil was very real to Calvin.[353] Satan, who represents the principality of evil, of which he is head, is God's adversary and humankind's. "If we are animated by a becoming zeal for defending the kingdom of Christ, we must necessarily have an irreconcilable war with him who conspires its ruin."[354] Yet Calvin maintained only a provisional dualism. Satan exists only by God's will. In fact, God exercises the faithful by allowing them to fight with the devil and his forces.[355] Calvin also speaks of human beings as slaves of Satan and death. Christians are those who are delivered from this captivity. A genuine aspect of the work of Christ is the conquest of Satan and the freeing of human beings from bondage to him.[356]

In the light of these metaphors the word "hero" is descriptive of the ethos of the Christian life. It is interesting to note that Calvin himself frequently uses the word. We are enjoined to cultivate a "spirit of invincible fortitude and courage, which may serve to sustain us under the weight of all the calamities we may be called to endure, so that we may be able to testify of a truth, that even when reduced to the extremity of despair, we have never ceased to trust in God."[357] Believers ought to be undaunted. Those who are followers of Nicodemus contrive a fiction for themselves.[358] Faith animates us to strenuous action in the same way as unbelief manifests itself by

---

[347]*CR* 55:363.
[348]*CR* 27:123; 33:254–255.
[349]*CR* 17:261.
[350]*CR* 6:41.
[351]Commentary on Psalm 18:44.
[352]*CR* 26:55.
[353]*CR* 33:57–58, 69, 327; 51:80, 99, 109.
[354]1.14.15. Cf. *CR* 25:627, 676, 678, 679.
[355]1.14.18.
[356]*CR* 28:581–582.
[357]*CR* 31:445. Cf. *CR* 23:112; 27:561; 31:657–658; 47:321; 48:94, 116.
[358]*CR* 50:57.

cowardice or cessation of effort. Lack of the heroic quality leads to sin. It is a matter of experience that poor people are led to crime more by fear of shame than by hunger.[359] Calvin condemns the timidity of Moses.[360]

The sources of heroism are faith and the Spirit of God. The fortitude of the saints in all ages is the work of faith.[361] Furthermore, the heroism of which Calvin speaks is not the hard fortitude of the Stoic, who is not touched with compassion.[362]

Paul Wernle has correctly written that the Calvinist ethic produces a particular type of person—the hero.[363] Yet it is not a secular heroism. It is a heroism of obedience to God, born out of confidence in the promises of God. "Although the whole world be set against the people of God, they need not fear, so long as they are supported by a sense of their integrity, to challenge kings and their counselors and the promiscuous mob of the people."[364]

Calvin's autobiographical notes in the introduction to the Psalms commentary clearly reveal the distinctive nature of this heroism.[365] It is a heroism which is the human response to God's gracious activity in human life and in the world.

---

[359]*CR* 24:61.
[360]*CR* 24:22, 29, 50.
[361]*CR* 31:59; 48:213, 389, 392; 55:168.
[362]*CR* 23:552.
[363]Calvin, p. 352. Cf. Fröhlich, op. cit., p. 26.
[364]*CR* 31:559.
[365]*CR* 31:19ff.

Chapter 2

The Christian Life
in Relation to Justification
by Faith Alone

A. Justification by Faith Alone

No doctrine in Calvin's *Institutes of the Christian Religion* stands alone. Each is a part of the whole. This is especially true of the doctrine of the Christian life or, more specifically, of regeneration. Calvin continually reminds his readers that the gift of the gospel is twofold: forgiveness of sin and renewal of life. These two gifts are the reverse sides of the one experience: salvation. Thus it is essential for each gift to be understood in the context of the other. There is no true knowledge of regeneration apart from a knowledge of justification by faith alone.

John Calvin regarded justification by faith alone as one of the central doctrines of Christian faith.[1] It is the "principal hinge by which religion is supported."[2] It is the substance of piety.[3] "Wherever the knowledge of it is taken away, the glory of Christ is extinguished, religion abolished, the church destroyed, and the hope of salvation utterly overthrown."[4] It is the foundation of true religion.[5] Calvin discusses this doctrine after he has treated the doctrine of repentance and the Christian life in the *Institutes,* but it is clear that justification by faith alone is the soil out of which the Christian life develops.[6]

Calvin's doctrine of justification by faith alone must always be predicated on his understanding of the divine claim on human life. Karl Holl has written that Martin Luther felt the wrath of God as

---

[1] Willy Lüttge has a historical discussion of the place which this doctrine has been given in Calvin's system by various Calvin scholars. (*Die Rechtfertigungslehre Calvins und ihre Bedeutung für seine Frömmigkeit* [Berlin: Reuther & Reichard, 1909], pp. 1–10.)
[2] 3.11.1.
[3] 3.15.7.
[4] *OS* 1:469.
[5] *CR* 23:688.
[6] 3.11.1.

no one had since the apostle Paul.[7] It was just this appreciation of the human plight before a holy God which made the doctrine of justification by faith alone not only intelligible but also intensely relevant to Luther and to his disciple John Calvin.[8] Calvin understood quite well that people can never appreciate this doctrine until they have known what it is to stand before the divine tribunal.[9] In this experience all subterfuges are swept aside. The innermost motives, the deepest recesses of self are clearly revealed. Before God's throne every person's soul is laid bare. Such is the judgment which awaits those who have been commanded to love God with all their hearts and their neighbors as themselves.

The Reformation made clear the absoluteness of the divine claim on human life.[10] Human standards must not be applied to God's claim. "In the first place, therefore, we should reflect that we are not treating of the righteousness of a human court, but of that of the heavenly tribunal; in order that we may not apply any diminutive standard of our own, to estimate the integrity of conduct required to satisfy the Divine justice."[11] One may speculate on the merit of works in the justification of human beings, but when one comes into the presence of God all these speculations are swept away. In order to get the right perspective one must keep one's eyes on God, the Judge of life, as he is described in the scriptures.[12]

The problem which stands at the very center of the divine-human relationship is, How can a person, in spite of sin, stand in confidence before a holy God? Calvin felt that there were two mutually exclusive answers to this question. The one answer is the righteousness of works; the other is the righteousness of faith. The righteousness of works Calvin believed to be beyond the ability of sinful people.[13] It

---

[7]*Gesammelte Aufsätze zur Kirchengeschichte* (Tübingen: J. C. B. Mohr [Paul Siebeck], 1923–28), 1:177.

[8]For a discussion of Calvin's indebtedness to Luther, cf. Wilhelm Niesel, "Luther und Calvin," *Reformierte Kirchenzeitung* (1931), 195–196.

[9]3.12.1.

[10]Paul Wernle, *Calvin,* vol. 3 of *Der evangelische Glaube nach den Hauptschriften der Reformatoren* (Tübingen: J. C. B. Mohr [Paul Siebeck], 1919), p. 15: "As sharply and clearly as only Luther did, he has recognized and experienced the way which alone leads to the evangelical faith of justification: the awareness of the absolute ideal, the standing before God, the true judge, the absolute honesty of self-recognition. This and nothing else has made him a reformer."

[11]3.12.1.

[12]Ibid.

[13]Divergent interpretations of the doctrine of original sin constitute the real watershed between Roman Catholic and Protestant theology. Luther congratulated Erasmus on going to the heart of the matter: "In this, moreover, I give you great praise. . . . You alone in pre-eminent distinction from all others have entered upon the thing itself; that is, the grand turning point

can be achieved only in the life which "discovers such purity and holiness, as to deserve the character of righteousness before the throne of God; or who, by the integrity of his works, can answer and satisfy the divine judgment."[14] Clearly this is beyond the power of fallen human beings, who are nevertheless confronted by the absoluteness of the divine claim. They must come as *poures mendiants* before God.[15]

The other way to stand confidently before God is the righteousness of faith, which is totally different from the righteousness of works. It was a basic conviction with Calvin that it would be easier to mix fire and water than to mix faith-righteousness and work-righteousness.[16] In the first place, the righteousness of faith, in distinction from that of works, is an imputed righteousness. Believers are righteous not in themselves, but through the righteousness of Christ, which is communicated to them by imputation by virtue of their participation in the life of the Redeemer. "Our righteousness is not in ourselves, but in Christ; and . . . all our title to it rests solely on our being made partakers of Christ; for in possessing him, we possess all his riches with him."[17]

The following statement is a comprehensive summary of Calvin's whole doctrine of faith-righteousness:

> Now you see how the righteousness of faith is the righteousness of Christ. That we may, therefore, be justified, the efficient cause is the mercy of God: Christ is the matter or material cause; the word and faith is the instrument or instrumental cause. Wherefore, faith is said to justify, because it is the instrument to receive Christ, in whom the righteousness is communicated unto us. After we are made partakers

---

of the cause; and have not wearied me with those irrelevant points about popery, purgatory, indulgences, and other like 'baubles,' rather than causes, with which all have hitherto tried to hunt me down, though in vain! You, and you alone saw, what was the grand hinge upon which the whole turned, and therefore you attacked the vital part at once; for which, from my heart, I thank you." (*Bondage of the Will,* tr. Henry Cole [London: T. Bensley, 1823], p. 376.)

Calvin wrote: "We must strenuously insist on these two points—first, that there never was an action performed by a pious man, which, if examined by the scrutinizing eye of Divine justice, would not deserve condemnation; and secondly, if any such thing be admitted, (though it cannot be the case of any individual of mankind,) yet being corrupted and contaminated by the sins of which its performer is confessedly guilty, it loses every claim to the Divine favour. And this is the principal hinge on which our controversy [with the Papists] turns" (3.14.11).

Cf. Council of Trent, Session 6: "Canons on Justification," Nos. 4 and 5 in Philip Schaff, *The Creeds of Christendom* (New York: Harper & Brothers, 1919), 2:111.

[14]3.11.2.
[15]*CR* 50:304.
[16]*CR* 50:208, 209; 3.11.13.
[17]3.11.23. Cf. *CR* 23:692; 49:60; 3.11.3.

of Christ, not only we ourselves are just, but our works are reputed just before God, namely, because whatsoever imperfection is in them, it is abolished or taken away by the blood of Christ.[18]

Quite clearly the righteousness of faith is not our own but that of Christ. Even after the process of regeneration is under way, the righteousness of fallen human beings can never take the place of the righteousness of Christ.

> Believers, therefore, even to the end of their lives, have no other righteousness than that which is there described. For the mediatorial office is perpetually sustained by Christ, by whom the Father is reconciled to us; and the efficacy of whose death is perpetually the same, consisting in ablution, satisfaction, expiation, and perfect obedience, which covers all our iniquities.[19]

A second distinction of faith-righteousness from work-righteousness is Calvin's identification of the former as forgiveness of sins.[20] Lüttge regards this as the fundamental element in Calvin's doctrine of justification.[21] In opposition to the Council of Trent, Calvin wrote that justification by faith alone is simply the forgiveness of sins.[22] "The righteousness of faith is a reconciliation with God, which consists solely in remission of sins."[23] Only remission of sins is put down for the cause of righteousness.[24] Lüttge has aptly pointed out the important role this concept plays, especially in the *Institutes* of 1536. Unquestionably Calvin is here writing out of his own living experience as truly as Luther did. Justification by faith alone was not for the Reformer abstract intellectualism; it was the living breath of life.

---

[18]*CR* 49:60. Cf. 3.14.17. Cf. Council of Trent, Session 6, Article VIII.

[19]3.14.11. Calvin's doctrine of the atonement needs to be subjected to new study. The *Institutes* and Catechism make indubitably clear that Calvin regarded penal satisfaction as a decisive element in the atonement. However, the atonement must not be limited to this one element, as is the tendency in circles which emphasize a forensic doctrine of justification. As previously noted, the idea of conquest of sin and the devil can be supported by passages from Calvin's writings. Calvin also in the discussion of the Christian life appeals to the life and example of Jesus.

[20]The Council of Trent denied that justification is merely forgiveness of sin (Session 6, Article VIII).

[21]Lüttge, op. cit., p. 87: "The interpretation of justification as forgiveness of sins, which to such great extent dominates the discussion, stands in the foreground as the guiding religious understanding of the teaching of justification in all editions of the *Institutes*. This meaning often also finds expression in comprehensive evaluation. And only next to it and very much in secondary rank is the idea of imputation drawn into the interpretation of justification."

[22]*CR* 7:447: "The verbal question is, What is justification? They deny that it is merely the forgiveness of sins, and insist that it includes both renovation and sanctification."

[23]3.11.21. Cf. *CR* 50:437.

[24]3.11.11.

The two concepts, imputation and forgiveness, are not contradictory. It has been easy to label the one as intellectualism and the other as genuine experience, but such an interpretation is hardly valid for the first Reformers. Despite occasional intellectualistic notes, imputation was no abstraction for Calvin. His understanding of the divine claim on human life and the absoluteness of the righteousness of God made it intensely relevant to actual life. Apart from imputation, forgiveness would have been unintelligible. Imputation means the price has been paid, that God in his freedom can forgive and still be just. Even in human relationships the guilt has to be borne by the forgiver before forgiveness can occur. Furthermore, imputation was no mechanical exchange of righteousness, but the consequence of the believer's union with the life of the Redeemer through faith.

Faith is the instrument by which the righteousness of Christ becomes humankind's and by which forgiveness is obtained. It is impossible to state in concise terms Calvin's doctrine of faith. It always reaches beyond human events, and when we try to imprison it by our logic it eludes us. Calvin briefly defined it: "We shall have a complete definition of faith, if we say, that it is a steady and certain knowledge of the Divine benevolence towards us, which being founded on the truth of the gratuitous promise in Christ, is both revealed to our minds, and confirmed to our hearts, by the Holy Spirit."[25] In the first place, faith exists only within the framework of knowledge. Calvin was vigorously opposed to the Roman Catholic notion of an implicit faith.[26] He would have nothing to do with wavering opinions.

> We see then that faith is not some cold and empty imagination, but that it extends much farther; for it is then that we have faith, when the will of God is made known to us, and we embrace it, so that we worship him as our Father. Hence the knowledge of God is required as necessary to faith.[27]

Yet faith is not to be identified with abstract knowledge. It is not knowledge of the human sciences.[28] Neither is it knowledge of bare facts.[29] It is not taught by the demonstration of reason.[30] It is not knowledge which people have of things that fall under their

---

[25] 3.2.7.

[26] *CR* 52:404. Cf. Thomas Aquinas, *Summa Theologica,* tr. English Dominican Province (London: Burns, Oates & Washbourne, 1937), II-II, Question 2, Articles 6–8, where Thomas considerably limits the notion of implicit faith.

[27] *CR* 42:331.

[28] *CR* 47:163.

[29] *CR* 48:2.

[30] 3.2.14.

senses.[31] The knowledge of faith consists more in certainty than in comprehension.[32] It is personal knowledge.

In the second place, the knowledge of faith centers in Jesus Christ. He is the object of faith. Calvin never wearied of making this point indubitably clear.[33] "Everything which faith ought to contemplate is exhibited to us in Christ. Hence it follows that an empty and confused knowledge of Christ must not be mistaken for faith, but that knowledge which is directed to Christ, in order to seek God in Christ."[34] Yet "faith is not a naked and a *frigid* apprehension of Christ, but a lively and real sense of his power, which produces confidence. Indeed, faith cannot stand . . . except it looks to the coming of Christ and, supported by his power, brings tranquillity to the conscience."[35] Faith is a knowledge of Christ which feels the power of his resurrection.[36] Faith is a lively, personal, not a naked, frigid apprehension of God's mercy and power in Jesus Christ.

Calvin also insisted that there is a mutual and perpetual relation between faith and the word of God.[37] Faith is bound by the personal claim of God, which, by the power of the Holy Spirit, confronts human beings in the Bible. This relationship of faith to the word of God saved Calvinism from the perils of undirected religious enthusiasm, but under the influence of a formal biblicism it sometimes turned faith into an abstract fideism.

Calvin declares that the faith about which he speaks involves the commitment of total personality. It is never mere assent. The affirmation which Divine Truth demands must come from the heart and from the affections, and not merely from the understanding.[38] It is the life of fellowship with God.[39] Lüttge has written that faith is the experience of forgiveness.[40] The essence of faith is unquestionably a human being's yes to God's gracious approach.[41] Yet the identifica-

---

[31]Ibid.

[32]Ibid.

[33]*CR* 7:451; 46:496; 48:388–389; 50:422; 51:200, 214.

[34]*CR* 51:183.

[35]*CR* 55:328.

[36]*CR* 52:50.

[37]3.2.6; *CR* 23:240, 313, 388, 689; 31:435; 37:285; 47:213, 354; 48:44, 327; 51:236; 55:45.

[38]3.2.8.

[39]Cf. Council of Trent, Session 6, Article VIII, which describes faith as one part of the life of fellowship with God, not as the life itself. Cf. *Summa Theologica,* II-II, Question 7, Article 2. Here Thomas describes faith as the first step in the life of purity.

[40]Lüttge, op. cit., p. 53.

[41]3.11.16: "The Scripture, when speaking of the righteousness of faith, leads us to something very different. It teaches us, that being diverted from the contemplation of our own works, we should regard nothing but the mercy of God and the perfection of Christ. For it states this to be the order of justification; that from the beginning God deigns to embrace sinful man with his pure and gratuitous goodness, contemplating nothing in him to excite mercy, but his

tion of faith and the experience of forgiveness is an oversimplification; but it is not incorrect. Faith is never merely *fiducia*, for it always involves fideistic elements which are the basis for the experience of *fiducia*. [42] In sum, Calvin's whole discussion of the subject emphasizes that the faith which justifies is an intensely personal act which involves the reorientation of the total personality.

Justification by faith alone has two very important results. It honors the glory of God and it preserves the believer's conscience in a placid composure and a serene tranquillity with regard to the divine judgment.[43] In the experience of justification by faith alone, believers cease their mad endeavor to put God in obligation to themselves. They no longer attempt to stand opposite God and bargain with him about their destinies. Justification by faith alone is the experience of willingly living out of the very hand of God, of accepting one's own life from the hands of Another. It involves the complete renunciation of all personal glory and the ascription of everything to God. It is just this experience of agreeing to accept one's life and destiny from the hand of God which gives to God the glory which is his due. As has been pointed out, the glory of God, according to Calvin's deepest understanding, is not the absolutism of an oriental monarch but the redemptive love of the cross, which is God's effort to heal the rupture in his relation with human beings, whom he has created in his image. It is the very nature of forgiving love which prohibits all attempts to deal with it on a bargaining basis. There is only one answer to forgiving love in human relations and that is a selfless gratitude. Even on this level one cannot buy or bargain with forgiving love. Calvin rightly saw that either it was this "letting one's self go into the arms of God," or it was the way of work-righteousness. This, it seems to me, is the essential content of Calvin's insistence that justification by faith alone gives God all the glory.

---

misery; (for God beholds him utterly destitute of all good works;) deriving from himself the motive for blessing him, that he may affect the sinner himself with a sense of his supreme goodness, who, losing all confidence in his own works, rests the whole of his salvation on the Divine mercy. This is the sentiment of faith, by which the sinner comes to the enjoyment of his salvation, when he knows from the doctrine of the gospel that he is reconciled to God; that having obtained remission of sins, he is justified by the intervention of the righteousness of Christ; and though regenerated by the Spirit of God, he thinks on everlasting righteousness reserved for him, not in the good works to which he devotes himself, but solely in the righteousness of Christ."

[42]The following sentence from the *Institutes* of 1536 clearly reveals the dependence of *fiducia* on *fides*: "Fiducia enim haec nostra est, quod Christus, filius Dei, noster est, nobisque datus: ut in ipso simus et nos filii Dei, regnique coelestis haeredes: Dei benignitate, non nostra arte, vocati in spem aeternae salutis" (*CR* 1:51).

[43]3.13.1.

In the second place, justification by faith alone gives to believers peace of conscience. They no longer have to worry about where they stand; they have given themselves to God. Justification by faith alone has reoriented life toward God in the only way which is ultimately important. The real question of life has been answered. Until this takes place, human beings are engaged in a losing battle which continually plagues them with the certainty of their defeat or drives them to lose themselves in some form of intoxication. As long as one seeks confidence in one's own works, one is continually thwarted by their imperfection. The only hope of peace comes when one fully believes that Jesus Christ is God's personal address to human needs and in this conviction surrenders life to God's mercy.[44] It was at just this point that Calvin felt that the Canons of Trent were inadequate. "The venerable Fathers will not allow Justifying Faith to be defined as the confidence with which we embrace the mercy of God as forgiving sin for Christ's sake."[45] Calvin felt that the purpose for which the gospel was preached was that human beings should know that God is their Father.[46] The Geneva Catechism of 1545 contained a good summary of what Calvin meant by confidence and peace before God.

> *Scholar:* That each of us should set it down in his mind that God loves him, and is willing to be a Father and the author of salvation to him.
> *Master:* But whence will this appear?
> *S:* From his word, in which he explains his mercy to us in Christ, and testifies of his love toward us.
> *M:* Then the foundation and beginning of confidence in God is to know him in Christ?
> *S:* Entirely so.[47]

Such in brief summary is Calvin's doctrine of justification by faith alone. It is basic in religion because it establishes a person's relationship with God. The doctrine of the Christian life always presupposes the fact that the Christian has been reconciled to God. Consequently, justification by faith alone is the precondition of all aspects of the ethical life.

---

[44] *CR* 7:604: "Peace of conscience, without which there is no salvation, exists only when there is an undoubting faith in acquittal. If everyone must confess before he can be forgiven, it is not for the will of man to define how far this necessity extends. Thus nothing is left but constant disquietude, and slow torture, and perplexing doubts, which will wear out the soul not less effectually than open murder." Cf. *CR* 7:456; 49:88; 50:481; 55:265.
[45] *CR* 7:478.
[46] *CR* 25:658.
[47] *CR* 6:11–12.

B. The Relation of Justification by Faith Alone to Sanctification

The relationship of justification by faith alone to sanctification is a crucial problem for Protestant theology. On the one side there is the ever present pitfall of antinomianism, and on the other side there is the constant temptation to lapse into some form of work-righteousness. Calvin was aware of these problems and was so concerned that no one misunderstand his doctrine of justification by faith alone as a form of antinomianism that he discussed the doctrine of repentance and the Christian life first, although logically justification should have received prior treatment.[48]

Calvin designates forgiveness and renewal as the two benefits which the gospel brings to humankind.[49]

> There is, therefore, a double washing. The first is that God does not ascribe our faults and our corruption to us, but receives us as his children. It is necessary that we be pure, but this is an imputed purity inasmuch as we borrow it from Jesus Christ. There is also an actual purity, or, as it is said, the goodness which God works in us. This shows itself by its effects, for God renews us by his Holy Spirit and corrects our evil affection. In short, he lives in us and rules us.[50]

Concerning the relationship of these two gifts of the gospel, Calvin is explicit on two points. First, they can never be separated.

---

[48]Calvin appears to have been very sensitive about the charge that justification by faith alone led to moral indolence. Note the vigor of this statement taken from his reply to Sadolet:

"We deny that good works have any share in justification, but we claim full authority for them in the lives of the righteous. For if he who has obtained justification possesses Christ, and, at the same time, Christ never is where his Spirit is not, it is obvious that gratuitous righteousness is necessarily connected with regeneration. Therefore, if you would duly understand how inseparable faith and works are, look to Christ, who, as the apostle teaches (1 Cor. 1:30), has been given to us for justification and for sanctification. Therefore, wherever that righteousness of faith is, which we maintain to be gratuitous, there also Christ is; and where Christ is, there also is the Spirit of holiness, who regenerates the soul to newness of life. On the contrary, where zeal for integrity and holiness is not in vigor, there neither is the Spirit of Christ nor Christ himself; and wherever Christ is not, there is no righteousness, nay, there is no faith; for faith cannot apprehend Christ for righteousness without the Spirit of sanctification.

"Since therefore, according to us, Christ regenerates to a blessed life those whom he justifies, and after rescuing them from the dominion of sin, hands them over to the dominion of righteousness, transforms them into the image of God, and so trains them by his Spirit into obedience to his will, there is no ground to complain that, by our doctrine, lust is left with loosened reins" (*OS* 1:470–471).

[49]3.11.1; 3.3.19; *OS* 1:60–61, 171.

[50]*CR* 46:359–360. Cf. 3.3.1; 3.3.19; 3.11.1; *OS* 1:60–61, 171; *CR* 7:425; 33:668; 47:191; 48:443; 50:199, 432–433, 437; 55:209, 307.

> The faithful are never reconciled to God without the gift of sanctifica-
> tion, yea, to this end are we justified, that afterward we might worship
> God in holiness of life. For Christ does not otherwise wash us with
> his blood, and by his satisfaction reconcile God to us, unless he makes
> us partakers of his Spirit, which renews us into a holy life.[51]

In the second place, these gifts must not be confused or confounded.
This is one of the points on which Calvin strongly opposed the
Council of Trent.

> The Fathers of Trent pretend that it [justification] is twofold, as if we
> were justified partly by forgiveness of sins and partly by spiritual
> regeneration; or, to express their view in other words, as if our righ-
> teousness were composed partly of imputation, partly of quality. I
> maintain that it is one, and simple, and is wholly included in the
> gratuitous acceptance of God. I . . . hold that it is without us, because
> we are righteous in Christ only.[52]

Calvin felt that the Papists overturned the whole doctrine of salvation by mingling and confounding pardon of sin and repentance.[53]
When justification is made to depend partly on repentance, there can
never be peace of conscience. Calvin was convinced that only when
they are neither confounded nor separated does salvation rest on a
secure foundation.[54] By this he meant, it seems to me, that justification and sanctification are two parts of one complex whole which,
for the sake of analysis, must be separated but which in actual life
are indissolubly united. Sanctification is a gradual process. Some
relics of sin remain in the righteous during the course of earthly life.
Justification, on the other hand, takes place for once and for all and
in a total manner. When it takes place, the justified may "boldly
appear in heaven, as being invested with the purity of Christ." Only
in this way can the righteous person's conscience be satisfied, for God
is not satisfied with any partial righteousness.[55]

    The relationship between justification and sanctification must not
be construed in any abstract and barren manner. The relation between the two gifts of the gospel is always dynamic and vital.[56]

---

[51]*CR* 49:104. Cf. *CR* 37:350; 45:112; 48:53, 111–112; 49:103, 137, 138, 144, 147, 331; 50:90;
52:90–91; 55:209, 305.
[52]*CR* 7:448.
[53]*CR* 37:350–351.
[54]*CR* 7:441–473.
[55]3.11.11.
[56]Lüttge, op. cit., p. 84: "From the strength of faith, from the forgiveness of sins experienced
in faith, and from the new position of man before God thus created—i.e., from the freedom
and joyful certainty of being a child of God—springs, by itself, ethical striving. This is very
often overlooked in characterizing Calvin. In this there lives, even though he coins different
formulas, the original strength of the Lutheran conception."

Justification provides the true foundation or the fertile soil out of which the true Christian life grows. Calvin regarded the confidence which comes from the experience of justification by faith alone as the only possible basis for real sanctification. As long as human beings are engaged in a tense and frantic search for salvation and standing before God, the moral life is impossible. Confidence before God is the indispensable milieu for the Christian life.

> They have made little proficiency in the gospel, whose hearts have not been formed by meekness, and among whom there does not yet reign that brotherly love which leads men to perform kind offices to each other. But this cannot be done before the consciences have been brought into a state of peace with God; for we must begin there, in order that we may also be at peace with men.[57]

> We cannot worship God in a proper manner without composure of mind. Those who are ill at ease, who have an inward struggle, whether God is favorable or hostile to them, whether he accepts or rejects their services—in a word, who fluctuate in uncertainty between hope and fear—will sometimes labor anxiously in the worship of God, but never will sincerely or honestly obey him. Alarm and dread make them turn from him with horror; and so, if it were possible, they would desire that there were no God.[58]

God does not accept coerced service. His service must be from *une affection pure et franche.* [59] The Christian life is always spontaneous.[60] The love of God is its commencement.[61] Justification by faith alone

---

[57]*CR* 36:66.

[58]*CR* 45:49. Cf. *CR* 49:268–269.

[59]*CR* 28:283. These statements certainly appear to be implicit denials of any mechanistic or deterministic interpretation of predestination. They are, as far as I can judge, irreconcilable with many of Calvin's formal definitions of the doctrine, as in 3.21.5. Cf. the section on predestination in the following chapter.

[60]*CR* 33:186; 51:57.

[61]*CR* 42:319: "The beginning of repentance is a sense of God's mercy; that is, when men are persuaded that God is ready to give pardon, they begin to gather courage to repent. Otherwise, perverseness will ever increase in them; however much their sin may frighten them, they will yet never return to the Lord. And for this purpose I have elsewhere quoted that remarkable passage in Psalm 130: 'With thee is mercy, that thou mayest be feared'; for it cannot be that men will obey God with true and sincere heart, unless a taste of his goodness allures them."

CR 37:289: "He shows that men cannot be led to repentance in any other way than by holding out assurance of pardon. Whoever, then, inculcates the doctrine of repentance without mentioning the mercy of God and reconciliation through free grace, labors to no purpose."

CR 43:71–72: "We have elsewhere said that men cannot be led to repentance unless they believe that God will be propitious to them; for all who think him to be implacable ever flee away from him, and dread the mention of his name. Hence, were anyone through his whole life to proclaim repentance, he could effect nothing unless he were to connect with this the doctrine of faith, that is, unless he were to show that God is ready to give pardon, if men only repent from the heart. These two parts, then, . . . ought not to be separated."

places human beings in the only possible position in the presence of God from which true goodness can spring. In sum, the gracious experience of forgiveness provides the inner dynamic which produces the true Christian life.

In addition to the experience of forgiveness of sins, Calvin speaks of faith as a source of the Christian life. In the last analysis it is another facet of the same experience which he calls forgiveness. "Repentance not only immediately follows faith, but is produced by it. . . . Those who imagine that repentance rather precedes faith, than is produced by it, as fruit by a tree, have never been acquainted with its power."[62] Nothing is more contrary to faith than torpor.[63] It was simply inconceivable to Calvin that faith would not issue forth in good works. In his *Antidote to the Council of Trent* he wrote: "It is therefore faith alone which justifies, and yet the faith which justifies is not alone. . . . Wherefore we do not separate the whole grace of regeneration from faith, but claim the power and faculty of justifying entirely for faith as we ought.[64] Faith can never be separated from love.[65] Calvin was particularly sensitive about those misinterpretations of his doctrine which applied "without works" to faith instead of justification.[66]

A third source of the Christian life which also, in the last analysis, is closely related to faith and forgiveness of sin is union with Christ.

> Both these branches of repentance [mortification and vivification] are effects of our participation in Christ. For if we truly partake of his death, our old man is crucified by its power, and the body of sin expires, so that the corruption of our former nature loses all its vigour. If we are partakers of his resurrection, we are raised by it to a newness of life, which corresponds with the righteousness of God.[67]

CR 48:71: "No man can be stirred up to repentance unless he have salvation set before him; but he who despairs of pardon, being, as it were, given over to destruction already, does not fear to run headlong against God obstinately."

[62]3.3.1. Cf. *CR* 52:433.

[63]*CR* 23:259.

[64]*CR* 7:477.

[65]*CR* 42:329–330; 55:360.

[66]*CR* 40:439: "Faith without works justifies, although this needs prudence and a sound interpretation; for this proposition, that faith without works justifies, is true and yet false, according to the different senses that it bears. The proposition that faith without works justifies by itself is false, because faith without works is void. But if the clause 'without works' is joined with the word 'justifies,' the proposition will be true, since faith cannot justify when it is without works, because it is dead, and a mere fiction. He who is born of God is just, as John says (1 John 5:18). Thus faith can be no more separated from works than the sun from its heat, yet faith justifies without works, because works form no reason for our justification; but faith alone reconciles us to God and causes him to love us, not in ourselves, but in his only-begotten Son."

[67]3.3.9.

The mystical union of the Christian to Christ means far more than conformity of example. By his Spirit, Christ pours power into those who are united with him by faith.[68] Being "ingrafted into the death of Christ, we derive from it a secret energy, as the twig does from the root."[69] The Christian "is animated by the secret power of Christ; so that Christ may be said to live and grow in him; for as the soul enlivens the body, so Christ imparts life to his members."[70] In short, the blessings of the Christian life do not become ours until we are united to Christ: "I attribute, therefore, the highest importance to the connection between the head and members; to the inhabitation of Christ in our hearts; in a word, to the mystical union by which we enjoy him, so that being made ours, he makes us partakers of the blessings with which he is furnished."[71]

Calvin was as vigorous a champion as Osiander of the Christian's union with Christ. His polemic against Osiander was directed at the latter's understanding of the nature of that union.[72] According to Calvin's understanding, Osiander taught a union of essence. Calvin maintained that we are united to Christ by the secret energy of his Spirit.[73] At times he also spoke of faith as the bond of union.[74] Union with Christ is historical, ethical, personal, not essential.

In the commentary on Galatians 2:20, he wrote that Christ lives in us in two ways: "The one life consists in governing us by his Spirit, and directing all our actions; the other, in making us partakers of his righteousness; so that, while we can do nothing of ourselves, we are accepted in the sight of God. The first relates to regeneration, the second to justification by free grace."[75]

These various sources of the moral life are summarized in the condition of sonship. The fact is frequently overlooked that the Fatherhood of God is a fundamental note in Calvin's theology.[76] If some statements of Calvin do not do justice to this concept, it is not because he did not vigorously assert the doctrine. The title of pater-

---

[68]*CR* 49:106.
[69]*CR* 50:199.
[70]Ibid.
[71]3.11.10.
[72]See W. Niesel, "Calvin wider Osianders Rechtfertigungslehre," *Zeitschrift für Kirchengeschichte* 46 (1927), 410–430, for the accuracy and the sources of Calvin's understanding of Osiander's doctrine.
[73]3.6.5.
[74]*CR* 51:52.
[75]*CR* 50:199.
[76]Cf. Émile Doumergue, *Jean Calvin, les hommes et les choses de son temps* (Lausanne: Georges Bridel & Cie., 1899–1927), 4:88–91); B. B. Warfield, *Calvin and Calvinism* (London: Oxford University Press, 1931), pp. 175–176.

nity, he wrote, belongs only to God.[77] There is not to be found a single father in the whole world who cherishes his children as tenderly as does God.[78] God loves human beings with a paternal love, and the true knowledge of God is knowledge of this love.[79] In a measure God is the father of all people by virtue of their creation in the image of God, but this relationship applies especially to those who belong to the body of Christ.[80] As a father, God seeks to draw his people to himself by gentleness, not by constraint.[81] God's goodness declares to all people that he wants to be a father to them, and this is sufficient reason to teach us that we ought to serve him.[82] Thus we may summarize the condition of the Christian life as sonship. "God reconciles us to himself in such manner that we serve him as a Father in holiness and righteousness."[83] The obedience we render to God is not the obedience of servility and constraint, but the obedience children render to a father who does not wish to subject them to rigor.[84]

The dominant motivation of the Christian life is gratitude.[85] The Christian ethic is the response of thankfulness. Ingratitude is the very nature of sin.[86] From this root spring idolatry and contempt of

[77] *CR* 26:138; 45:625–626.

[78] *CR* 42:327.

[79] *CR* 27:542; 28:501–502; 33:74.

[80] *CR* 43:37; 45:28; 54:403: "Even this is not solely according to the Spirit, but in all things and by all things, God must be recognized and honored as the unique Father. It is true that the apostle, in the Epistle to the Hebrews, asserts that he is the God of our souls, and compares him with fathers of the flesh, but in all events, according to our bodies, God must be our Father. For although we are begotten by our earthly fathers according to nature, God has nonetheless made us and created us. And this is a miracle which truly merits being noted: that when God creates a creature such as man, he gives man his form. There, now, God displays fine wisdom, really and truly, in that our bodies are mirrors in which we can contemplate his work. And thus (as I have already touched on), God will be the father of our bodies as well as of our souls, but most of all he wants to be our spiritual father."

[81] *CR* 26:532; 27:60; 28:253.

[82] *CR* 25:689; 26:602; 27:34; 28:281; 33:87, 287, 693; 50:262.

[83] *CR* 45:139. Cf. 3.17.6.

[84] *CR* 50:657–658. Cf. *CR* 28:346: "So here is a father who humbles himself of his authority. And why? Because he much prefers that his children serve him openly, rather than having to force them by extreme strictness. Note well, then, that all the promises contained in the Holy Scripture are, as such, witness to the paternal love of our God: and in this is shown that he looks out for our well-being and salvation, as it pleases him to accommodate himself to us, and to do this. And by this the law of God is rendered more gracious to us, when we vow in observing it that we are not disappointed with a good reward, truly much more ample than we could have wished for."

[85] *CR* 6:53–54; 23:29–30, 570; 24:157, 166, 169, 195, 210, 222, 223, 232, 233–234, 237, 244, 247, 560; 25:305, 488; 26:124, 159, 185, 256, 271, 424, 445, 612, 616; 27:20, 33; 28:484; 31:48, 226, 290, 438; 33:152, 361; 36:47, 104, 106, 317; 37:121; 40:122, 384; 48:69, 152; 49:233–234; 50:85, 451.

[86] Günter Gloede, *Theologia naturalis bei Calvin* (Stuttgart: W. Kohlhammer, 1935), p. 98,

God.[87] The ravages of Satan in the world are the just reward of this ingratitude.[88]

Calvin continually exhorts human beings to meditate on God's goodness. They should declare the acts of God's kindness and thus testify to their gratitude. Moreover, from past events and benefits received, the godly can reason that God will take care of them in the future. Hope of the future is based on the experience of God's goodness in the past.[89] The goodness of God should inflame us with an "ardent" affection to serve him.[90] We are condemned before God if we do not profit from his gifts in such a manner as to be incited to honor and serve him.[91]

God's mercy in redeeming us is a special incentive to the Christian life. God's people must look on him as their Redeemer and live a life which corresponds to the mercy they have received.[92] Calvin wrote: "[Jonah] knew that God was merciful, and there is no stronger stimulant than this to stir us on when God is pleased to use our labor: and we know that no one can with alacrity render service to God except he be allured by his paternal kindness."[93]

Calvin repudiated servile fear as the motivation of the Christian life.[94] If we are constrained to keep the commandments by fear, we are far from true obedience.[95] When fear prevails in our hearts, we are as it were lifeless; but when hope animates us, there is vigor in the whole body so that alacrity appears.[96] In short, servile fear is full

---

speaks of "Das Wesen der Sünde als Undankbarkeit." Yet it must be kept in mind that unbelief is the prior sin. Concerning Adam's fall Calvin wrote: "Infidelity, therefore, was the root of that defection. But hence sprang ambition, pride, and ingratitude" (2.1.4).

[87] *CR* 26:252, 665–666.

[88] *CR* 48:381.

[89] *CR* 31:582. Cf. *CR* 23:494, 503; 26:455–456: "Here, in sum, is what we have to remember about this passage: that each of us thinks of all the blessings he has received from the hand of God, and which we are daily still receiving from him: and that they incite us to continue to strive to come to him, and that we learn, in everything and by everything, to pay homage to him. Because we profane all his benefits if we do not bring them to this end—that he be honored and glorified by us. Moreover, as for the benefits of this world, let us recognize that our Lord knowingly limits our possession of them, and gives us the meager portion he does, only that we might cling to him all the more. For we ought to see that he treats us gently and supports us, in order to spur us and entreat us that much more to come to him."

[90] *CR* 28:384.

[91] *CR* 28:497–498.

[92] *CR* 32:47. Cf. *CR* 49:100, 317; 52:61.

[93] *CR* 43:265.

[94] *OS* 1:379: "Now, true piety does not lie in fear, which voluntarily flees the judgment of God, and moreover dreads it, but it consists rather in a pure and true zeal which loves God completely as a father and reveres him as Lord, embraces his justice, and fears offending him more than death." *CR* 43:258.

[95] *CR* 55:361. Cf. *CR* 24:115.

[96] *CR* 44:71.

of perverseness.[97] It is interesting to note that Calvin specifically repudiated the fear theory of the origin of religion. "False indeed is what is said, that fear is the cause of religion, and that it was the first reason why men thought there were gods: this notion is indeed wholly inconsistent with common sense and experience. But religion, which has become nearly extinct, or at least covered over in the hearts of men, is stirred up by dangers."[98]

Nevertheless, a certain sort of fear remains in the relation of the Christian to God. Calvin did not understand the Father-child relationship to mean that a person can operate with God on a "pal" or "old chum" basis. He could even say that the source of repentance is fear excited by a true sense of the divine reprobation.[99] Threats stimulate the regenerate, but they alarm the reprobate.[100] In general, however, Calvin did not use the word "fear" in these cases in the sense of horror or servility. He said: "I understand 'fear' in general to mean the feeling of piety which is produced in us by the knowledge of the power, equity, and mercy of God."[101] Thus Calvin distinguished between servile and filial fear.[102] Fear in the filial sense Calvin believed to be fully compatible with hope and trust.[103] Fear is an awe which appropriately corresponds to the difference between Creator and creature. Yet, despite his good intentions on this matter, some statements are difficult to understand in any other sense than that of cringing fear.[104] In general Calvin thought of God as both Father and Lord. Christians can rest confidently in his fatherly love, but at the same time they must never forget that God is their sovereign

---

[97]*CR* 43:230.

[98]*CR* 43:212.

[99]*CR* 7:470. Cf. *CR* 23:290, 463; 24:108, 120; 25:232; 3.3.5.

[100]*CR* 25:23. Cf. *CR* 43:230–231.

[101]*CR* 31:406.

[102]3.2.27: "Now, the assertion of John, that 'there is no fear in love, but perfect love casteth out fear, because fear hath torment,' is not at all repugnant to what we have advanced. For he speaks of the terror of unbelief, between which and the fear of believers there is a wide difference. For the impious fear not God from a dread of incurring his displeasure, if they could do it with impunity; but, because they know him to be armed with vindictive power, they tremble with horror at hearing of his wrath. . . . But the faithful . . . fear his displeasure more than punishment, and are not disturbed with the fear of punishment, as though it were impending over them, but are rendered more cautious that they may not incur it. . . . This [fear of unbelievers] is commonly called a servile fear, in opposition to a filial fear, which is ingenuous and voluntary."

[103]*CR* 31:406.

[104]E.g., *CR* 23:463. Wernle, *Calvin,* p. 233, believes that Calvin derived his early doctrine of repentance in particular from fear, and though he corrected this in later works, he did not do so radically enough. I think there is truth in the contention that Calvin did not fully correct this thought, but Wernle probably overdoes it.

Lord.[105] As a matter of fact, they can only truly perceive the Lordship of God when they know him as their Father. It is the experience of fatherhood which makes sin appear so terrible. For this reason Calvin could root the Christian life in love and trust and at the same time speak of its origin in fear and sorrow over sin. Apart from the experiences of love and trust, fear and sorrow would lead not to God but to despair. No person genuinely hates sin who has not been captivated by a love of righteousness.[106]

C. The Place of Good Works in the Christian Life

A knowledge of justification by faith alone and of the sources of the moral life provides a background for an interpretation of the place of good works in Calvin's theology. As previously indicated, Calvin was sensitive to the Roman charges that his doctrine undermined good works.[107] He himself was convinced that he fought not against good works but against a false understanding about them.[108]

Calvin was primarily concerned to strike down at the very roots all optimism about good works. He was never flattered by the external appearance of morality. "However beautiful and splendid the works of men may appear, yet unless they spring from the living root of the heart, they are nothing better than a mere pretense."[109] Until the heart is right, no external work can be good. In the background there is always Calvin's perception of the rigor of the divine judgment. This one fact upsets all the subtle arguments of the advocates of the merit of works.[110]

It was a further conviction with Calvin that no heart is ever right until a reconciliation has been effected between God and a human being. Consequently no works which arise from unregenerate hearts are good.[111] Until a person is reconciled to God, not a single spark

---

[105]This dialectic in Calvin's definitions of piety and religion may be noted: "By piety, I mean a reverence and love of God, arising from a knowledge of his benefits" (1.2.1). "It [religion] consists in faith, united with a serious fear of God, comprehending a voluntary reverence, and producing legitimate worship agreeable to the injunctions of the law" (1.2.2).

[106]3.3.20.

[107]Cf. 3.16.1.

[108]*CR* 52:48.

[109]*CR* 31:411–412. Cf. *CR* 40:455; 44:113.

[110]3.12.1.

[111]3.14.1: "For the further elucidation of this subject, let us examine what kind of righteousness can be found in men during the whole course of their lives. Let us divide them into four classes. For either they are destitute of the knowledge of God, and immerged in idolatry; or, having been initiated by the sacraments, they lead impure lives, denying God in their actions, while they confess him with their lips, and belong to Christ only in name; or they are hypocrites,

of goodness can be found in that person. To be sure, the unregenerate produces works which reveal some external splendor; but God, whose sight penetrates to the secret spring of works, knows the disposition from which they proceed.[112]

This unequivocal disavowal of the value of the works of the unregenerate does not mean that Calvin did not appreciate whatever excellencies may appear in unbelievers. "I am not so at variance with the common opinion of mankind, as to contend that there is no difference between the justice, moderation, and equity of Titus or Trajan, and the rage, intemperance, and cruelty of Caligula, or Nero, or Domitian; between the obscenities of Tiberius and the continence of Vespasian."[113] Indeed God confers favors on unbelievers who practice such virtues. These virtues hold society together. They are in real truth the gifts of God. Nevertheless, they are a mere "image" of true virtue.[114]

The reason the virtues of the unregenerate are mere images of true virtues is the fact that they proceed from evil hearts.

> They perform these good works of God very improperly; being restrained from the commission of evil, not by a sincere attachment to true virtue, but either by mere ambition, or by self-love, or by some other irregular disposition. . . . Besides, when we remember that the end of what is right is always to serve God, whatever is directed to any other end, can have no claim to that appellation. Therefore, since they regard not the end prescribed by Divine wisdom, though an act performed by them be externally and apparently good, yet, being directed to a wrong end, it becomes sin.[115]

These statements accentuate Calvin's basic conviction that a person must stand in the right position before God before that person's life can be really good. This true position before God, the *sine qua non* of the moral life, is the selfless affirmation of the forgiving love of God.

When a person is reconciled to God, that person is in a position to do good works. Yet even then it is only the prevailing inclination of the regenerate person to submit to God's will and promote his glory.[116] Even the best of the regenerate person's "performances are

---

concealing the iniquity of their hearts with vain disguises; or, being regenerated by the Spirit of God, they devote themselves to true holiness."

[112]3.14.1.

[113]3.14.2.

[114]Ibid.

[115]3.14.3.

[116]3.14.9: "We admit, that when God, by the interposition of the righteousness of Christ, reconciles us to himself, and having granted us the free remission of our sins, esteems us as righteous persons, to this mercy he adds another blessing; for he dwells in us by his Holy Spirit,

tarnished and corrupted by some carnal impurity and debased by a mixture of some alloy." Not a single action of any saint, if judged by its intrinsic worth, deserves any reward except shame.[117] The works of a person, as well as of one's self, must be justified by faith alone.[118] It is only on the basis of justification by faith alone that works are entitled to any reward or value.[119]

The works of a Christian, although inadequate in themselves to be meritorious in the sight of God, are by God's grace far from valueless. It was Calvin's conviction that God in his grace takes the "good" works of his children and gives them both value and reward.[120] The Geneva Catechism made it plain that "good" works are not useless.

> *Master:* We are not therefore to think that the good works of believers are useless?
> *Scholar:* Certainly not. For not in vain does God promise them reward both in this life and in the future. But this reward springs from the free love of God as its source; for he first embraces us as sons, and then burying the remembrance of the vices which proceed from us, he visits us with his favor. . . .
> *M:* Hence it follows that faith is the root from which all good works spring, so far is it from taking us off from the study of them.[121]

Calvin's insistence that the works of the righteous do have value goes beyond the concept of mere reward. It carries the conviction that good works have a place in God's work and are not accidental factors in the passage of history. Calvin would disavow any theory which declares good works valuable simply because they contribute to the social welfare. Good works have value essentially because they belong to the glory of God. This is to say that they are part of God's gracious redemption of humanity, which is the truly real fact in human history.

In summary, justification by faith alone is the presupposition of the Christian life. By putting the believer in the proper position before God, it provides the soil out of which the Christian life grows.

---

by whose power our carnal desires are daily more and more mortified, and we are sanctified, that is, consecrated to the Lord until real purity of life, having our hearts moulded to obey his law, so that it is our prevailing inclination to submit to his will, and to promote his glory alone by all possible means."

[117]3.14.9. Cf. *CR* 24:19, 434; 48:243–244.

[118]*CR* 7:458; 50:65, 489; 3.14.11ff.

[119]3.11.2; *CR* 50:65.

[120]3.16.2; *CR* 7:484–485, 481–482, 597–598; 23:128, 728–729; 27:209; 33:187–188; 38:187.

[121]*CR* 6:49–50.

The dynamic character of this doctrine is revealed in Calvin's appeal to confidence before God, the experience of forgiveness, faith, union with Christ—all factors involved in justification by faith alone—as sources of the moral life. In general, these various sources are summarized in the condition of sonship. The obedience of Christians is the free obedience of children to their father. The works of believers are never meritorious in themselves, but the works of Christians are supported by the grace of God, who not only rewards them but also assures to them an effective place in the historical process.

Chapter 3

The Christian Life
in Relation to Providence
and Predestination

According to John Calvin, Christians are humble but confident. They are not thereby split personalities, because their confidence is founded on something wholly outside of themselves—God. In themselves human beings are nothing. Sin whittles down their noblest thoughts, and the seeds of death within them finally come to fruition and carry them back to dust, from whence they came. On every side their lives are disorder, and their best efforts cannot integrate their disjointed personalities. All of this Christians know, and they are therefore humble. On the other hand Christians know that they were made for life with God. Although this fellowship has been broken by humankind's own rebellion, God himself has restored it. God's mercy is more powerful than the fact of people's sinfulness. In spite of their sin, they are children of the heavenly Father, in whom infinite power is united with infinite love. Such is the confidence which belongs to Christians. This religious sentiment Calvin describes in the theological language of providence and predestination.

Apart from the quiet confidence that life is lived out of the fatherly hand of God, Calvin's life and writings are unintelligible. No statement is more characteristic than the one with which Calvin greeted his banishment from Geneva: "Well indeed! If we had served men, we should have been ill rewarded, but we serve a great master who will recompense us."[1]

The Psalms commentary is one of Calvin's finest works, precisely because it gave to him a genuine opportunity to enter into the experiences of the Hebrew saints, who also had trusted God for everything. He would not have called the Psalter "the anatomy of all the parts of the soul" if he had not found there the sentiments of his own soul.[2] The conviction that his own life reproduced many of the experiences

---

[1] *CR* 21:226–227.
[2] *CR* 31:15.

of David induced Calvin to put into the preface of this commentary many of the most personal items he ever wrote.[3] This confidence about life in the face of every earthly calamity was woven into the very fiber of Calvin's teachings about the Christian life. He attacked the Romanists because they destroyed confidence about salvation, and he took issue with the astrologists because they put human destiny in the hands of a blind and ruthless fate.[4] The Christian way, he maintained, is the life of sonship with a heavenly Father.

A. The Doctrine of Providence and Its Relation to the Christian Life

Providence is God's activity in governing and preserving his creation. In the *Institutes* of 1539 Calvin discusses it in the same chapter with predestination. He located this chapter after the teaching on the Apostles' Creed and justification by faith, which indicates that he approached it *a posteriori* from the experience of the Christian community. Logically he should have discussed it in relation to the doctrines of God and creation. In the final edition of the *Institutes* he separates predestination and providence, and providence is then discussed in relation to the doctrines of God and creation. This change in position does not mean that Calvin wished to separate the doctrine of providence from the teaching on salvation. Providence is, of course, much broader than salvation and includes within its orbit those who do not belong to the community of the elect, as well as that part of creation which is below and above the human in the scale of existence. Nevertheless, Calvin's whole development of the doctrine reflects his conviction that God is a father of his children. This is true for all people in the sense that God is the Creator of all, but in a special sense it applies only to those who belong to the body of Jesus Christ.[5] Thus, almost at every point, the doctrine of providence presupposes the gracious activity of God in the salvation of human beings.

The source of Calvin's doctrine is primarily neither logic nor

---

[3]With the exception of a few of his letters.

[4]1.16.2; *CR* 7:478.

[5]*CR* 43:37: "We hence see that God's providence extends to all mortal beings; but yet not in an equal degree. God has ever known all men so as to give them what is needful to preserve life. . . . Then as to the necessities of life, he performs the office of a Father toward all men. But he has known his chosen people because he has separated them from other nations that they might be like his own family."

CR 6:94: "Neque enim filiorum loco nos habet Deus, nisi quatenus Christi sumus membra."

CR 9:289: "Nempe quia paternum eius favorem in spem aeternae salutis non experiuntur alii, nisi quos sibi gratos reddit in filio unigenito."

speculation, but the religious conviction of a believer who takes God very seriously. It is the expression of faith in the infinite power and the infinite love of God—a basic element in Calvin's theology.[6] Come what may, either in logic or in history, the Geneva Reformer steadfastly refused to surrender one iota of this conviction. His own life was hard. Diseases ravaged his body, and on every side he met theological and political opposition. Yet he maintained that God tenderly cared for him. One secret of his political success lies in the fact that he did not succumb to the temptation to make life secure by trusting in the things of the world.[7] There were certainly many occasions when Calvin could not square his faith in God's providential care for the world with logic, but on these occasions this man of logic willed to trust the love and justice of God. This is not to say that Calvin was an apostle of an irrationalistic fideism. On the contrary, he sometimes tended in the opposite direction. Fundamentally, he refused to sacrifice the indubitable facts of his religious experience for the sake of his own logic and preferred to believe that these facts which the human mind could not put together stood in full rational coherence in the mind of God. It is true that some of his attempts to maintain the apparently antithetical facts of God's all-embracing activity and humankind's responsibility are harsh and crude, but this harshness is more apparent when Calvin, nettled by the barbs of his opponents or the demands of logic, attempts to give his doctrine a pattern of full rational coherence. Consequently, if one wishes to penetrate into the real significance of Calvin's thought on providence, one must approach it as a doctrine of faith and not as an *a priori* rationalization of God's relationship to the world. Calvin himself never fails to warn his readers that this is the only profitable approach to the subject.

> We ought to contemplate Providence, not as curious and fickle persons are wont to do, but as a ground of confidence and excitement to prayer. When he informs us that the hairs of our head are all numbered, it is not to encourage trivial speculations, but to instruct us to depend on the fatherly care of God which is exercised over these frail bodies.[8]

It was utterly preposterous to Calvin that anyone should think that God had created the world and then left it to run itself or to be guided by a set of impersonal motions which he had fixed to govern it. Such thoughts he described as "frigid" and "jejune." Believers have nothing more dreadful to fear than that Satan should fascinate them into thinking that God sits idly in his heaven and does

[6]Cf. *CR* 31:464, 590–593.
[7]E.g., he was never tempted by money. *CR* 21:813.
[8]*CR* 45:290. Cf. 1.17.1, 12; *CR* 53:553ff.

nothing.[9] God is not devoted to ease and self-satisfaction.[10] When God is thought of as shut up in heaven, he is no longer God but an idol.[11] Indeed, Christians are especially distinguished from the heathen by their conviction that the divine power is perpetually present in the world no less than it was present in the creation of the world.[12]

When faith has learned that God is the creator of all things,

> it should immediately conclude that he is also their perpetual governor and preserver; and that not by a certain universal motion, actuating the whole machine of the world, and all its respective parts, but by a particular providence sustaining, nourishing, and providing for everything which he has made. . . .[13]

> God [is] the Arbiter and Governor of all things, who, in his own wisdom, has, from the remotest eternity, decreed what he would do, and now, by his own power, executes what he has decreed.[14]

Such is the language by which Calvin defined his doctrine of providence. God is creator, governor, preserver, arbiter of the whole world.

Calvin's doctrine of providence is characterized by its emphasis on the continual, efficacious activity of God in the totality of his creation; that is, everything which is not God. God is never aloof from his creation, and on Calvin's principles any aloofness of God from creation would be the annihilation of that creation.[15] He could agree with Zwingli's statement that nature is God when properly interpreted, though he preferred the more cautious wording that nature is an order prescribed by God.[16] Thus Calvin rejected any notion of a universal providence which limits God's governance of the world to his preservation of an order of nature. Providence means God's peculiar care over every one of his works.[17] God has not merely infused some power into nature, but he immediately and continually cares for every person or thing.[18] Indeed, it is principally necessary for the pious person to contemplate this particular care of God which extends to so small a matter as the numbering of the hairs of the

---

[9]1.16.3; *CR* 42:339.
[10]*CR* 31:99.
[11]*CR* 31:136.
[12]1.16.1.
[13]Ibid.
[14]1.16.8.
[15]*CR* 23:16.
[16]1.5.5.
[17]1.16.4.
[18]*CR* 8:348: "The knowledge of a general and universal Providence is vague and confused unless at the same time we hold the belief and indulge the contemplation that God covers, under the wings of his care, each single one of his creatures."

head.[19] This immediate, all-embracing activity of God in his creation was, to Calvin, a profound religious conviction "which the rule of piety dictates to us."[20] Consequently he could write with all the enthusiasm of religious feeling:

> Let us then hold this doctrine, that nothing is done except by God's command and ordination, and, with the Holy Spirit, regard with abhorrence those profane men who imagine that God sits idly as it were on his watchtower and takes no notice of what is done in the world, and that human affairs change at random, and that men turn and change independently of any higher power. Nothing is more diabolical than this delirious piety; for as I have said, it extinguishes all the acts and duties of religion; for there will be no faith, no prayer, no patience, in short, no religion, except we believe and know that God exercises such care over the world, of which he is the Creator, that nothing happens except through his certain and unchangeable decree. . . .
>
> Let us then learn not to subject God to our judgment, but adore his judgments, though they surpass our comprehension; and since the cause of them is hid from us, our highest wisdom is modesty and sobriety. . . . In a word, as far as the heavens are from the earth, so great is the difference between the works of God and the deeds of men, for the ends . . . are altogether different.[21]

Calvin was not satisfied to state that providence comprehends the whole of creation. He was specifically concerned with the many ways in which it covers the whole of human existence. On the natural level, as noted above, what we call the order of nature is really the activity of God. Likewise, all spiritual beings are embraced in the activity of God. Even the devil can do nothing apart from the will of God. The wicked fulfill the purposes of God as well as the godly. Thus all moral beings are enclosed in the net of divine providence.[22]

The fact that providence includes both the natural order and the activity of moral beings means that God's activity is particularly manifested in history. Calvin continually advised his readers to look for God's activity in the events of the times.[23] Such admonitions were

---

[19] 1.17.6.

[20] Ibid.

[21] *CR* 39:589–590.

[22] 1.18.1; *CR* 43:344–345.

[23] *CR* 23:529: "Also our own indolence hinders us from perceiving God, with the eyes of faith, as holding the government of the world, because we either imagine fortune to be the mistress of events, or else, adhering to near and natural causes, we weave them together and spread them as veils before our eyes. Whereas, therefore, scarcely any more illustrious representation of divine providence is to be found than this history furnishes, let pious readers carefully exercise themselves in meditation on it, in order that they may acknowledge these things which, in appearance, are fortuitous, to be directed by the hand of God."

not theoretical admonitions to the people of Geneva. Living in an exposed city, the citizens of Geneva, many of whom were already refugees for conscience' sake, were well aware of the political movements which continually jeopardized their very existence. When Calvin counseled his hearers to look to God for defense against armies of enemies, the people of Geneva understood well what he meant.[24]

Furthermore, Calvin saw the hand of God in the configurations of society. God exalts some above others.[25] He gives riches to some and poverty to others.[26] Thus providence takes in the whole gamut of human existence. Nevertheless, the special locus of providence is the church.[27] Here God's fatherly care is uniquely revealed. "We must hold fast to the principle that, while God rules all men by his providence, he honors his elect with his peculiar care and is watchful for their deliverance and support."[28] In his own interpretation of biblical history, Calvin is careful to point out the care with which God watches over the activities of his church.[29]

Calvin's disavowal of all forms of deism brought him to the very brink of pantheism. He avoided this pitfall by an equally emphatic doctrine of the transcendence of God. From what has been said, it is clear that Calvin did not interpret the transcendence of God in terms of the aloofness of God from his world. God and creation are, of course, totally different in the sense that the one is self-existent being and the other created being. This distinction between Creator

---

[24]*CR* 26:64. Cf. *CR* 26:18–19: "Moreover, note that this must serve as consolation. Because if we know that God has called us to the place where we are, and that we live there by serving him, we have a promise that when we are assailed, no matter what forces our enemies have or how much it seems that it is a tempest which must lose all and ruin all, nevertheless we will be sustained by the hand of God. We will be sustained when our Lord thus takes us under his protection and declares that, if we live in a country under his guidance, this is how we must be assured and how we can vex all our enemies. But when it pleases God to leave us, it is done. No great force would be necessary to defeat us. So, therefore, let us learn to put ourselves always on the side of God and pray that he will be our defense. And when we see many efforts rise against us, may we have refuge in what he has promised us, and may we wait to be helped by him as needed. This is how this doctrine must be applied for our use, in order that we do not think that God only shows to princes what they have to do, because the common people are consoled when they see that God keeps them like his flock and his pasture."

[25]*CR* 26:95.

[26]*CR* 25:17–18; 26:95; 1.16.6.

[27]*CR* 8:349: "For though God thus shows himself the Father and Judge of the whole human race, yet, as the church is his sanctuary in which he resides, he there manifests his presence by clearer and brighter proofs; he there shows himself as the Father of his family and condescends to grant a nearer view of himself, if I may so speak. . . . In a word, the church is the great workroom of God wherein, in a more especial manner, he displays his wonderful works; and it is the more immediate theater of his glorious providence."

[28]*CR* 24:24. Cf. 1.17.1.

[29]*CR* 24:15, 17, 24, 25, 36, 68, 120.

and creature is one of the most emphatic articles in the whole of Calvin's theology.[30] Under no circumstances can these two categories of being be mixed. The horror with which Calvin repulsed the subtly pantheistic notions of Servetus is sufficient evidence of this. Although this distinction is always paramount for Calvin, he never interpreted it to mean that history and creation are ever removed from the all-embracing activity of God. Fundamentally Calvin describes the divine transcendence in terms of freedom. The language and atmosphere of sovereign freedom dominate everything Calvin wrote on the subject of providence. On the human level the most apt category we have to summarize the nature of divine activity is personality. Of course, any human category is insufficient in the light of the distinction between Creator and creature, but Calvin continually uses the language of personality to express what he means by providence. The following statement, for example, is unintelligible apart from personal activity:

> My present design is to refute that opinion, which has almost generally prevailed, which, conceding to God a sort of blind and uncertain motion, deprives him of the principal thing, which is his directing and disposing, by his incomprehensible wisdom, all things to their proper end.[31]

God *moderatur, tenet, dirigit, disponit.* Thus he is immanent in creation in terms of will and purpose.

The sovereign freedom of God's activity is not irresponsible. On this point Calvin left no doubt. God's will is never arbitrary. It is the perfect expression of his character, which is justice and love.[32] Frequently the justice of God is beyond human comprehension. Human beings must always realize that they have to deal with their Creator in the matter of providence and must accordingly reverence his secret judgments.[33] "So it must be concluded, that while the turbulent state of the world deprives us of our judgment, God, by the pure light of his own righteousness and wisdom, regulates all those commotions in the most exact order, and directs them to their proper end."[34] We must

> account his will the only rule of righteousness, and most righteous cause of all things. Not, indeed, that absolute will which is the subject of the declamation of sophists, impiously and profanely separating his

---

[30]Cf. V. Hepp, "De Soevereiniteit Gods," *Second International Conference of Calvinists* (Amsterdam: Martinus Nijhoff, 1935), p. 15.

[31]1.16.4.

[32]Cf. p. 128 in this chapter.

[33]1.17.2.

[34]1.17.1.

justice from his power, but that providence which governs all things, from which originates nothing but what is right, although the reasons of it may be concealed from us.[35]

The very heart of Calvin's doctrine lies in the conviction that infinite power and infinite love are united in God.[36]

Calvin was careful to distinguish, in theory at least, the free personal governance of God from all forms of impersonal determinism, from any "necessity arising from a perpetual concatenation and intricate series of causes, contained in nature."[37] "It is one thing to imagine a necessity which is involved in a complicated chain of causes, and quite another thing to believe that the world, and every part of it, is directed by the will of God."[38] "What God decrees, must necessarily come to pass; yet it is not by absolute or natural necessity."[39]

The religious significance of the doctrine of providence inheres precisely in Calvin's conviction that it is the expression of the powerful and loving personality of God. Calvin was constantly aware of the religiously deadening effect of second or natural causes when believers do not see beyond them to the First Cause, God.[40]

The intensely personal and religious character of Calvin's doctrine of providence is revealed in what he wrote about prayer. Prayer, which is familiar intercourse between God and pious people, is the means by which people lay hold of the riches reserved for them by their heavenly Father. "Prayer digs out those treasures, which the gospel of the Lord discovers to our faith."[41] Believers are enjoined to pray for those things which they are entitled to expect from the Lord.[42]

Quite clearly God could discharge all the gifts of providence without human prayers, but to discharge providence in this mechanical sort of way would be to destroy the personal confidence and trust which is prayer. Prayer is appointed not for the sake of God, but for

---

[35]1.17.2.

[36]*CR* 31:464: "That our faith may rest truly and firmly in God, we must take into consideration at the same time these two parts of his character—his immeasurable power, by which he is able to subdue the whole world unto him, and his fatherly love, which he has manifested in his word. When these two things are joined together, there is nothing which can hinder our faith from defying all the enemies which may rise up against us, nor must we doubt that God will succor us, since he has promised to do it; and as to power, he is sufficiently able also to fulfill his promise, for he is the God of armies."

[37]1.16.8.

[38]*CR* 45:289–290.

[39]1.16.9.

[40]*CR* 23:20.

[41]3.20.2.

[42]Ibid.

the sake of human beings. Here are the reasons Calvin gave for prayer:

> Yet it highly concerns us assiduously to supplicate him, that our heart may be always inflamed with a serious and ardent desire of seeking, loving, and worshipping him, while we accustom ourselves in all our necessities to resort to him as our sheet anchor. Further, that no desire or wish, which we should be ashamed for him to know, may enter our minds; when we learn to present our wishes, and so to pour out our whole heart in his presence. Next, that we may be prepared to receive his blessings with true gratitude of soul. . . . Lastly, that use and experience itself may yield our minds a confirmation of his providence in proportion to our imbecility.[43]

In the realm of practical living, the doctrine of providence stands in opposition to all ideas of chance and fortune. Nothing happens at random or as the result of ineluctable fate. Every event depends on God's secret providence.[44] As far as Calvin was concerned, chance and fortune did not belong to the vocabulary of religious people. The pious live their lives under the persuasion that every event is known to and controlled by the will of God.

> If any one falls into the hands of robbers, or meets with wild beasts; if by a sudden storm he is shipwrecked on the ocean . . . , carnal reason will ascribe all these occurrences, both prosperous and adverse, to fortune. But whoever has been taught from the mouth of Christ, that the hairs of his head are all numbered, will seek further for a cause, and conclude that all events are governed by the secret counsel of God.[45]

The doctrine of providence also stands in opposition to the notion that the world is ruled by a "perpetual law of nature. For nothing would exceed the misery of man, if he were exposed to all the motions of the heaven, air, earth, and waters."[46] The pious person is always careful not to make an idol out of God's benefits, that is, second causes.[47] God's power is not tied down to agents which he uses.[48] Second causes have only what they borrow from the First Cause, and consequently Calvin continually insists that the eyes of the pious be directed to God.[49] The rising of the sun is not from the blind instinct of nature, but from the activity of God. The seasons

---

[43] 3.20.3.
[44] *CR* 40:687.
[45] 1.16.2.
[46] 1.16.3.
[47] *CR* 26:600.
[48] *CR* 23:17; 1.16.2.
[49] *CR* 23:20, 22.

come and go in order, but there is sufficient variation to convince one that every year, month, and day is governed by a new and particular providence of God.[50] The laws of nature are faithful only because God is faithful. As Calvin said, "The order of nature is nothing else than the obedience which is rendered to him [God] by every part of the world."[51]

On the human level Calvin maintained with equal insistence that providence does not nullify the decisions and acts of human beings. He was as fully aware as any of his opponents that he could not put the all-embracing activity of God and human responsibility together in a pattern of full rational coherence. Both factors were real to his religious faith and experience, and he refused to compromise either.

> The eternal decrees of God form no impediment to our providing for ourselves, and disposing all our concerns in subservience to his will. The reason of this is manifest. For he who has fixed the limits of our life, has also intrusted us with the care of it; has furnished us with means and supplies for its preservation. . . . Now, it is evident what is our duty. If God has committed to us the preservation of our life, we should preserve it.[52]

It is the consolation of believers to cast their cares on the bosom of God only if they perform their own duties. It is a perversion to make the providence of God an excuse for negligence and sloth.[53] In a nutshell, Calvin's teaching is that providence must not be "contemplated abstractly by itself, but in connection with the means which he [God] employs."[54]

The importance of the doctrine of providence for practical Christian living is abundantly emphasized in Calvin's writings. He continually ascribes human failures in the art of living to lack of living faith in the power and love of God working in an all-embracing providence.[55] As the Psalms commentary reveals, it was his conviction,

---

[50] 1.16.2.

[51] *CR* 36:29.

[52] 1.17.4.

[53] *CR* 24:22.

[54] 1.17.4.

[55] *CR* 31:271: "Certainly we find that all our fears arise from this source, that we are too anxious about our life, while we do not acknowledge that God is its preserver. We can have no tranquillity, therefore, until we attain the persuasion that our life is sufficiently guarded because it is protected by his omnipotent power."

CR 8:350–351: "Now, a much more appropriate and effectual remedy for all these evils is to hold our minds under the constant consideration in what manner and to what end the providence of God should be contemplated. The first end is that it may keep us free from all presumptuous confidence and hold us fast in the fear of God, and also may stir us up to continual prayer. A second end is to bring us to rest on God, with still and peaceful minds,

confirmed in his own experience, that the Christian life is only possible when it is lived out of the fatherly hand of God. The Christian life is a paradox: relaxation on the one hand, intensity of effort on the other. As has been seen, the doctrine of justification provides a basis for relaxation as well as the motive for the intensity of activity in the matter of a person's basic relationship to God. In the vast area of human experience in which a person has to adjust to the varied events of existence, providence also provides a basis for the paradox. On the one hand it enables the believer to rest peacefully in the all-powerful mercy of God, regardless of what happens; and on the other hand it enables the believer to face the world with unwavering confidence and energy. As Calvin himself said, "the necessary consequences of this knowledge are gratitude in prosperity, patience in adversity, and a wonderful security respecting the future."[56]

Faith in divine providence enables the believer to face danger not rashly but without fear. The program of the Christian in the face of danger is threefold. First, the Christian resorts directly to the Lord. Second, the Christian applies to immediate use whatever means of help may offer themselves. Finally, as a person prepared for any event, the Christian proceeds with intrepidity wherever the Lord commands.[57] Nothing can be safer than to make God the protector of life, for he is sufficient to meet every need in the way which pleases him.[58] All fears arise from the fact that human beings do not acknowledge God as the preserver of their lives.[59] As a matter of fact, Calvin was convinced that "there can be no security felt unless we satisfy ourselves of the truth of a divine superintendence and can commit our lives and all that we have to the hands of God."[60]

---

and to teach us to despise, in all courage and security, the dangers which surround us on every side and the numberless deaths which constantly threaten us from every quarter."

CR 31:673: "We no doubt all agree in admitting that the world is governed by the hand of God; but were this truth deeply rooted in our hearts, our faith would be distinguished by far greater steadiness and perseverance in surmounting the temptations with which we are assailed in adversity. But when the smallest temptation which we meet with dislodges this doctrine from our minds, it is manifest that we have not yet been truly and in good earnest convinced of its truth."

CR 32:144: "Besides, the joy here mentioned arises from this, that there is nothing more calculated to increase our faith than the knowledge of the providence of God, because without it we would be harassed with doubts and fears, being uncertain whether or not the world was governed by chance."

Cf. *CR* 43:510; 31:590–593.

[56]1.17.7.
[57]*CR* 23:441.
[58]*CR* 26:64, 682; 31:629; 36:431; 37:15–16; 40:637; 47:384.
[59]*CR* 31:271.
[60]*CR* 31:590.

In the sphere of human relations, belief in the sovereignty of God has similar revolutionary effects.

> When we suffer injuries from men, forgetting their malice, which would only exasperate our grief and instigate our minds to revenge, we should remember to ascend to God, and learn to account it a certain truth, that whatever our enemies have criminally committed against us, has been permitted and directed by his righteous dispensation.[61]

When Joseph turned his eyes to God, he forgot the injuries his brethren had committed and voluntarily administered clemency to them.[62] Furthermore, a living faith in God's governance enables believers to face enemies unafraid because they know that the hearts of human beings are guided by the secret inspiration of God.[63] Thus providence takes personal antagonism and fear out of human relations and enables the pious to love their enemies because their own well-being does not depend on destroying their enemies in a malicious way. Calvin, of course, recognized times when there should be lawsuits, wars, and punishment for heresy; but he always insisted that the element of personal advantage should be kept out of such proceedings,[64] even though he may not have always measured up to his theory.

Divine providence is also an antidote to fear and anxiety about the physical needs of human existence. These, too, are in the hands of God.

> And certainly we do no small dishonor to God when we fail to trust that he will give us necessary food or clothing; as if he had thrown us on earth at random. He who is fully convinced that the Author of our life has an intimate knowledge of our condition will entertain no doubt that he will make abundant provision for our wants. Whenever we are seized by any fear or anxiety about food, let us remember that God will take care of the life which he gave us.[65]

While the devout accept their life directly out of the hands of God, they do not overlook inferior causes. They feel and readily acknowledge their obligation to these causes and endeavor to return their generosity as occasion permits.

> He will reverence and praise God as the principal Author of benefits received, but will honour men as his ministers. . . . If he suffer any loss either through negligence or through imprudence, he will conclude

---

[61]1.17.8.
[62]Ibid.
[63]*CR* 24:49.
[64]4.20.11–18.
[65]*CR* 45:210.

that it happened according to the Divine will, but will also impute the blame of it to himself. . . . But it is principally in regard to things future that he will direct his attention to inferior causes of this kind. For he will rank it among the blessings of the Lord, not to be destitute of human aids which he may use for his own safety; he will neither be remiss, therefore, in taking the advice, nor negligent in imploring the help, of those whom he perceives to be capable of affording him assistance; but, considering all the creatures, that can in any respect be serviceable to him, as so many gifts from the Lord, he will use them as the legitimate instruments of the Divine providence. . . . But he will not place his confidence in external helps to such a degree as, if possessed of them, securely to rely on them, or, if destitute of them, to tremble with despair. For his mind will always be fixed solely on the Divine providence, nor will he suffer himself to be seduced from a steady contemplation of it, by any consideration of present things.[66]

This living faith in the fatherly love of God is what Calvin meant by patience, a virtue he regarded very highly.

Ignorance of the providence of God is the cause of all impatience, and . . . this is the reason why we are so quickly, and on trivial accounts, thrown into confusion, and often, too, become disheartened because we do not recognize the fact that the Lord cares for us. On the other hand, we learn that this is the only remedy for tranquillizing our minds—when we repose unreservedly in his providential care, as knowing that we are not exposed either to the rashness of fortune, or to the caprice of the wicked, but are under the regulation of God's fatherly care. In fine, the man that is in possession of this truth, that God is present with him, has what he may rest upon with security.[67]

Calvin specifically rejected the notion that patience is either hardness or helpless resignation. It is living faith in the loving and omnicompetent activity of God.[68] This is the context in which Calvin develops his doctrines of self-denial, cross bearing, and meditation on the future life.

---

[66]1.17.9.

[67]*CR* 52:60–61.

[68]*CR* 33:93–94: "Here we see, first, that those who are patient have some affliction, that they feel angry and anguished in their heart, for if we were like a tree trunk or a rock, there would be no virtue in us. A man who has no comprehension of his pain, would he be worthy of praise? We see a poor insane person who laughs and mocks the whole world, and yet he is at the brink of the tomb; friends, it is because he has no feeling of his illness. This, therefore, does not merit being held or reputed as virtue, because it is more a stupidity: wild animals don't feel anything, but they are not virtuous because of it. Therefore, note that the word 'patience' does not mean that men are weary, that they have no sadness, that they are not angry when they feel some affliction. Rather, virtue means that they are able to mitigate and maintain some propriety, that they will not stop glorifying God in the midst of their sorrow, that they will not be troubled with anguish and so dissipated as to leave everything there; but they will fight against their feelings until they can make way for God's will and conclude as Job did, and say, this is just."

Calvin's insistence on the immediacy of God's Lordship in all creation confronts us with two problems. First, providence as Calvin expounded it invests some events with too much significance and ties the transcendent to the finite. Second, Calvin's exposition robs the created order of its reality and integrity. Neither conclusion was Calvin's intention, but in practice this was the consequence of ascribing every falling leaf without adequate qualification to the specific will of God. Theology as a reflective discipline has to give more attention to the natures, structures, and energy systems of the created order than Calvin, the preacher, did.

B. The Doctrine of Predestination and Its Relation to the Christian Life

Calvin approached the doctrine of predestination from the viewpoint of practical Christianity. For him it was an article of faith, not merely a matter of dogmatic or historical interest.[69] His point of departure was not the doctrine of God but the practical problems involved in the existence of the church.[70] Thus, whatever may be the current status of the problem, predestination for Calvin was intimately tied up with the everyday experience of Christian faith. He also saw it as a part of the wider mystery of the incongruities of existence, the mystery not only of why the gospel is not preached equally to all, but also of why one mother can nurse her baby and another cannot.

Calvin did not hesitate to describe predestination as an "illustrious doctrine"[71] which is "productive of the most delightful benefits."[72] In one of his strongest statements on predestination, *De Aeterna Dei Praedestinatione,* he included the following paragraph as to its practical application to life:

> This great subject is not, as many imagine, a mere thorny and noisy disputation, nor a speculation which wearies the minds of men without any profit, but a solid discussion, eminently adapted to the service of the godly: because it builds us up soundly in the faith, trains us to humility, and lifts us up into an admiration of the unbounded goodness of God toward us; while it elevates us to praise this goodness in our highest strains. For there is not a more effectual means of building up faith than giving our open ears to the election of God, which the Holy Spirit seals upon our heart while we hear, showing us that it stands

---

[69]Paul Jacobs, *Prädestination und Verantwortlichkeit bei Calvin* (Kassel: J. G. Oncken Nachf., 1937), p. 15.
[70]*OS* 1:86; *CR* 22:46; 3.21.1.
[71]*CR* 8:306.
[72]3.21.1.

in the eternal and immutable good will of God toward us; and that, therefore, it cannot be moved or altered by any storms of the world, by any assaults of Satan, by any changes, or by any fluctuations or weaknesses of the flesh. For our salvation is then sure to us, when we find the cause of it in the breast of God. Thus, when we lay hold of life in Christ, made manifest to our faith, the same faith being still our leader and guide, our sight is permitted to penetrate much farther and to see from what source that life proceeded. Our confidence of salvation is rooted in Christ and rests on the promises of the gospel. But it is no weak prop to our confidence, when we are brought to believe in Christ, to hear that all was originally given to us of God; and that we were as much ordained to faith in Christ, before the foundation of the world, as we were chosen to the inheritance of eternal life in Christ.[73]

It is clear beyond dispute that Calvin himself was convinced of the relevance of the doctrine of predestination to the actual living of the Christian life, but it is not so clear that his exposition of the doctrine was always faithful to this conviction. Although this study is not concerned with the doctrine of predestination as such, but with its relation to the Christian life, we cannot accept Calvin's own assertions on the subject without asking to what extent his exposition of the doctrine bears out these assertions. Does predestination as expounded by Calvin build up the confidence of Christians in their adoption and in the divine love and power which undergird the Christian life? Is predestination a "practical" doctrine which "edifies,"[74] or is it a speculative and rationally satisfying unraveling of the mystery of the divine mercy? We shall attempt to find at least a partial answer to this question by investigating the development of the doctrine from 1536 to 1559 and its place in Calvin's theology, the answers which the Reformer gave to objections which were raised against it, and the relation of the doctrine to the revelation of God in Jesus Christ.

The position Calvin gave to predestination in his theology is an important factor in interpreting its relationship to the Christian life.

---

[73]*CR* 8:260. Cf. *CR* 8:275: "For our security and God's omnipotence are equal: the former not being less than the latter. Wherefore, amid all the violent assaults, all the various dangers, all the mighty storms, and all the shakings, convulsions, and agitations with which we have to contend, the continuance and perpetuity of our standing lie in this: that God will constantly defend that which he has decreed in himself concerning our salvation, by the omnipotent power of his arm. If any one of us but look into himself, what can he do but tremble? For all things shake, to their center, around us, and there is nothing more weak and tottering than ourselves. But since our heavenly Father suffers not one of those whom he gave to his Son to perish, as great as is his power, so certain is our confidence and so great our glorying. And his omnipotence is such that he stands the invincible vindicator of his own gift."
[74]Cf. p. 26 in the Introduction.

Consequently, an outline review of the development of the doctrine in the various editions of the *Institutes* and the catechisms is a necessary preliminary step in assessing its real significance. Calvin's whole method and set of mind prohibit the possibility that he threw the various doctrines of his theology together without regard for logical order. Therefore, we can suppose that he always placed certain doctrines in specific places because he had good reasons for doing so. In the light of this fact, the location of predestination in the various systematic works is very revealing.[75]

In the *Institutes* of 1536 predestination does not appear as an independent teaching. Nevertheless, it is certainly present in this edition; and even though reprobation is not defined, it is hardly true to say that this doctrine is not also recognized.[76] The most significant fact about the doctrine in the 1536 *Institutes* is that it is approached from a practical and a religious point of view, that is, from the viewpoint of one who stands within the religious community.

Predestination undercuts all confidence in work-righteousness and lays bare the source of human salvation. It is the negation of all merit and places salvation solely in the mercy of God. It means that salvation is rescue and not achievement. This is to say that predestination is implicit in any real doctrine of forgiveness or justification by faith alone. To be elected in Christ is to be forgiven. Such is Calvin's first approach to predestination in the *Institutes* of 1536.[77] It was a way of saying that any feverish attempt to bargain with God is sheer futility. Salvation is the out-reaching love of God which lays hold of human beings. In this sense justification by faith and predestination embody the same doctrine.

The primary locus of the doctrine, however, is found in the teaching on the church. The church is the whole number of the elect who are united to Christ.[78] This catholic society is one; for as there is one

---

[75]The four major steps in the systematic development of predestination are the *Institutes* of 1536, the Catechism of 1537, the Romans commentary and the *Institutes* of 1539, and the final edition of the *Institutes* in 1559.

[76]Jacobs, op. cit., p. 61, finds fifteen references to election and three to reprobation in this edition.

[77]*OS* 1:63: "Quale autem istud est fundamentum? An quod Iesus Christus initium fuit nostrae salutis et quod viam nobis aperuit, cum nobis meruit occasionem merendi? Minime. Sed quod in eo electi ab aeterno sumus ante mundi constitutionem, nullo nostro merito, sed secundum propositum beneplaciti Dei, quod eius morte ipsi a mortis damnatione redempti ac liberati a perditione sumus, quod in ipso adoptati a patre sumus, in filios et haeredes, quod per ipsius sanguinem patri reconciliati, quod illi a patre in custodiam dati sumus ne unquam pereamus aut excidamus, quod ita illi inserti iam vitae aeternae quodammodo sumus participes, in regnum Dei per spem ingressi."

[78]*OS* 1:86.

head, there must be one body.[79] The consequences of election are justification, sanctification, and glorification.[80] The fact that this society has its origin and existence in the election of God means that it is secure from all the wiles of the world, the flesh, and the devil.

> Moreover, since the church consists of the people elected by God, it is not possible for those who are truly its members to perish finally, or be destroyed by evil forces. For their salvation depends on so sure and solid a foundation that, even though the whole world be thrown out of its orbit, it cannot fail or fall to pieces. They may waver and fluctuate and even fall down, but they will not be bruised, because the Father supports them. . . . Hence, those whom the Father elects he surrenders into the protection and care of his son Christ that none of them should perish, but that they might be all restored on the final day. Under such good protection they can both wander and totter, but they surely cannot be lost.[81]

There are signs of election, but these are not sufficient for human beings to distinguish between the elect and the nonelect. This distinction is the prerogative of God alone. The consequences of the doctrine for church discipline are far-reaching, and they separate Calvin from the Roman Catholics on the one hand and from the Anabaptists on the other.[82] Human beings cannot restrict the mercy of God either by sacramentalism or by ethical requirements. Excommunication is provisional and extends only to the works of a person, not to one's selfhood.

Thus Calvin expounds predestination as the divine basis of the existence and salvation of the Christian community. Election takes place in Christ, and it has for its security the eternal will of God. It is the mystery of the divine mercy; and it must always remain

---

[79]Ibid.

[80]*OS* 1:86–87.

[81]*OS* 1:87.

[82]*OS* 1:90: "Plus licentiae ne nobis in iudicando arrogemus, nisi volumus Dei virtutem limitare ac misericordiae eius legem dicere, cui quoties visum est, pessimi in optimos mutantur, alieni inseruntur, extranei cooptantur in ecclesiam; ut sic hominum opinionem eludat et temeritatem retundat, ne sibi iudicandi ius, supra quam decet, usurpare audeant. Danda potius opera, ut mutuo candore alter de altero quam poterit optime fieri, sentiamus, alii aliorum facta ac dicta vicissim in optimam partem accipiamus, non ut suspicaces solent, oblique ac sinistre torqueamus. Quod si qui ita perversi sunt, ut de se bene sentiri non permittant, eos tamen in manum Dei committamus bonitatique commendemus, meliora de his sperantes, quam videmus. Sic enim fiet, ut et mutua aequitate ac patienta nos sufferentes, pacem ac caritatem alamus, nec stolide irrumpentes in secretiora Dei iudicia, errorum tenebris nos involvamus. Ut uno verbo absolvam: non personam ipsam, quae in manu atque arbitrio Dei est, in mortem addicamus, sed tantum qualia sint cuiusque opera, aestimemus ex lege Dei, quae boni et mali regula est."

a mystery, free from all human efforts to master or circumscribe it.

In the Catechism of 1537 a special section devoted to predestination is located after the teaching on the law and before the teaching on soteriology.[83] Thus the doctrine is oriented about the subject of salvation and not around the doctrine of God. The point of departure is the very practical fact that some people hear the word of God and profit from it and others do not. This is somewhat different from the *Institutes* of 1536, which took its point of departure more from within the community of the elect. Nevertheless, it remains an ecclesiological problem.

The word of God takes root only in the hearts of those whom the Lord, by his eternal election, has predestined to be his sons and daughters and heirs of the celestial kingdom. The reason he shows mercy to some and the rigor of his judgment to others is known only to himself. Both the elect and the nonelect serve to exalt the glory of God. In order to confirm their own salvation, believers must not attempt to penetrate the mysteries of heaven but must turn their gaze toward Christ, who is the pledge and ground of their election. Christ is not only a mirror through which the will of God is represented to us, but a pledge by which it is revealed and confirmed to us.

Thus in 1537 Calvin had begun a systematic development of double election. The stage was set for the more elaborate development of the doctrine in the next edition of the *Institutes.*

The next step in the development of the doctrine is found in the *Institutes* of 1539, which clearly reflect the study that went into the Romans commentary, which was completed the same year. Predestination, which is greatly elaborated from the small beginnings of 1536, occupies an independent section in this edition.

Double predestination was fully developed in 1539, before Calvin was engaged in any of his great controversies on the subject.[84] Two factors were chiefly responsible for this development. The first was Calvin's loyalty to what he believed to be the teaching of the Bible, and especially of Romans. The second factor was the logical demand of the doctrine of election. The very fact of election seemed to involve necessarily the fact of reprobation.

In 1539 the chapter on predestination was located after the discussion of faith, the Apostles' Creed, and justification by faith. It was placed before the chapters on prayer, the sacraments, and the

---

[83]*OS* 1:390–391.

[84]Although Calvin was not engaged at this time in any of his great controversies on the subject, the treatment in 1539 is, in places, of a definitely argumentative character. Some of the harshest statements which he ever wrote are contained in some of his answers to objections which could be raised against the doctrine.

church. Thus Calvin gave the doctrine a strong soteriological orientation. He also combined the discussion of predestination with that of providence, but he had little to say about the relation of the two. A brief statement indicates that they are two parts of the same thing.[85] Predestination determines a person's status in relation to salvation, and providence rules in all other things.

It is significant to note that the definition of predestination which remained in the *Institutes* of 1559 as Calvin's considered opinion on the subject first appeared in the 1539 edition:

> Predestination we call the eternal decree of God, by which he has determined in himself, what he would have to become of every individual of mankind. For they are not all created with a similar destiny; but eternal life is foreordained for some, and eternal damnation for others. Every man, therefore, being created for one or the other of these ends, we say, he is predestinated either to life or to death.[86]

This formal definition appears to be a coldly speculative unraveling of the mystery of the divine mercy.[87] As will later be indicated, it is difficult to harmonize this definition with some of Calvin's more existential statements concerning the doctrine. The fact that it appeared in the 1539 edition and remained in the final edition of the *Institutes* as Calvin's settled opinion is all the more significant.

The exposition of the doctrine in 1539 is essentially that which is found in the final edition of the *Institutes* in 1559. This last edition is much longer, but its increase in length is due to (1) explanatory notes involving quotations, (2) refutation of objections which were raised against the doctrine, (3) statements which aim for greater precision of thought, and (4) a broader biblical basis, as Calvin now frequently appeals to the Gospel of John as well as to Romans.

The most significant change in the final edition of the *Institutes* is the separation of the doctrines of providence and predestination. Predestination is now placed at the conclusion of the section on soteriology.[88] This represents the fourth change Calvin made in the

---

[85]*CR* 1:861: "Hic autem locus duobus membris continetur. Prius enim expediendum, qualiter intelligi debeat, quod hominum alii ad salutem, alii ad damnationem praedestinantur. Deinde quum aeterna quoque rerum omnium dispensatio ex Dei ordinatione pendeat, quomodo providentia illius regatur hic mundus declarandum."

[86]3.21.5.

[87]Cf. Emil Brunner, *The Divine-Human Encounter,* tr. Amandus W. Loos (Philadelphia: Westminster Press, 1943), pp. 123–127.

[88]Cf. J. Köstlin, "Calvins Institutio nach Form und Inhalt," *Theologische Studien und Kritiken* 41 (1868), 469: "We can comprehend this treatment of predestination in the system of the *Institutes* only if Calvin saw it not merely as a matter of popular Christian instruction but also as the task of a scientific Christian dogmatics. The matter of Christian interest for Calvin was indeed not the eternal decree itself, toward which saving faith should direct itself, but much

location of the doctrine, and apparently he was convinced that this was where it belonged. From the viewpoint of a spectator or of logic, predestination certainly belongs at the beginning of a system, as the Westminster Assembly clearly understood. Calvin did not give predestination this place. He discussed it after the fact of salvation, not before it. When predestination is placed before salvation, it tends to undercut Christology and soteriology. Calvin was aware of this danger, and it was his intention to avoid it. The fact that he neither wholly succeeded nor wholly failed in achieving this purpose, as will be seen, makes an evaluation of his doctrine very difficult.

In the development of the doctrine, Calvin takes notice of four major objections to predestination. In the first place, people inquire by what right the Lord is angry with creatures who have not provoked him by any previous offense. To devote to destruction whom he pleases is more like the caprice of a tyrant than the just sentence of a judge.[89] Calvin gives two answers to this question, and the first has served as the basis of the prevalent notion that he was a Scotist in his doctrine of God.[90]

> How exceedingly presumptuous it is only to inquire into the causes of the Divine will; which is in fact, and is justly entitled to be, the cause of every thing that exists. . . . For the will of God is the highest rule of justice; so that what he wills must be considered just, for this very reason, because he wills it.[91]

The assertion that Calvin maintains "the Scotist idea of the irresponsibility of the divine will" is serious.[92] If Calvin understood predesti-

---

more the present offering of salvation in Christ, with the present experience of salvation and the present directives of God primarily to the subject, or that which the subject realizes from the presently working God. We furthermore can comprehend it only if Calvin did not just see it as a matter of popular Christian instruction, but if he also saw it as the task for scientific Christian dogmatics to start from, and to stay with, that which is the next object of interest."
[89]3.23.2.
[90]Cf. R. L. Calhoun, *Lectures on History of Christian Doctrine* (New Haven, Conn.: Printed for private distribution, 1948), 3:335–336, for a discussion of Scotist doctrine on this point.
[91]3.23.2. Cf. *CR* 25:110; Williston Walker, *John Calvin* (New York: G. P. Putnam's Sons, 1906), p. 418; Reinhold Seeberg, *Textbook of the History of Doctrines,* tr. Charles E. Hay (1904, rev.; Philadelphia: Lutheran Publication Society, 1905), 2:398.
[92]Seeberg, op. cit., p. 397. This charge has been vigorously refuted by many Calvin scholars: (1) By A. Lecerf, *Introduction à la dogmatique réformée* (Paris, 1931), 1:250; also in "L'exposition Jean Calvin et la réforme française," *Bulletin de la Société de l'histoire du protestantisme français* 84 (1935), 202–203; also in "Reports," *Second International Conference of Calvinists,* pp. 25ff. (2) By P. Barth, "Calvin," *RGG* 1:1432: "One should also notice that Calvin rejects the late-scholastic thought of *potentia absoluta* (of the "absolute power" of God) and of the *Deus exlex* (the lawless God) with greatest determination"; also in "Die biblische Grundlage

nation to be a groundless and arbitrary fact, it places in question his whole understanding of the gospel and puts him closer to Muhammad than to Christ. One fact is clear: the ground of predestination does not lie in the elect. "For the assertion, that God purposed in himself, is equivalent to saying, that he considered nothing out of himself, with any view to influence his determination."[93] "If, therefore, we can assign no reason why he grants mercy to his people but because such is his pleasure, neither shall we find any other cause but his will for the reprobation of others."[94] "He reprobates . . . from no other cause than his determination."[95] These statements leave it beyond question that the ground of predestination is in God alone; and if they are taken by themselves, they have an arbitrary sound. Calvin himself frequently lets them stand alone, and he has himself to blame that critics have seized on these passages and called his doctrine the caprice of a tyrant.[96]

In general, however, Calvin did not let these statements stand alone, but closely related them with what he believed about the character of God. In 1559 he added some qualifying sentences to the assertion that it is presumptuous to inquire into the causes of the Divine will. He said:

> Yet we espouse not the notion of the Romish theologians concerning the absolute and arbitrary power of God, which, on account of its profaneness, deserves our detestation. We represent not God as lawless, who is a law to himself; because, as Plato says, laws are necessary to men, who are the subjects to evil desires; but the will of God is not

der Prädestinationslehre bei Calvin," in *De l'élection éternelle de Dieu,* ed. Martinus Nijhoff (Geneva: Éditions Labor et Fides, 1936), p. 37. (3) By Émile Doumergue, *Jean Calvin, les hommes et les choses de son temps* (Lausanne: Georges Bridel & Cie., 1899–1927), 4:119ff.

Warfield vigorously refuted this interpretation and made the following observation on its source: "The vogue of this remarkable misrepresentation of Calvin's doctrine of God is doubtless due to its enunciation (though in a somewhat more guarded form) by Ritschl (*Jahrbb. für deutsche Theologie,* 1868, xiii, pp. 104 sq.). Ritschl's fundamental contention is that the Nominalistic conception of God, crowded out of the Roman Church by Thomism, yet survived in Luther's doctrine of the enslaved will and Calvin's doctrine of twofold predestination (p. 68), which presuppose the idea of 'the groundless arbitrariness of God' in His actions. Calvin was far from adopting this principle in theory or applying it consistently. He is aware of and seeks to guard against its dangers (p. 106); but his doctrine of a double predestination (in Ritschl's opinion) proceeds on its assumption: 'In spite of Calvin's reluctance, we must judge that the idea of God which governs this doctrine comes to the same thing as the Nominalistic *potentia absoluta*' (p. 107)." (*Calvin and Calvinism* [London: Oxford University Press, 1931], p. 155.)

[93] 3.22.3.
[94] 3.22.11.
[95] 3.23.1.
[96] Cf. *CR* 24:363.

only pure from every fault, but the highest standard of perfection, even the law of all laws.[97]

The emphatic affirmation that God's power cannot be separated from his character occurs repeatedly in Calvin's writings.[98] He understood the inadequacy of human thought, which has to distinguish between love and justice and wisdom and power in the being of God, but he was convinced that in God all of these things are one.[99] "There is such a close connection between the goodness of God and his Deity, that his being God is not more necessary than his being good."[100] Calvin asserted that God loves his children as a father;[101] yet he rigorously circumscribed God's fatherhood at times and attributed frightful deeds to God without blinking an eye.[102] A fair

---

[97] 3.23.2. Cf. Thomas Aquinas, *Summa Theologica,* tr. English Dominican Province (London: Burns, Oates, & Washbourne, 1937), Part I, Question 25, Article 5.

[98] *CR* 31:387: "Nothing, therefore, can be more preposterous than to imagine that there is in God a power so supreme and absolute (as it is termed) as to deprive him of his righteousness." Cf. *CR* 34:341–342.

CR 40:291: "For God was never willing to be disjoined from his word, because he himself is invisible and never appears otherwise than in a mirror."

CR 24:49: "Nevertheless I do not suppose him to be without law; for although his power is above all laws, still, whatever he does must be perfectly right; and therefore he is free from laws, because he is a law to himself and to all."

CR 33:371: "Here we are admonished to attribute to God this honor: that he is the source of all fairness and justice, and that it is impossible for him to do anything which is not good and just. Some attribute omnipotence to God; however, they don't recognize him to be a just God, as they should, because we cannot separate one from the other. We must not imagine that in God there are things which can be divided one from the other. It is true that we must distinguish between God's wisdom, goodness, justice, and power; but inasmuch as he is God, all these things must be in him, and they are his essence. Now, let us keep from imagining an absolute power in God, as if he governed the world like a tyrant, that he used excess or cruelty, but know that in having everything under his hand, having infinite power, making all things, yet he remains just. Now it is true that God's justice is hidden from us in part, that we don't understand it: but that is all the more his power. And that being so, can we measure it by our senses or our minds? Certainly not. And thus it is that when we speak of God's justice, note that it can 'not yet' be fully and manifestly known to us, yet must we love it."

CR 33:540: "Now, however, what if we do not attribute to God an absolute power, as the doctrines of the papacy name it. That is a detestable and diabolic thing. In their schools they do confess that God, with his absolute power, could strike down the angels and damn them: but they call that the absolute power of God, an unjust and tyrannical power. Guard against imagining God as a tyrant, because he does all things with fairness and justice. However, he has his design, which is hidden from us; and moreover, we must love his justice when it is not known to us and our mind and our senses cannot perceive it. Because when it is said that "all things are possible in God," first of all we must think of what his nature is, and then we must come to his will."

[99] *CR* 38:371.

[100] 2.3.5.

[101] *CR* 42:327.

[102] *CR* 24:363: "Nam propheta exclamans beatos fore qui allident parvulos eius ad lapidem, commendat carte iustam Dei vindictam. Itaque hoc quoque loco, si nobis non videtur rationi

interpretation of Calvin's theology must take both assertions into account. It seems to me that Calvin was clearly aware of the danger of exalting the will of God above his character and genuinely sought to avoid this danger. Nevertheless, he did not always succeed in his intention. His failures are at least in part the result of his working principles of biblical interpretation and an almost irresistible tendency to enlarge speculatively on the biblical materials as in the passage referred to above.[103]

Calvin also gave a second answer to the charge that predestination is the caprice of a tyrant. "As we are all corrupted by sin, we must necessarily be odious to God, and that not from tyrannical cruelty, but in the most equitable estimation of justice."[104] By sin human beings have forfeited all right to the love and mercy of God.

The second objection asks how God can condemn persons for that which he has imposed on them. "Were they not, by the decree of God, antecedently predestined to that corruption which is now stated as the cause of condemnation?"[105] Calvin answers this objection with a difficult paradox.

> Their perdition depends on the Divine predestination in such a manner, that the cause and matter of it are found in themselves. For the first man fell because the Lord had determined it was so expedient. The reason of this determination is unknown to us. Yet it is certain that he determined thus, only because he foresaw it would tend to the just illustration of the glory of his name. Whenever you hear the glory of God mentioned, think of his justice. For what deserves praise must be just. Man falls, therefore, according to the appointment of Divine Providence; but he falls by his own fault.[106]

Calvin refused to attempt to solve the problem by claiming that God merely permitted Adam's sin. He considered this a theological quibble. Rather than compromise with what he regarded as basic truth, he let the extreme paradox stand. "Man falls . . . according to the appointment of Divine Providence, but he falls by his own fault." He could not put the two ideas together, so he let them stand in sheer contradiction. It was at this point that Calvin said, *"Decretum quidem horribile, fateor."*[107]

---

consentaneum totam impiorum sobolem e mundo exterminari, sciamus Deum iure suo fraudari quamdiu proprio sensu metimur immensam illam altitudinem, quam angeli ipsi cum admiratione adorant. Quanquam tenendum est Deum numquam fuisse passurum ullos infantes occidi, nisi quos iam reprobasset ac destinasset aeternae morti."
[103]Ibid.
[104]3.23.3.
[105]3.23.4.
[106]3.23.8.
[107]3.23.7.

The third objection states that predestination makes God a re-
specter of persons. Calvin answers that God does not have regard to
what the world sees in a person, that is, riches, power, nobility,
elegance on the one hand, and poverty, ignoble birth, slovenliness on
the other.

> God looks not at man, but derives his motive to favour him from his
> own goodness. God's election of one man, therefore, while he rejects
> another, proceeds not from any respect of man, but solely from his
> own mercy; which may freely display and exert itself wherever and
> whenever it pleases.[108]

The fourth objection contends that predestination undermines ethics. "Its establishment would destroy all solicitude and exertion for
rectitude of conduct."[109] Calvin countered with the assertion that the
object of election is holiness of life.[110] Predestination, instead of ham-
pering ethical activity, provides the true motivation for moral living.[111] "If the object of election be holiness of life, it should rather
awaken and stimulate us to a cheerful practice of it, than be used as
a pretext for slothfulness."[112] "That God has elected us and that he
now calls us to holiness are two things which are joined together and
are inseparable."[113] Predestination involves responsible moral living,
and there is not any predestination apart from this moral responsibility. Indeed, election is the source of the moral life. "Holiness,
purity, and every excellence that is found among men are the fruit
of election. . . . Holiness and purity of life flow from the election of
God."[114]

Election is ratified when the Spirit of God governs people's

---

[108]3.23.10.

[109]3.23.12.

[110]*CR* 55:450: "But as he has chosen us and calls us for this end, that we may be pure and
spotless in his presence, purity of life is not improperly called the evidence and proof of
election, by which the faithful may not only testify to others that they are the children of God,
but also confirm themselves in this confidence, in such a manner, however, that they fix their
solid foundation on something else. . . .

"The import of what is said is that the children of God are distinguished from the reprobate
by this mark, that they live a godly and a holy life, because this is the design and end of election.
Hence it is evident how wickedly some vile unprincipled men prattle, when they seek to make
gratuitous election an excuse for all licentiousness, as though, forsooth! we may sin with
impunity because we have been predestinated to righteousness and holiness!" Cf. *CR* 58:44,
61, 73, 75, 98, 99; 49:312–313; 52:162, 205–206.

[111]Karl Holl, "Johannes Calvin" *Calvinreden* (Tübingen: J. C. B. Mohr [Paul Siebeck], 1909),
p. 11: "The faith in election with him is not a resting point which stops the working of man.
Just as he has realized God as the eternally creating one in the world, through men working
in men, so he derives from the idea of predestination a motivation for restless (doing) activity."

[112]3.23.12.

[113]*CR* 51:270; 8:107.

[114]*CR* 51:147.

hearts.[115] However, it is easy to exaggerate moral living as a sign of election.[116] Calvin always placed the primary emphasis on the experience of faith, from which true morality proceeds. Under no circumstances can human beings determine whether other persons are elect—an important fact for church discipline. Election must always remain the mystery of the divine mercy.[117]

A crucial factor in evaluating any Christian doctrine is its relation to the revelation of God in Jesus Christ. One of the most important elements in Calvin's doctrine of predestination is the assertion that believers are elected "in Christ." In 1537 Calvin wrote that Christ is the pledge of our election[118] and this same idea is found in many of his later works.[119]

The God who elects is the same God who was in Christ. The Christ who performs the deeds of salvation is the eternal Christ who is the register of election.[120] He is the mirror in which election can be understood.[121] For this reason Calvin contended that it is not permissible to consider predestination abstractly, in relation to God the Father alone.[122] As Christ "is the Father's eternal Wisdom, immutable Truth, and determined Counsel, we have no reason to fear the least variation in the declarations of his word from that will of the Father, which is the object of our inquiry; indeed he faithfully reveals it to us, as it has been from the beginning, and will ever continue to be."[123] Calvin's doctrine of predestination must not be

---

[115]*CR* 58:73. Cf. 4.1.8: "We ought to acknowledge as members of the church all those who by a confession of faith, an exmplary life, and a participation of the sacraments profess the same God and Christ with ourselves."

[116]*CR* 36:116: "True . . . , we derive confirmation from works, but we must not begin at them; for this is the distinction between the elect and reprobate, that the elect simply rely on the word but do not disregard works, while ungodly men scorn and disdain the word, though men speak a hundred times; and yet they continually and eagerly call on him for works." Cf. *CR* 51:650.

[117]4.12.9.

[118]*OS* 1:391.

[119]*CR* 51:269–270. Also cf. *CR* 7:47; 8:49–50, 58, 95; 51:147; 3.24.5.

[120]*CR* 51:269: "And the Holy Scriptures also call the election of God the book of life. As I have already said, Jesus Christ serves as the account book, and we are engraved in Him, and that God recognizes us as his children."

CR 51:269: "Jesus Christ, who is like the true account book."

CR 51:270: "Jesus Christ . . . is a pledge to us, as much for our election as for the hope of our salvation and all the spiritual blessings which come from that source and fountain of God's free love."

3.22.7: "He [Christ] claims . . . the right of election, in common with the Father."

[121]*CR* 7:47; 42:127.

[122]3.24.5.

[123]3.24.5. Cf. T. F. Torrance, "Predestination in Christ," *Evangelical Quarterly* 13 (April 15, 1941), 109: "Just because Christ is therefore the author and the instrument of election, we may not think of it in any deterministic sense, but in terms of the way our Lord treated men when he himself was on earth."

separated from his teaching on the Trinity. He did not intend to drive a wedge between the decree of election and Christ, though it cannot be said that he always succeeded in avoiding this error.

Election in Christ also means that human beings are chosen by God apart from anything in themselves. Jesus Christ is the only source of election.[124]

Finally, the notion of election in Christ stands, at least by intention, in strong opposition to a speculative approach to the doctrine. In order to understand election, the starting point is Christ, not the eternal will of God abstractly considered.[125]

> They are madmen, therefore, who seek their own salvation or that of others in the whirlpool of predestination, not keeping the way of salvation which is exhibited to them. Nay more, by this foolish speculation they endeavor to overturn the force and effect of predestination; for if God has elected us to this end, that we may believe, take away faith, and election will be imperfect. But we have no right to break through the order and succession of the beginning and the end, since God, by his purpose, hath decreed and determined that it shall proceed unbroken. Besides, as the election of God, by an indissoluble bond,

---

[124]*CR* 8:95; 51:147; 58:49–50.

[125]*CR* 8:306–307: "Now I would by no means hurry men away to the secret election of God that they might, with open mouth, expect salvation from thence. But I would exhort them to flee directly to Christ, in whom salvation is set forth before our eyes. This salvation, had it not been revealed in Christ, would have forever remained hidden in God. For whoever walks not in the plain way of faith, to him the election of God can be nothing but a labyrinth of destruction. Wherefore, if we would enjoy the certain remission of our sins, if our consciences would rest in a sure confidence of eternal life, if we would call on God as our heavenly Father without fear, we must by no means make our beginning with the investigation of what God decreed concerning us before the world began. Our contemplation must be what God, of his fatherly love, has revealed to us in Christ, and what Christ himself daily preaches to us through his everlasting gospel. Our deepest search and highest aim must be to become the sons of God, and to know that we are such. But the mirror of free adoption, in which alone we can behold so high and unspeakable a blessing, is Christ the Son, who came down to us from the Father for the very end that, by engrafting us into his body, he might make us heirs of the kingdom of heaven; of which kingdom he is himself the earnest and the pledge. And as, moreover, this inheritance was once obtained for us by the blood of Christ and remains consigned to us on the sacred pages of the everlasting gospel, so the knowledge and possession of it can be attained in no other way than by faith. In a word, I not only now freely confess, but everywhere inculcate in all my writings, both that the salvation of men is inseparably connected with their faith and that Christ is the only door by which any man can enter the kingdom of heaven; and also, that tranquil peace can be found nowhere but in the gospel. Moreover, I have ever taught that whoever shall turn aside even the shortest step from the gospel of Christ, and from faith therein, can do nothing but lose himself in doubts, ambiguities, and perplexities; and that the more confidently anyone attempts to break in upon and penetrate those profound mysteries of God's secret counsel, without the gospel and faith therein, will ever, in so doing, get so much the farther and farther from God. Wherefore, that the children of God, notwithstanding their election by God before all worlds, are to walk by faith, I deny not, but constantly affirm." Cf. 3.24.5.

draws his calling along with it, so when God has effectually called us to faith in Christ, let this have as much weight with us as if he had engraven his seal to ratify his decree concerning our salvation. For the testimony of the Holy Spirit is nothing else than the sealing of our adoption. To every man, therefore, his faith is a sufficient attestation of the eternal predestination of God, so that it would be a shocking sacrilege to carry the inquiry farther; for that man offers an aggravated insult to the Holy Spirit, who refuses to assent to his simple testimony.[126]

Those who by faith truly participate in Jesus Christ are able to assure themselves that they belong to the eternal election of God and are his children.[127]

Let no one, then, seek confidence in his own election of God, anywhere else than "in Christ": unless, indeed, he would blot out and do away with the "book of life," in which his name is written. God's adoption of us "in Christ" is for no other end than that we should be considered his children. Now the scripture declares that all those who believe in the only-begotten Son of God are the children and heirs of God. Christ . . . is the clear glass in which we are called upon to behold the eternal and hidden election of God: and of that election he is also the earnest. But the eye, by which we behold that eternal life which God sets before us in this glass, is faith! And the hand by which we lay hold of this earnest and pledge is faith! If any will have the matter more plainly

---

[126]*CR* 47:147.

[127]*CR* 8:114. Cf. *CR* 42:127–128: "The original of our election is in God; however, he gives us a copy of it through faith so that that predestination, which would have been incomprehensible to us, is written in our hearts, as if God had had it copied there. Now this copy is not left to be the authentic instrument, for it is signed with the blood of our Lord Jesus Christ and sealed by the Holy Spirit, as St. Paul says. Therefore, now we see, as the Holy Scripture shows us, two articles. The first is that God has elected and predestined us by his eternal counsel before the creation of the world. The second is that we are made certain of it, that he has given to us a good witness and assured us of it, that we might see, when he copies his will, that free adoption which he has given to us—which he has written in our hearts, which he has signed with the blood of his Son, whom he has sealed with the virtue of his Holy Spirit, who is the earnest and pledge of our election."

CR 42:130–131: "Now we must come to what I have already touched on, which is that we have abundance which God has given us by faith, because if a man wants to be assured of his status, he doesn't have to take the city register and have it in his house, for what good would that do? But he would be content to have assurances and signs, and the register would remain in the hands of the city and the community. If this would be done for human beings and earthly creatures, I say, what will it be in the kingdom of God and his celestial glory? For that reason we do not have to go and take God's register to be certain of our election, but we will be content that he has given us a good document and by faith he has borne witness to us that he has adopted us as his children. . . . When our God (who is infallible truth) writes our names, not on paper, but in our souls, not with pen and ink, but with his own Son's blood, and then does not seal it with wax, but by virtue of his Holy Spirit; when (I say), he gives us such assurance as this, and we do not take advantage of all that, what ingratitude would that be?"

stated, let them take it thus: Election precedes faith, as to its Divine order; but it is seen and understood by faith.[128]

In his *Antidote to the Council of Trent,* Calvin wrote: "What else, good sir, is a certain knowledge of our predestination than that testimony of adoption which scripture makes common to all the godly?"[129]

These statements indicate that predestination must be interpreted in the light of God's revelation in Jesus Christ and that the doctrine is closely related to the experience of faith. This exposition points up the existential character of the doctrine and its relevance to the confidence and joy which undergird the Christian life. Nevertheless, Karl Barth has written that one of the most serious objections which can be raised against Calvin's doctrine is that his electing God is not the God which is revealed in Jesus Christ.[130] There is a considerable amount of evidence to support this judgment. For example, Calvin does not hesitate to speak of the damnation of infants.[131] Again, he writes that although God could save people, he does not because he has predestined them to destruction.[132] Even Calvin's deliberate definition of predestination in the *Institutes* (3.21.5), with its assertion that some persons are created for destruction, is hardly compatible with these assertions of the close relation of the doctrine to the revelation of God in Jesus Christ.

One fact is clear from this brief and far from exhaustive review of Calvin's doctrine of predestination. No simple yes or no answer is possible to the question, Is Calvin's doctrine of predestination a practical doctrine which edifies, or is it a rationalistic and speculative attempt to unravel the mystery of the divine mercy? Calvin's exposition of the doctrine does, in a measure, support his assertion of its relevance to the Christian life: (1) Predestination is located at the conclusion of the section on soteriology, not in the more logical position nearer the beginning of the system. (2) Predestination is "in Christ," which means that it not only takes place on account of Christ but also is performed by Christ. It is the personal act of the Triune God. (3) It is indissolubly united with vocation. On its deepest level, vocation is the experience of faith. When Calvin interprets predestination in this way, it is unquestionably relevant to the Christian life.

The problem lies in the fact that Calvin's exposition of the doctrine

---

[128]*CR* 8:318.
[129]*CR* 7:479.
[130]Karl Barth, *Die Kirchliche Dogmatik* (Munich: Chr. Kaiser, 1932–38), II/2, 19.
[131]*CR* 24:363; 8:309.
[132]3.24.14.

is not consistent. Several contradictions have already been pointed out. This confusion in Calvin's thought is further revealed in the fact that he uses at least three sets of terms to describe the doctrine. The first set is of a mechanistic nature, that is, of cause and effect.[133] This is especially true of his formal definitions of the doctrine, which seem to do violence to the personal relationship which Calvin frequently asserts is the true bond between God and humankind. A second group of terms is of a more organic nature: ground and consequence, foundation, and so on.[134] A third group of terms recognizes the mystery which surrounds God's choice of people and speaks of it in personal terms.[135] Only the last two sets of terms agree with the insight which placed the doctrine at the conclusion of the section on soteriology or which described the Christian life as the deeply mutual and personal response of human beings to God's love.[136]

The most active critics of Calvin's doctrine of predestination have been the Barthians. As previously noted, Karl Barth has objected that Calvin's electing God is not the God revealed in Jesus Christ.

---

[133]*CR* 36:138; 3.21.5.

[134]*CR* 54:50: "Because it is the foundation of our salvation. How can we build and support the building when the foundation is ruined?" Cf. *CR* 58:38, 199. Calvin speaks of good works as the *fruit* of election. Holiness *flows* from election. *CR* 51:147.

[135]Election, choice, and call are all personal words which Calvin uses in this connection.

[136]A statement by F. W. Camfield, written from the viewpoint of Barthian theology, is well worth quoting here: "The idea of predestination has given endless trouble to theology. It must always contain its problems and to discuss them here would take us too far afield. But the root of the trouble is mainly this, that predestination has been regarded as if it were human and rational causality made absolute. It has been only poorly perceived that predestination points to a mode of causality which is of a totally different kind from the rational, indeed it implies a complete break with it. It means, as we have said, that the ground of the relation between the believer in his faith and the object ρf that faith is to be found in God alone. The relation which is set up between a man and Christ and which we call faith springs out of a relation immanent in the Eterρal Godhead. It is the relation between the spirit and the Son. A predestination which meant the absolutising of the causation which we know, would be a purely rational idea, and one entirely removed from revelation. A predestination acting like a fate on human life, making thus the relation between man and Christ an unfree and therefore less than a personal one, could have nothing to do with predestination in Christ. It would simply be determinism at its highest pitch, for arbitrary and coercive will is the worst form of determinism. For this reason Luther and Calvin gave warning against abstracting the idea of predestination and treating it rationally, though it cannot be said that they always kept in mind their own warning. But they very rightly inserted that it was a dangerous thing to think about predestination except 'in Christ.' Rational causality in all its forms, whether in that of logical process, or natural law, or coercive will, has this characteristic that it excludes freedom and is incapable of setting up a truly personal relation. It treats men as things, not as persons; thus it does not truly *choose* them. Predestination is causality of a wholly other kind. So far from excluding freedom it implies it and creates it. Just because it sets up in human life a relation which has its ground in an eternal relation to God, a relation which is supremely personal, the relation between the Son and Spirit, it is the great charter and guarantee of freedom." (*Revelation and the Holy Spirit* [London: Elliot Stock, 1933], pp. 94–95.)

As was observed, there is considerable evidence to support this objection. At the Calvinist Congress in Geneva in 1936, the Barthians also raised questions as to the use of temporal terminology in the description of the acts of God. Lecerf took the traditional Calvinist position that the "pre" before "destination" indicates the point of view God wants people to take.[137] Nevertheless, when Calvin speaks of predestination as a decree which is made at one point in time and executed at a later point, it appears that violence is done to the eternity of God.[138] Calvin himself did not feel obligated to give the "fore" in "foreknowledge" a meaning which involved time sequence, for "foreknowledge" was defined as an eternal act.[139] Furthermore, Calvin sometimes interpreted the phrase "before the foundation of the world" to mean that God chose humankind not on the basis of anything in the elect, but solely out of his divine mercy.[140] Consequently it would seem that the traditional Calvinists have been too impatient with the Barthian criticism of Calvin at this point.

Another criticism which Peter Barth raised at this same Congress was that Calvin gave too large a place to experience as a source of knowledge in the exposition of the doctrine.[141] In the *Congregation on Election* Calvin did speak of experience as a source of knowledge about election,[142] and the same fact was implicit in other treatments of the doctrine.[143] Calvin's own experience was frequently bitter. In France his brethren were persecuted. In Geneva he was engaged in a running battle with the less religiously inclined portion of the population. It seems legitimate to ask if this experience did not lead to too much interest in the *selection* among people and to incite the judgment that few are elected.[144]

The inconsistencies which run through Calvin's doctrine of predestination reveal, it seems to me, the basic tension between Calvin the exegete of scripture and Calvin the rationalizer and systematizer of scriptural truths.[145] An example of Calvin's speculative extension

---

[137]A. Lecerf in *D'élection éternelle de Dieu,* ed. Martinus Nijhoff (Geneva: Éditions Labor et Fides, 1936), p. 179.

[138]Cf. 3.21.7; 3.14.1; 3.24.11.

[139]3.21.5.

[140]*CR* 51:267: "For he said 'Before the creation of the world' to exclude all regard and dignity that men would be able to claim, as we are always inclined to attribute to ourselves I do not know what, and we cannot stand to be reduced to nothingness."

[141]P. Barth, "Die biblische Grundlage der Prädestinations lehre bei Calvin," in *De l'élection éternelle de Dieu,* ed. Martinus Nijhoff (Geneva: Éditions Labor et Fides, 1936), p. 44.

[142]*CR* 8:94.

[143]E.g., 3.21.1.

[144]3.22.7.

[145]The same type of speculative extension of biblical data can be found in Luther's *Bondage of the Will.* Zwingli's discussion of the subject is more speculative and rationalistic than is true

of the scriptural material (Ezekiel 33:11) can be seen in the following passage from the *Institutes:*

> A passage is produced from Ezekiel, where God says, "I have no pleasure in the death of the wicked, but that the wicked turn from his way and live." If this is to be extended to all mankind, why does he not urge many to repentance, whose minds are more flexible to obedience than those of others, who grow more and more callous to his daily invitations? Among the inhabitants of Nineveh and Sodom, Christ himself declares that his evangelical preaching and miracles would have brought forth more fruit than in Judea. How is it, then, if God will have all men to be saved, that he opens not the gate of repentance to those miserable men who would be more ready to receive the favour? Hence we perceive it to be a violent perversion of the passage, if the will of God, mentioned by the prophet, be set in opposition to his eternal counsel, by which he has distinguished the elect from the reprobate.[146]

Calvin's commentary on Ezekiel did not extend to the thirty-third chapter, but he did comment on a similar passage from Ezekiel 18:23: "Have I any pleasure at all that the wicked should die? said the Lord God: and not that he should return from his ways and live?" The following comments reveal a different approach and emphasis from the passage in the *Institutes,* but even in this passage the tension is revealed in the closing sentences.

> He confirms the same sentiment in other words, that God desires nothing more earnestly than that those who were perishing and rushing to destruction should return into the way of safety. And for this reason not only is the gospel spread abroad in the world, but God wished to bear witness through all ages how inclined he is to pity. For although the heathen were destitute of the law and the prophets, yet they were always endued with some taste of this doctrine. Truly enough they were suffocated by many errors; but we shall always find that they were induced by a secret impulse to seek for pardon, because this sense was in some way born with them, that God is to be appeased by all who seek him. Besides, God bore witness to it more clearly in the law and the prophets. In the gospel we hear how familiarly he addresses us when he promises us pardon (Luke 1:78). And this is the knowledge of salvation, to embrace his mercy which he offers us in Christ. It follows, then, that what the prophet now says is very true, that God wills not the death of a sinner, because he meets him of his own accord and is not only prepared to receive all who fly to his pity, but he calls them toward him with a loud voice when he sees how they

---

in the case of either Luther or Calvin. Cf. "Sermon on Providence of God," *Latin Works of Huldreich Zwingli,* tr. S. M. Jackson (Philadelphia: Heidelberg Press, 1922), 2:128ff.
[146] 3.24.15.

are alienated from all hope of safety. But the manner must be noticed in which God wishes all to be saved, namely, when they turn themselves from their ways. God thus does not so wish all men to be saved as to renounce the difference between good and evil; but repentance, as we have said, must precede pardon. How, then, does God wish all men to be saved? By the Spirit's condemning the world of sin, of righteousness, and of judgment, at this day, by the gospel, as he did formerly by the law and the prophets (John 16:8). God makes manifest to mankind their great misery that they may betake themselves to him: he wounds that he may cure and slays that he may give life. We hold, then, that God wills not the death of a sinner, since he calls all equally to repentance and promises himself prepared to receive them if they only seriously repent. If anyone should object, then there is no election of God, by which he has predestinated a fixed number to salvation, the answer is at hand: the prophet does not here speak of God's secret counsel, but only recalls miserable men from despair, that they may apprehend the hope of pardon and repent and embrace the offered salvation. If anyone again objects, this is making God act with duplicity, the answer is ready, that God always wishes the same thing, though by different ways, and in a manner inscrutable to us. Although, therefore, God's will is simple, yet great variety is involved in it, as far as our senses are concerned. Besides, it is not surprising that our eyes should be blinded by intense light, so that we cannot certainly judge how God wishes all to be saved, and yet has devoted all the reprobate to eternal destruction, and wishes them to perish.[147]

Paul Jacobs, in his study of Calvin's doctrine of predestination, found a marked difference in the exposition of the doctrine in Calvin's systematic writings and in his preaching. In his sermons he rarely referred to reprobation.[148] Bauke was correct in detecting the rationalistic form of Calvin's systematic thought, but he erred in not perceiving that the rationalistic form also affected the content.[149] Furthermore, neither the form of Calvin's thought nor his theological method is consistently the same in all of his writings.

C. The Problem of Human Responsibility

Calvin's doctrine of providence and predestination raises serious problems in regard to human responsibility and freedom. If these

---

[147]*CR* 40:445–446. Cf. his exegesis of same passage in the polemic against the doctrine of Pighius *CR* 6:371.

[148]Paul Jacobs, *Prädestination und Verantwortlichkeit bei Calvin* (Kassel: J. C. Oncken Nachf., 1937), p. 148. Emil Brunner goes too far when he asserts that Calvin never preached reprobation. (*The Divine-Human Encounter,* tr. Amandus W. Loos [Philadelphia: Westminster Press, 1943], p. 126.) Cf. *CR* 58:42.

[149]Hermann Bauke, *Die Probleme der Theologie Calvins* (Leipzig: J. C. Hinrichs, 1922).

doctrines do annihilate human responsibility and freedom, then the Christian life is nothing more than the gyrations of marionettes.

Calvin's understanding of human responsibility always presupposes his doctrine of the human will. According to his meager psychology, the human soul has two faculties which relate to the problem of human responsibility—the understanding and the will. The office of the understanding is to discriminate between objects, and the function of the will is to choose and follow what the understanding shall have pronounced to be good.[150]

> Without perplexing ourselves with unnecessary questions, it should be sufficient for us to know that the understanding is, as it were, the guide and governor of the soul; that the will always respects its authority, and waits for its judgment in its desires.[151]

The condition of the first human was such that he could continue in a life of fellowship with God or turn his back on God.

> The primitive condition of man was ennobled with those eminent faculties; he possessed reason, understanding, prudence, and judgment, not only for the government of his life on earth, but to enable him to ascend even to God and eternal felicity. To these was added choice, to direct the appetites, and regulate all the organic motions; so that the will should be entirely conformed to the government of reason. In this integrity man was endued with free will, by which, if he had chosen, he might have obtained eternal life. . . . Adam, therefore, could have stood if he would, since he fell merely by his own will; but because his will was flexible to either side, and he was not endued with constancy to persevere, therefore he so easily fell. Yet his choice of good and evil was free; and not only so, but his mind and will were possessed of consummate rectitude, and all his organic parts were rightly disposed to obedience, till destroying himself, he corrupted all his excellencies.[152]

Calvin positively ascribes to original man the power of contrary choice. Adam's will was flexible to either side. He could have stood, if he would. Calvin regarded it as an important question whether the

---

[150]It is interesting to note the difference between paragraphs 1.15.7 and 1.15.8. In the first paragraph the will is completely determined by the understanding. In the following paragraph the will is given a much more independent place. The first paragraph was written in 1539 and the second in 1559. This may be an example of Platonic influence on Calvin's thought, which was more pronounced in the early years. However, the confusion of thought on this point existed in 1539, as 2.2.26 indicates.

[151]1.15.7.

[152]1.15.8.

fatal wound in human nature was there originally or was derived from an extraneous cause.[153] In as vigorous language as possible Calvin affirmed that human sinfulness proceeds from human acts, not from God.[154] Human corruption is an adventitious quality or accident, not a substantial property originally innate.[155] Nevertheless, Calvin could also write: "The first man fell because the Lord had determined it was so expedient."[156]

> They [those who object to Calvin's doctrine of predestination] maintain, that he [Adam] was possessed of free choice, that he might be the author of his own fate, but that God decreed nothing more than to treat him according to his desert. If so weak a scheme as this be received, what will become of God's omnipotence, by which he governs all things according to his secret counsel, independently of every person or thing besides?[157]

These quotations put in sharp relief two basic convictions of Calvin's theology. On the one hand, he had to hold to the complete sovereignty of God. This is to say that he could admit of no power which stood over against God, unless God willed that it so stand. The contention that God merely permitted some power to stand over against him he regarded as a subterfuge.[158] On the other hand, he was equally certain that God is not the author of sin, that Adam fell by his own decision. Calvin, admittedly, could not put these two elemental convictions together, but he was unwilling to sacrifice either for the sake of rational coherence. The result was a certain instability in his exposition of the doctrine which led to exaggerated statements that, taken by themselves, gave the impression that he made God the author of sin.

After the fall the human will was enslaved by sin. Adam was not merely the progenitor but also the root of all humankind, and therefore the race was necessarily vitiated in his corruption.[159] By sin the human will became the slave of sin. On the level of civil polity, domestic arts, and all the mechanical and liberal sciences, Calvin seems to allow human beings some freedom and some competence of understanding. On closer analysis, however, it appears that even these virtues are attributed to the working of the Spirit of God,

---

[153]It is important to note that Calvin discusses the necessity of the will in the section on man and not in the section on providence. The subject is discussed in the chapter on providence but only in an incidental way.

[154]2.1.10.

[155]2.1.11.

[156]3.23.8.

[157]3.23.7.

[158]3.23.8.

[159]2.1.6.

except that the Spirit in these cases does not sanctify. Confronted with the examples of persons who by the light of nature have been eminent for noble actions, Calvin remarks that we ought "to remember, that amidst this corruption of nature there is some room for Divine grace, not to purify it, but internally to restrain its operations."[160]

On the spiritual level, the enslaved will can in no sense repair the ruptured relationship with God. People have turned their backs on God, and they cannot find their way back to him unless God draws them.[161]

Calvin sought to maintain both the slavery of the will and human responsibility by distinguishing between the function of will as will and its capacity to choose between the good and the evil. Everywhere this premise is implicit in his writings. Adam's sin did not destroy the will. "There still remains the faculty of will, which with the strongest propensity is inclined to and rushes into sin; for when man subjected himself to this necessity, he was not deprived of his will, but of soundness of will."[162] On this basis Calvin insisted that people sin necessarily, but voluntarily.[163]

> We must therefore observe this grand point of distinction, that man, having been corrupted by his fall, sins voluntarily, not with reluctance or constraint; with the strongest propensity of disposition, not with violent coercion; with the bias of his own passions, and not with external compulsion: yet such is the pravity of his nature, that he cannot be excited and biassed to any thing but what is evil.[164]

Few people have ever maintained the responsibility of humankind more emphatically than Calvin. When he was confronted by the Spiritual Libertines, who held to a pantheistic determinism which made God the author of sin, he vigorously asserted human freedom.

---

[160] 2.3.3.

[161] 2.2.12.

[162] 2.3.5.

[163] *CR* 6:279: "Si coactioni opponitur libertas, liberum esse arbitrium, et fateor, et constanter assevero: ac pro haeretico habeo, quisquis secus sentiat. Si hoc, inquam, sensu liberum vocetur, quia non cogatur, aut violenter trahatur externo motu, sed sponte agatur sua, nihil moror."

CR 6:280: "Coactionem et violentiam tollimus, quia pugnet cum natura voluntatis, nec simul consistat. Liberum autem negamus, quia propter ingenitam homini pravitatem ad malum necessario feratur, nec nisi malum appetere queat. Atque hinc colligere licet, quantum sit necessitatis et coactionis discrimen. Neque enim hominem dicimus invitum trahi ad peccandum, sed quoniam vitiosa sit eius voluntas, sub peccati iugo teneri captivam, ideoque necessario male velle. Ubi enim servitus, illic necessitas. Sed plurimum interest, voluntariane sit servitus, an coacta. Nos autem non alibi statuimus peccandi necessitatem quam in vitio voluntatis: unde spontaneam esse ipsam sequitur. Nunc vides spontaneum et necessarium simul convenire posse."

[164] 2.3.5.

He pointed out to them "three wretched consequences" of their doctrine which attributed "to man no free will, any more than if he were a stone":

> The first of these is that there would no longer be any difference between God and the devil, for indeed the God which they made for us would be an idol, worse than the devil in hell. The second is that men would no longer have any conscience to avoid evil, but as beasts would follow their sensual appetites without any discretion. The third is that everything would have to be judged as good, whether it be lechery, murder, or larceny; and the most wicked crimes that one can imagine would have to be considered praiseworthy works.[165]

Calvin is speaking of free will in the sense of an uncoerced will. In the *Institutes* he also admits that the will is free in this sense but objects to using the term "free will" to describe its voluntary character. The term free will is too noble to be applied to so insignificant a quality of the will.[166] Apparently the context determined how insignificant this quality was.

In regeneration the human will always retains its integrity as will.

> When he [Augustine] observes that the will is not taken away by grace, but only changed from a bad one into a good one, and when it is good, assisted; he only intends that man is not drawn in such a manner as to be carried away by an external impulse, without any inclination of his mind; but that he is internally so disposed as to obey from his very heart.[167]

This change of will is effected internally by the Spirit and externally by the Word. "By his spirit illuminating their minds and forming their hearts to the love and cultivation of righteousness, he makes them new creatures. By his word he excites them to desire, seek, and obtain the same renovation."[168] Calvin uses a number of words to describe what the Spirit does in the act of regeneration.[169] But he does

---

[165]*CR* 7:186.

[166]2.2.7.

[167]2.3.14.

[168]2.5.5.

[169]2.3.6: "Therefore God begins the good work in us by exciting in our hearts a love, desire, and ardent pursuit of righteousness; or, to speak more properly, by bending, forming, and directing our hearts towards righteousness; but he completes it, by confirming us to perseverance."

2.5.15: "Hence it appears that the grace of God, in the sense in which this word is used when we treat of regeneration, is the rule of the Spirit for directing and governing the human will. He cannot govern it unless he correct, reform, and renovate it; whence we say that the commencement of regeneration is an abolition of what is from ourselves; nor unless he also excite, actuate, impel, support, and restrain it; whence we truly assert, that all the actions

not tell how the Spirit does this work without doing violence to the will. This is the mystery of the divine election. Calvin displays little curiosity about the matter and contents himself with what he regards as the fact. He was equally convinced that this work of the Spirit is so done that "there is no reason why we may not justly be said to perform that which the Spirit of God performs in us, although our own will contributes nothing of itself, independently of his grace."[170]

Calvin endeavored to maintain the facts and the mystery which unified the facts. He did not regard this mystery as irrational, but as beyond the comprehension of human intelligence, particularly intelligence which is partially vitiated by sin. Furthermore, Calvin was sure that the mystery of the divine-human relationship is not unintelligible to experience and that the reality of that which cannot be captured by human logic is verified in the experience of the saints.

Calvin does make two suggestions which illuminate the relationship of God and humankind in connection with these problems. First, in all of his operations God deals with human beings as persons and not as things. In his tract against the Libertines Calvin wrote:

> Satan and the wicked are not such instruments of God that they do not work as well on their own part. For it is not necessary that we imagine that God needs a wicked man as a stone or as a trunk of wood, but he uses him as a reasonable creature, according to the quality of his nature which he has given him. When, therefore, we say that God works through the wicked, that does not prevent them from working also on their own part.[171]

In his reply to Bolsec Calvin explicitly disavowed the use of necessitarian language in describing God's relation to human beings.[172]

---

which proceed from this are entirely of the Spirit. At the same time, we fully admit the truth of what Augustine teaches, that the will is not destroyed by grace, but rather repaired; for these two things are perfectly consistent—that the human will may be said to be repaired, when, by the correction of its depravity and perverseness, it is directed according to the true standard of righteousness; and also that a new will may be said to be created in man, because the natural will is so vitiated and corrupted, that it needs to be formed entirely anew."

[170] 2.5.15.

[171] *CR* 7:188.

[172] Ibid. Cf. *CR* 31:412: "Moreover, it appears from other places of scripture that it is the peculiar office of the Holy Spirit to engrave the Law of God on our hearts. God, it is true, does not perform his work in us as if we were stones or stocks, drawing us to himself without the feeling or inward moving of our hearts toward him. But as there is in us naturally a will, which, however, is depraved by the corruption of our nature, so that it always inclines us to sin, God changes it for the better, and thus leads us cordially to seek after righteousness, to which our hearts were previously altogether averse. Hence arises that true freedom which we obtain when God frames our hearts, which before were in thralldom to sin, unto obedience to himself."

God does not force people.[173] Admittedly, this does not solve the problem, but it gives us warrant for attempting to find in human relations some analogy for the operation of God in people's hearts. If one wants some clue to the operation of the Spirit in the elect, one may find it in the deepest of personal experiences—love. In every experience of true love there is a sort of election which lays hold of another person, but in such a way that violence is not done to that person's will. Indeed, true freedom is the gift of grace.[174] The problem of Calvin's theology at this point is the apparent inconsistency between some of his statements on predestination and his assertion that God always deals with human beings as persons and not as things.

The other suggestion Calvin makes is the diversity of intention between the work of God and evil people in any particular event.

> The wicked man is moved either by avarice, or ambition, or envy, or cruelty, to do what he does; and he does not take into consideration any other end. He is rightly judged evil since the nature of works is determined by their source, which is the affection of the heart, and the end to which they are directed. But with God it is different. He exercises his justice for the salvation and preservation of the righteous, directs his goodness and grace toward the faithful to chastise those who deserve it. Therefore it is necessary to discern between God and men in order to contemplate in a single deed his justice, his goodness, his judgment; and on the other hand, such great mischief of the devil and of the unfaithful.[175]

The case of Job was a favorite illustration which Calvin used in this connection.[176] Here God, the Chaldeans, and the devil took part

---

[173]*CR* 8:182: "As for me, he slanders me falsely, saying that I have written that God forces man to sin. In the first place, the phrase 'God forces' is not my language but the jargon of priests, which I have never used. After this, it is impudent spite to say that I have even applied the word sin to God or to his will. Too well have I said that God's will as supreme cause is necessary in all things. But I stated when and where God disposes for himself, and moderates everything he does with such fairness and justice that the most wicked are forced to glorify him, and that his will is neither a tyranny nor a pleasure without reason, but rather it is the true rule of all good. Moreover, I have notably expressed and declared that men are not compelled to do either good or evil, but that those who do good do it from a frank desire that God give them his Holy Spirit. Those who do evil do it of their natural desire, which is corrupt and bad."

[174]2.3.14. Cf. Alfred de Quervain, *Calvin, sein Lehren und Kämpfen* (Berlin: Furche, 1926), p. 58: "Freedom does not lie in man's nature; it rests in God. He alone frees, and our freedom is his gift, no principle of a system, no goal of development. His holy will does not coincide with the law of our own nature; it never comes of the natural law of man, not even of the religious one."

[175]*CR* 7:189. Cf. *CR* 43:502; 48:46.

[176]1.18.1 Cf. *CR* 33:49. "Thus we may say with truth and propriety that Joseph was sold by the wicked consent of his brethren and by the secret providence of God. Yet it was not a work common to both, in the sense that God sanctioned anything connected with or relating to their

in the same event, yet in such a way that each acted according to the motivation of his own heart. The end which each had in view was different from that of the others.

In sum, the confidence which characterizes the Christian life finds its theological basis in providence and predestination. Providence is the loving care of an omnicompetent heavenly Father. Predestination is the personal election of a loving God which calls forth faith in his children. Yet the power of God which is manifest in providence and predestination acts upon people in such a way that their personalities are neither coerced nor destroyed. Calvin's theological statement of this doctrine, it seems to me, is in many ways inadequate, as has been noted. Sometimes it comes close to a speculative determinism which undercuts all personal existence. Yet, as important as this fact is, it is also necessary to remember that Calvin was endeavoring to give expression to a doctrine which, as he said, is a testimony to our adoption, and not a speculative unraveling of the mystery of the divine mercy. His understanding of the Christian life is unintelligible apart from the confidence and humility which come from the conviction that the life of faith is undergirded by the power of God. Furthermore, it is this living conviction that God works in and through human life which largely accounts for the creativity of Calvinism in history.

---

wicked cupidity, because while they were contriving the destruction of their brother, God was effecting their deliverance from on high. Whence also we conclude that there are various methods of governing the world. This truly must be generally agreed, that nothing is done without his will because he governs the counsels of men, and sways their wills and turns their efforts at his pleasure, and regulates all events. But if men undertake anything right and just, he so actuates and moves them inwardly by his Spirit that whatever is good in them may justly be said to be received from him; but if Satan and ungodly men rage, he acts by their hands in such an inexpressible manner that the wickedness of the deed belongs to them, and the blame of it is imputed to them."

Chapter 4

The Christian Life in Relation to History and the Transhistorical

The Christian life is a life of hope. In this world the life of the godly is hidden, and their salvation is invisible.[1] Paul takes it for granted that so long as we live in this world our salvation stands in hope.[2] The forces of sin contradict the life in which Christians believe, both in their own hearts and in the world.[3] For this reason Calvin was convinced that faith cannot stand unless it is firmly founded on the promises of God.[4] The Christian warfare is sustained by hope.[5] The holy fathers were animated by the hope of a better life, and they did not give way to fatigue before death.[6] Lot is an example for us all, when in the midst of destruction he laid hold of the promises of God.[7]

Hope places history in tension with that which is beyond history.

---

[1] *CR* 45:371.

[2] *CR* 45:155.

[3] 3.25.1: "In a word, above and below, before and behind, we are beset by violent temptations, which our minds would long ago have been incapable of sustaining, if they had not been detached from terrestrial things, and attached to the heavenly life, which is apparently at a remote distance. He alone, therefore, has made a solid proficiency in the gospel who has been accustomed to continual meditation on the blessed resurrection."

[4] *CR* 22:59. The relation of faith and hope is well described in his passage from the Catechism of 1537: "Thus Faith believes that God is real; Hope awaits the opportune time for him to demonstrate his reality. Faith believes that God is our Father; Hope believes that he will always act as such toward us. Faith believes that eternal life is given to us; Hope awaits the time when it will be revealed. Faith is the foundation on which Hope is supported; Hope nourishes and entertains Faith."

[5] *CR* 51:154. Cf. *CR* 49:242: "For no man will cheerfully, and with a quiet mind, submit himself to bear the cross, but he who hath learned to seek for his felicity out of the world, that with the consolation of hope he may mitigate and qualify the bitterness of the cross; but because both these are far above our strength, we must be earnest in prayer, and beseech God continually, that he suffer not our hearts to faint, fall to the ground, or be broken with adversity."

[6] *CR* 23:321.

[7] *CR* 23:273; 26:224.

Life within history is always not yet completed. It looks to its fulfillment beyond history. This tension between life as not yet completed and life as fulfilled energizes the whole of Christian existence and drives it forward. It gives zest and purpose to life. The peculiar character of Christian existence is just this tension between two worlds, and paradoxically it is this tension which integrates the Christian personality. Hope is tension between life as it now is and life as God promises it shall be.

The tension between heaven and earth which constitutes the Christian hope can be broken from either side. When the meaning of life is confined to history, the result is secularism. The heavenly city is built on earth. This has been the case wherever Calvinism has become identified with the capitalistic spirit. The virtues of frugality and industry were always given a strong eschatological setting by the Genevan Reformer, but his posterity sometimes dropped the eschatology.

Life's meaning can also be confined to that which is beyond history, thereby denying any real significance to the historical process. According to this view, progress is not possible in history, but in escape from history. Martin Schulze, whose study pointed out the strongly eschatological character of Calvin's theology, concludes that the Genevan Reformer was guilty of this otherworldly asceticism. According to Schulze, Calvin differs from Luther in that for Calvin, salvation was essentially a matter of expectation, thereby giving an ascetic turn to the Christian's relation to the world.[8] Meditation on the future life, conceived in an otherworldly sense, Schulze says, is the dominant idea in Calvin's whole theology. Even the doctrine of humankind is treated from the viewpoint of the immortality of the soul.[9] This otherworldly coloring of Calvin's theology has two important consequences. In the first place, Calvin did not rise above Catholic monachism as a life ideal.[10] This is to say that

---

[8]*Meditatio futurae vitae; ihr Begriff und ihre beherrschende Stellung im System Calvins* (Leipzig: T. Weicher, 1901), p. 1: "In both regards Calvin diverges from Luther. The treasure of salvation with him is mainly an object of expectation, and the attitude toward the world receives in this connection a turn to the ascetic."

[9]Ibid., p. 65.

[10]Ibid., p. 18: "After all this, it must be said: Calvin has not overcome the monkish idea of life in principle. Of course, he was far from speaking for a presumably higher morality outside the calling. But on the other hand, he has not achieved a positive appreciation of it. As long as this miserable life endures, it is only the outer form, in which the Christian is not to set value on his deeds; it is the school in which one has to learn and to practice self-denial. The actual task of the Christian life remains in the calling to die to the world. The meaning of this task, of course, is for him an unendingly deeper one, and in the striving for its solution a much purer one, than in monasticism."

Calvin failed to give positive value to life in history. In the second place, Calvin's understanding of life is essentially that of the *Phaedo.* [11]

If Schulze's thesis is correct, then Calvin did not maintain the tension between the historical and the transhistorical. History is a meaningless process which is to be endured for the sake of that which is beyond history. Schulze can quote texts from the *Institutes* to establish his thesis. For example, "there is no medium between these two extremes; either the earth must become vile in our estimation, or it must retain our immoderate love."[12] On the other hand, there are equally striking passages which affirm the real value of historical existence. God himself has given human beings the various blessings of historical life not merely to satisfy the necessities of life, but also to provide pleasure and delight for humankind.[13] Thus the problem is to set in proper balance Calvin's evaluation of the historical and the transhistorical. In other words, the problem is to see Calvin's eschatology in the light of other factors in his theology. Schulze attempted to make eschatology the "central" doctrine by which all other doctrines were interpreted. As has been the case with other attempts to reduce Calvinism to one central doctrine, the result was a misinterpretation of the whole theology.[14]

A. History

Calvin does not depreciate history as such. His strictures against history are directed against history as sinful existence. The sinful nature of history is, however, an accidental quality; therefore a careful distinction must be made between what Calvin has to say about history as sinful existence, and history as such. For history as such Calvin had genuine appreciation.

In the first place, history is a sphere in which God works and in which people live. Consequently it is a potential source of knowledge about God and people and their relations with each other. The importance of history for religious knowledge is one of the distin-

---

[11]Ibid., p. 81. "Calvin's view of life resembles that which is here essentially outlined after the *Phaedo.* The correspondence extends even to the peculiarities of expression and representation, as I have shown. The matter in my thought is such that we would have to assume Plato's direct influence on Calvin in this respect even if the latter nowhere referred to the former."
[12]3.9.2.
[13]3.10.2.
[14]Hermann Bauke, *Die Probleme der Theologie Calvins* (Leipzig: J. C. Hinrichs, 1922), p. 4; Émile Doumergue, *Jean Calvin, les hommes et les choses de son temps* (Lausanne: Georges Bridel & Cie., 1899–1927), 4:305ff.

guishing features of Calvin's epistemology. He placed far more emphasis on it than on speculative reasoning, though the two methods are not exclusive.

History, however, is not an independent source of religious knowledge. It is a valid source of knowledge only when it is interpreted in the light of the Bible.[15] Furthermore, it is faith alone which perceives the operations of God.[16] God is infinitely more than history, and consequently no one can master God by knowing history. God is always the revealer of himself, never the object of human investigation. Nevertheless, the knowledge of God which we gain from history is not worthless. "For although God does not declare to us what he is about to do, yet he intends us to be eyewitnesses of his works, and prudently to weigh their causes, and not to be dazzled by a confused beholding of them, like unbelievers, who seeing, see not, and who pervert their true design."[17]

Although history in general is a valuable source of knowledge of God and humankind, this is especially true of the history of the church.

> This is the chiefest praise that a profane history has, namely, that it is the mistress of life. If that narration of famous deeds, which only teaches men what they ought to follow, or what they ought to eschew, in their common actions, deserves such a title, of how great praise are the divine histories worthy, which do not only frame the outward life of man that he may win praise by virtue, but also (which is more) which declare unto us that God, from the beginning, has always had a special regard of his church (and faithful congregation), that he has been always a most just revenger of all wrongs done unto those that have betaken themselves unto his tuition and have committed themselves unto his custody; that he has showed himself favorable and merciful unto most miserable and wretched sinners; and, lastly, by teaching us faith, raised us high above the heavens.[18]

The value of history is manifold: "It becomes the faithful to be employed in reflecting on the histories of all times, that they may always form their judgment from the scripture of the various de-

---

[15]*CR* 49:86: "The heathen have truly called a history the mistress of life; but, as it comes from them, no man can safely profit in it. Only the scripture rightly challenges that preeminence; for, first, it prescribes general rules to which we may bring every history for trial, that it may serve to our profit. Second, it clearly discerns what deeds are to be followed, and what are to be avoided. And, as for doctrine, wherein it is chiefly conversant, . . . it shows the providence of the Lord, his justice and goodness toward his own, and his judgments toward the reprobate."

[16]*CR* 25:447.

[17]*CR* 23:258.

[18]*CR* 48:7.

structions which, privately and publicly, have befallen the ungodly."[19] Faith is confirmed by the study of the works of God in
history.[20] Recollection of some event in which God's power has been
manifested for his people supports one with "invincible firmness."[21]
History reminds us that all of life stands under death, that there is
no immortality on earth; and thereby it restrains immoderate attachment to riches.[22] It reveals human infirmity and the grace of God,
which relieves this infirmity.[23] History animates the godly with good
hopes and everywhere reflects God's paternal care.[24] The recollection
of one's past life should stimulate one to repentance.[25]

The importance of history, however, extends far beyond the personal life of the Christian. It serves as a criterion of the morality of
society and offers a vantage point for judgment.[26]

Calamities and other crises which befall human beings should be
subjected to careful study by the faithful in order to discover the
meaning of these events. Calvin would, of course, object to any easy
rationalization of history, especially those rationalizations which
exempt the interpreter from the judgment of God. On the other
hand, he would equally object to the indifference with which a scien-
tifically-minded modern Christian dismisses history without any theological reflection.

> It is when God sends some calamity upon the world that we realize
> it is not without cause that he is irritated. For if we recognize the
> offenses and transgressions which have been committed, it is necessary
> that we come to this conclusion: God is showing himself a judge
> who punishes sin. Now is it only for those who endure the blows?
> No, for God wishes to show in general his just vengeance, in order
> that one learn to humble himself before him, that one walk in fear of
> him, that one no longer allow himself to provoke him. In brief, all
> the chastisements which we see in the world should serve to teach
> us.[27]

---

[19]*CR* 23:257.
[20]*CR* 45:79; 23: 583–584.
[21]*CR* 24:181.
[22]*CR* 23:106, 190.
[23]*CR* 23:286, 504.
[24]*CR* 42:582; 58:18.
[25]*CR* 55:271.
[26]*CR* 36:22: "Yet it is of high importance to us to compare the behavior of men of our own
age with the behavior of that ancient people; and from their histories and examples we ought
to make known the judgments of God; such as that what he formerly punished he will also
punish with equal severity in our own day, for he is always like himself. Such wisdom let godly
teachers acquire, if they would wish to handle the doctrine of the prophets with any good
result."
[27]*CR* 26:113.

In addition to calamities which in scientific terminology are ascribed to natural causes, Calvin also insisted that matters of political and social significance should be subjected to the same theological scrutiny. In other words, they should not be interpreted by mere political and sociological criteria, but also by the revelation of God which we have in the Bible. Calvin does not neglect the former, but he does consider the latter as the decisive norm of interpretation.[28]

The fact that history is a valid and important source of religious knowledge is not a final assessment of its meaning, but it is a step toward a positive evaluation of the historical process. Unless there were some meaning to the historical process, it would be foolish to put so great an emphasis on it as the sphere in which human beings come to know themselves and their God. This emphasis distinguishes Calvin from those who give primary attention to the rational processes to the exclusion of events and acts. For him acts and events were as real as rational processes. There is a rational pattern of existence and of history which is partially intelligible to humankind's fallen reason, but Calvin always tried to balance actual events against any speculative apprehension of that rational structure.

In the second place history is important because it is the sphere in which human beings use or misuse God's gifts. One of the most emphatic points in Calvin's whole theology is that creation is good. There is no opposition between nature as such and grace. Calvin would have nothing to do with any doctrine of a superadded gift. Schulze's thesis that Calvin did not rise above the monkish retreat from the world contradicts his doctrine of creation. Calvin distinguished between creation as such and creation insofar as it has been distorted by sin, but he does not always indicate this distinction. His failure to make clear this distinction provides the basis for Schulze's thesis.

In the use of God's creation, Calvin sought to avoid the extreme of severity on the one hand and the extreme of license on the other.

---

[28]*CR* 26:25–26: "When we see a healthy people, strong and well-fortified towns, ... and when it is brought down by enemies, yet must we think that God has worked there. And thus we must learn to reflect on his judgments in all the revolutions in the world. And as much as these things are troubling, know that God rules over all. It is true that men are unruly, and that they go around in confusion, and when they move, and relocate, it seems that God is excluded: but all that they plot will not stop God from turning everything to such an end as he has designated in his wisdom. And therefore, as I have already said, we should not think that fortune dominates in this world, but should know that God has reserved for himself the superintendency to bring all, even the dissensions that men undertake, to such an end as he will have ordered, and to punish the sins of those who offend him, to humble those who exalt themselves too much, and to suppress his blessings when he sees that men are profane. This is what we must take note of."

He explicitly rejected austerity as a way of holiness[29] and did so for two reasons. In the first place, he understood too well that religion is a personal matter and that ceremonies and externals do not necessarily touch a person's relationship with God.[30] Calvin would have nothing to do with "fanatics" who would make poverty the only gate to heaven. Poverty, he rightly understood, sometimes involves more temptations than riches.[31] Asceticism is not religion. In the second place, austerity in life is an abuse of God's gifts. A passage concerning dress illustrates this point:

> But it would be an immoderate strictness wholly to forbid neatness and elegance in clothing. If the material is said to be too sumptuous, the Lord has created it; and we know that skill in art has proceeded from him. Then Peter did not intend to condemn every sort of ornament, but the evil of vanity, to which women are subject. Two things are to be regarded in clothing, usefulness and decency; and what decency requires is moderation and modesty.[32]

Timothy was rebuked because excess severity of living was a fault with him.[33]

Furthermore, the gifts God has provided for humankind minister not merely to the necessities of human life but also to human pleasure and delight.

> But shall the Lord have endued flowers with such beauty, to present itself to our eyes, with such sweetness of smell, to impress our sense of smelling; and shall it be unlawful for our eyes to be affected with

---

[29]3.10.1.

[30]*CR* 52:299: "This is a very necessary warning; for the world will always lean to the side of wishing to worship God by outward services, which is an exceedingly dangerous imagination. But—to say nothing about the wicked opinion of merit—our nature always disposes us strongly to attribute more than we ought to austerity of life, as if it were no ordinary portion of Christian holiness. . . . But godliness is profitable for all things. That is, he who has godliness wants nothing, though he has not those little aids; for godliness alone is able to conduct a man to complete perfection. It is the beginning, the middle, and the end of Christian life; and therefore, where that is entire, nothing is imperfect. Christ did not lead so austere a manner of life as John the Baptist; was he, therefore, in any way inferior? Let the meaning be thus summed up. We ought to apply ourselves altogether to piety alone, because when we have once attained it, God asks nothing more from us; and we ought to give attention to bodily exercises in such a manner as not to hinder or retard the practice of godliness."

CR 45:14: "We must not on this ground imagine that the worship of God consists in the abstinence from wine, as apish copyists select some part of the actions of the fathers for an object of imitation. Only let all practice temperance; let those who conceive it to be injurious to drink wine abstain of their own accord, and let those who have it not endure the want with contentment."

[31]*CR* 23:189.

[32]*CR* 55:254.

[33]*CR* 52:320.

the beautiful sight, or our olfactory nerves with the agreeable odor? ... In a word, has he not made many things worthy of our estimation, independently of any necessary use?[34]

Calvin's appreciation of the good things of life stands in sharp contrast to asceticism. His own life was no doubt severe in the light of present-day standards; but he did not, like some persons of his age, wear a hair shirt. There is no indication that he was ever seriously tempted to become a monk. As early as 1531 he had little sympathy for such practices as a way of holiness.[35] Calvin's repudiation of Catholic monachism is explicit and unequivocal.

Calvin also sought to avoid the extreme of licentiousness, as well as that of austerity. The blessings of earthly life are not an end in themselves but are a means to prepare human beings for the enjoyment of eternal happiness.[36] The essence of life, according to Calvin, inheres in fellowship with God. God's blessings of food and clothing are designed as aids to this fellowship. Intemperance transforms the means of fellowship into the end of life itself. Thus those who become "slaves of the palate" are drawn off from their duty and from the obedience and fear of God.[37] Everything in life must be evaluated with reference to fellowship with God, in which human life consists.[38] Consequently, Calvin regarded the ability to be satisfied with

---

[34] 3.10.2. *CR* 23:545: "Should any one object that a frugal use of food and drink is simply that which suffices for the nourishment of the body, I answer: although food is properly for the supply of our necessities, yet the legitimate use of it may proceed further. For it is not in vain that our food has savor as well as vital nutriment; but thus our heavenly Father sweetly delights us with his delicacies. And his benignity is not in vain commended in Psalm 104:15, where he is said to create wine that makes glad the heart of man. Nevertheless, the more kindly he indulges us, the more solicitously ought we to restrict ourselves to a frugal use of his gifts."

CR 32:90: "In these words we are taught that God not only provides for men's necessity and bestows on them as much as is sufficient for the ordinary purposes of life, but that in his goodness he deals still more bountifully with them by cheering their hearts with wine and oil. Nature would certainly be satisfied with water to drink, and therefore the addition of wine is owing to God's superabundant liberality."

[35] *CR* 10(b): 10. The letter which is the source of this reference is dated 1531 by the editors of the *Corpus Reformatorum*. Jacques Pannier dates it several years later in his *Recherches sur l'évolution religieuse de Calvin jusqu'à sa conversion* (Strasbourg: Librairie Istra, 1924), pp. 33ff.

[36] *CR* 36:47–48. Cf. *CR* 36:111: "Men were not born to eat, drink, and wallow in luxury, but to obey God, to worship him devoutly, to acknowledge his goodness, and to endeavor to do what is pleasing in his sight. But when they give themselves up to luxury, when they dance, and sing, and have no other object in view than to spend their life in the highest mirth, they are worse than beasts; for they do not consider for what end God created them, in what manner he governs this world by his providence, and to what end all the actions of our life ought to be directed."

[37] *CR* 40:550.

[38] *CR* 32:412: "Better it were at once to perish for want than have a mere brute satisfaction and forget the main thing of all, that they and they only are happy whom God has chosen

little or with plenty, so long as fellowship with God remained unimpaired, as the true proof of temperance.[39] Temperance is not a quantitative term but is the ability to make all of life contribute to communion with God.

The very nature of this problem makes it impossible to set fixed and precise rules to govern the human use of God's blessings.[40] As has been repeated over and over, the relation of the Christian to God is a personal relationship; and personality cannot be circumscribed by laws. Love, which is the essence of personal relationships, is singularly free from regulations. In God's dealing with people there is all the freedom of a father who deals with his children.[41]

Although Calvin does not prescribe exact rules for guidance in the use of God's gifts in this life, he does formulate certain general principles which are useful in guiding the individual conscience in its course of action. The decision must always be that of the individual, however.[42]

The first principle which Calvin laid down is "that the use of the gifts of God is not erroneous, when it is directed to the same end for which the Creator himself has created and appointed them for us; since he has created them for our benefit, not for our injury."[43] It is an inhuman philosophy which allows no use of the divine beneficence except that which is absolutely necessary, for it despoils human beings of their sense and reduces them to a senseless block.[44] Calvin was convinced that there was no sin in being a real human being. Human emotions and appetites are good, and they are evil only when

---

for his people. We are to observe this that while God in giving us meat and drink admits us to the enjoyment of a certain measure of happiness, it does not follow that those believers are miserable who struggle through life in want and poverty, for this want, whatever it be, God can counterbalance by better consolations."

[39]*CR* 40:551.

[40]3.10.1.

[41]*CR* 31:378: "With respect to the temporal blessings which God confers upon his people, no certain or uniform rule can be established. There are various reasons why God does not manifest his favor equally to all the godly in this world. He chastises some, while he spares others. . . . But in general, he humbles all of them by the tokens of his anger, that by secret warnings they may be brought to repentance."

[42]It may be objected that Calvin was legalistic in practice. Calvin certainly believed that excess is wrong and that in many cases that which constitutes excess can be clearly recognized. By present-day standards what he regarded as excess may be more or less normal. However, in any such assessment of Calvin, it must be remembered that Geneva was not unique because of sumptuary legislation. Men were burned for heresy and sumptuary legislation was on the books long before Calvin ever arrived at Geneva. It was not sumptuary legislation which made Geneva "the most perfect school of Christ on earth." Cf. Henri Naef, *Les origines de la réforme à Genève* (Geneva: A. Jullien, 1936), pp. 216ff.

[43]3.10.2.

[44]3.10.3.

they are abused. "The perfect purity of his [Christ's] nature did not extinguish the human affections; it only regulated them that they might not become sinful through excess."[45] Against all asceticism, Calvin set the principle that God's gifts are to be used for the purposes for which he gave them.

On the other hand, Calvin was opposed to intemperance; and he found four general principles to aid people in avoiding this pitfall. In the first place, "it will be one check . . . if it be concluded, that all things are made for us, in order that we may know and acknowledge their Author, and celebrate his goodness towards us by giving him thanks."[46] If the body is stupefied by dainties or inflamed with passions by abundance, or if by virtue of sumptuous apparel one esteems oneself and despises others, then quite clearly one is not giving thanks.

A second means by which intemperance can be checked is meditation on the future life. As indicated previously, meditation on the future life must not be conceived in the sense of otherworldly speculation. It is essentially a life of communion with God. It is the apprehension of the fact that the essence of life inheres in this fellowship and not in such things as wealth or power or pleasure. The meditation on the future life has two implications as regards the use of the things of this life:

> The first is, "that they that have wives be as though they had none; and they that buy, as though they possessed not; and they that use this world, as not abusing it"; according to the direction of Paul; the second, that we should learn to enjoy penury with tranquillity and patience as well as to enjoy abundance with moderation.[47]

The use of this world as though one used it not Calvin interprets to mean that God not only prohibits "intemperance in eating . . . , ambition . . . , fastidiousness in our furniture, our habitations, and our apparel, but every care and affection, which would seduce or disturb us from thoughts of the heavenly life, and attention to improvement of our souls."[48] Furthermore, meditation on the future life places life in balance so that a person is neither ashamed of poverty nor proud of wealth. Life does not consist in the abundance a person possesses. Calvin rightly perceived that the person who is proud of a splendid garment will be ashamed of a mean garment. Pride and shame arise from the same unbalanced attitude toward life. The

---

[45]*CR* 31:227–228.
[46]3.10.3.
[47]3.10.4.
[48]Ibid.

reason for this imbalance in life is the failure to meditate on the future life.[49]

The third principle which enables a person to avoid intemperance is stewardship. All things which are given to us by the divine goodness and appointed for our benefit are entrusted to our care, and someday we all must give an account of our stewardship.[50] Calvin does not permit us to claim anything as our own, fee simple. Everything, even life itself, is a trust from God. The same God who grants his gifts as trusts demands frugality and charity in their use.

The fourth principle is the doctrine of vocation.[51] Vocation has a twofold significance for Calvin. In the first place, "every individual's line of life . . . is, as it were, a post assigned to him by the Lord."[52] Consequently, every person is responsible to God for the performance of a task.[53] Every work is a sacred trust. There is "no employment so mean and sordid (provided we follow our vocation) as not to appear truly respectable and be deemed highly important in the sight of God."[54] In the second place, vocation places a limit on ambition and the mad scramble of people for position and honor. God has assigned the people particular duties in different spheres of life to prevent universal confusion as a result of human folly and temerity.[55] No one should seek to transgress the limits of one's call-

---

[49] *CR* 49:420: "All things that are connected with the enjoyment of the present life are sacred gifts of God, but we pollute them when we abuse them. If the reason is asked, we shall find it to be this, that we always dream of continuance in the world, for it is owing to this that those things which ought to be helps in passing through it become hindrances to hold us fast. Hence, it is not without good reason that the apostle, with the view of arousing us from this stupidity, calls us to consider the shortness of this life, and infers from this that we ought to use all the things of this world as if we did not use them. For the man who considers that he is a stranger in the world uses the things of this world as if they were another's, that is, as things that are lent us for a single day. The sum is this, that the mind of a Christian ought not to be taken up with earthly things or to repose in them, for we ought to live as if we were every moment about to depart from this life."

[50] 3.10.5.

[51] 3.10.6.

[52] Ibid.

[53] *CR* 7:81: "Vocation is the principal part of the human life and that which is the most important before God."

[54] 3.10.6.

[55] *CR* 52:163–164: "This is the purport of what he adds immediately afterward—to do your own business: for we commonly see that those who intrude themselves with forwardness into the affairs of others make great disturbance and give trouble to themselves and others. This, therefore, is the best means of a tranquil life, when everyone, intent on the duties of his own calling, discharges those duties which are enjoined on him by the Lord and devotes himself to these things: While the husband-man employs himself in rural labors, the workman carries on his occupation, and in this way everyone keeps within his own limits. So soon as men turn aside from this, everything is thrown into confusion and disorder. He does not mean, however, that everyone shall mind his own business in such a way as that each one lives apart, having

ing. "He that is in obscurity will lead a private life without discontent, so as not to desert the station in which God has placed him."[56] Thus Calvin condemned a social restlessness which gives ambition or personal gain a dominant priority in life. The culture in which Calvinism has found its strongest expression has always placed its greatest emphasis on the doctrine of calling in the sense of zealously performing one's work to the best of one's ability, but has soft-pedaled Calvin's use of the doctrine as a limitation on ambition.

Vocation does not mean that any work is acceptable before God.[57] Calvin was very clear that only those forms of life which agree with God's will are acceptable. Nor does the doctrine mean that people cannot change their work once they have begun in a specific trade, but a change in work must not be undertaken rashly.[58] Calvin's purpose was to reduce the role of pride and selfishness in social activity. A person's position in society must be determined by some other motive than personal aggrandizement. It is easy to see the value of the doctrine of vocation not only to society but also to personal living. The difficulty in the doctrine lies in the fact that there is no short and easy way to determine clearly what is one's calling. Calvin gives little specific instruction, and in the last analysis it is always a matter which must be decided by individuals as they stand in the presence of God. On the negative side, Calvin could clearly

---

no care for others; but he has merely in view to correct an idle levity which makes men noisy bustlers in public, who ought to lead a quiet life in their own houses."

[56]3.10.6.

[57]*CR* 49:415–416: "A calling in scripture means a lawful mode of life, for it has a relation to God as calling us, lest anyone should abuse this statement to justify modes of life that are evidently wicked or vicious. But here it is asked whether Paul means to establish any obligation, for it might seem as though the words conveyed this idea, that everyone is bound to his calling, so that he must not abandon it. Now it were a very hard thing if a tailor were not at liberty to learn another trade, or if a merchant were not at liberty to betake himself to farming. I answer that this is not what the apostle intends, for he has it simply in view to correct that inconsiderate eagerness which prompts some to change their condition without any proper reason, whether they do it from superstition or from any other motive. Further, he calls everyone to this rule also, that they bear in mind what is suitable to their calling. He does not, therefore, impose on anyone the necessity of continuing in the kind of life which he has once taken up, but rather condemns that restlessness which prevents an individual from remaining in his condition with a peaceable mind, and he exhorts that everyone stick by his trade, as the old proverb goes. . . . And hence we infer, not merely that it is owing to the providence of God that there are different ranks and stations in the world, but also that a regard to them is enjoined by his word."

[58]*CR* 49:414: "The sum is this, that in external things you must not rashly abandon the calling on which you have once entered by the will of God. And he begins with circumcision, respecting which many at that time disputed. Now, he says that with God it makes no difference whether you are a Gentile or a Jew. Hence he exhorts everyone to be content with his condition. It must always be kept in view that he treats only of lawful modes of life, which have God as their approver and author."

point out that any calling which is motivated by pride and selfishness is no calling from God.

In the third place, history has positive value for Calvin because it is the sphere in which human beings grow in fellowship with God. As has been previously noted, creation in the image of God means that the highest human good consists in communion with God.[59] Apart from the fall, history would presumably be important as the sphere in which fellowship develops and deepens. After the fall history is important because it is the sphere in which this fellowship is restored and developed. The image of God is reconstructed in history, but this reconstruction of the image finds its full fruition beyond history—in eternity. Thus the onward movement of sanctification in history is eternally important. On the negative side, the destruction of the image also has eternal significance.

The development of fellowship with God has social as well as individual significance. The life of sonship is life in community. There is within history the community of the elect which seeks to realize God's will on earth. Calvin did not identify the kingdom of God with any earthly kingdom, but he did quite clearly believe that the kingdom exists in and through history and that it is visible to the eyes of faith. The kingdom of God is also closely related to the church, and Calvin had no hesitation in calling the people of God to warfare against and conquest of all earthly evils. Indirectly his writings reveal a genuine optimism about the conquest of social evil.[60] Always the activities of God's people are undergirded by the power and promises of God.[61]

Calvin took note of the fact that pagans frequently despair of life. They see no reason for joy on the day of birth. Calvin would have nothing to do with any such view. Pagans know only the misery of this world, but Christians know the source of this misery. In evaluating the significance of life the point of departure must be the original creation, where God's goodness is abundantly manifest.[62] God placed human beings in the world that he might be a Father to them and give them manifold expressions of his fatherly love. Through this love God chooses to draw them to himself. Such is the meaning of human life as God ordained it. Sin throws human life into disorder, but it does not annihilate its purpose. In spite of sin God continually seeks to draw people to himself by his gentleness and his love. It is

---

[59]2.2.1.

[60]J. T. McNeill, *Christian Hope for World Society* (Chicago: Willett, Clark & Co., 1937), pp. 111–112.

[61]*CR* 58:19–20. See the next chapter for further discussion of these ideas.

[62]*CR* 33:144.

only base ingratitude which refuses to rejoice in the goodness of God in human life.[63]

Schulze contends that Calvin taught that human beings should long for death. Certainly this is not the whole truth. Calvin made abundantly clear that love for this life is not wrong in itself. It is wrong only when it distorts the very being of life itself—fellowship with God. When love for this world does distort a person's relation with God, then life itself is destroyed.[64] Calvin faced the question of an otherworldly religion which longs for death as an escape from the evil of the world, and he answered it with a decisive no. Death is desirable only insofar as it is the end of the torments of sin.

> Now if one raises a question here, whether it is lawful to desire death—the answer may be briefly this: that death is not to be desired on account of weariness of life, this is one thing—and by weariness of life I understand that state of mind, when either poverty, or want, or disgrace, or any such thing, renders life hateful to us. But if any, through weariness on account of his sins and hatred to them, regrets his delay on earth, and can adopt the language of Paul, "Miserable am I; who will free me from the body of this death?" (Rom. 7:24), he entertains a holy and pious wish, provided the submission to which I have referred be added, so that this feeling may not break forth in

---

[63]*CR* 33:143–144: "Pagans spoke thus because their senses could not attain to where God leads us by his word, because they looked for nothing more in life than to be, not only to drink and to eat, but also to be honored, to be worthy for each to follow his course. However, we have the Holy Scriptures, which show us that because God, putting us here on earth, made us in his image, we have to recognize the nobility and dignity that he has given us above all creatures. And it is not only that God made us in his image and likeness, but also that his glory would shine in us; I pray you, is that not a reason to rejoice, to magnify him? Moreover, as long as we have food and drink in this world, we have evidence that God is our Father. Why does the earth produce substance? In order to nourish us; it is not by chance, but God has ordered it thus. And why? Because he wants that much to be a father to us. So here are the means to feed us here on earth, such is the approval of our God's paternal love. Should we not esteem such blessings; can we even honor them as they ought to be honored? But there is even more—that God wants to prepare us here on earth in the hope of heavenly life, to give us a taste of it. He calls us there, he wants to be served and honored by us, in order that we recognize that we are his and that he has accepted us to be in his house and in his family. When all these things have been seen, should not we truly magnify the favor he has done us by putting us here in this present life?" Cf. *CR* 26:450; 33:145, 146, 164, 213; 34:465.

[64]*CR* 47:289: "In short, to love this life is not in itself wrong, provided that we only pass through it as pilgrims, keeping our eyes always fixed on our object. For the true limit of loving life is when we continue in it as long as it pleases God, and when we are prepared to leave it as soon as he shall order us, or—to express it in a single word—when we carry it, as it were, in our hands and offer it to God as a sacrifice. Whoever carries his attachment to the present life beyond this limit destroys his life; that is, he consigns it to everlasting ruin. For the word 'destroy' does not signify to lose, or to sustain the loss of something valuable, but to devote it to destruction."

opposition to the will of God; but that he who has such a desire may still suffer himself to be detained by his hand as long as he pleases.[65]

Thus history is of positive value for at least three reasons. It is the sphere in which God works and reveals himself. It is the sphere in which human beings can make use of the gifts God has given to them. It is the sphere in which people grow and develop in fellowship with God. Negatively, it is the sphere in which human beings reject this fellowship and eternally destroy themselves.

B. The Transhistorical

The meaning of history, however, is not absolute. It has value only so long as it contributes to human fellowship with God, which transcends history and finds its fruition beyond history. For this reason Calvin could write that "there is no medium between these two extremes; either the earth must become vile in our estimation, or it must retain our immoderate love."[66] The point Calvin is making in this extravagant statement is that earthly existence must not be allowed to eclipse the eternal life for which human beings were created. Earthly existence and eternal life do not necessarily stand in opposition.[67] The opposition arises only when earthly existence is made the whole of life. History can serve eternal ends and thereby attain eternal significance.

Calvin was an unceasing opponent of secularism. On every side he saw people measuring life in terms of that which they could see, taste, touch, and handle. He was everywhere confronted with the prevalent conviction that happiness consists in the abundance of what one possesses.[68] Consequently, one of the most emphatic notes of Calvin's preaching was the call to meditation on the future life.[69] By this he did not mean otherworldly speculation but actual participation in a

---

[65]*CR* 43:269. Cf. *CR* 33:295.

[66]3.9.2.

[67]*CR* 51:94–95: "Moreover, this comparison is always true, that we sow when we apply our labor and industry to this or to that. We should thus look closely at ourselves, and we should know that even though God wants us to gather wheat and wine in this world for the nourishment of our bodies, he still calls us higher and he does not want us to be retained here. Let us learn by this method to be called to seek what God rules, and what he governs, so that we may be fully brought to him and to his justice; and let us learn that the worries of this transitory life are not at all here to weigh us down, as we have already shown: that this must only be an accessory of the essential point we should arrive at, that is to say, at the kingdom of God."

[68]*CR* 31:202: "We see how mankind, without well thinking what they are doing, pursue with impetuous and ardent affections the transitory things of this world; but in thus catching at the empty shadow of a happy life they lose true happiness itself."

[69]*CR* 23:353, 355, 382, 430, 580; 31:62–63, 488–490.

life of fellowship with God. The good things of life are tokens of God's paternal love which seeks to draw people to himself; but when the good things of life are taken as a means of destroying this fellowship, then history becomes not merely valueless but a means of destruction.

It was Calvin's conviction that life is reduced to the level of the beast when it is robbed of the hope of eternal life.[70] For this reason he frequently advised consideration of the transitory character of human existence and the certainty of death.[71] Fortunately, human perfection and happiness do not consist in these things over which death exercises dominion, but in godliness, in fellowship with God.[72] Consequently the realization that this fellowship is brought to fruition beyond history in the resurrection is a constant spur to greater enthusiasm for the glory of God.[73] The miseries of earthly existence are accidental qualities of human life and will be eliminated at death.[74] The whole of Calvin's theology is dominated by this eschatology which on one side carries the promise that sin and evil shall be conquered and on the other the hope for the completion of humankind's salvation.

It is this eschatology which enabled the Calvinists to be brave in the face of danger and active in the work of the Lord. No matter how much the evils of life may have tormented them they knew that these evils would be eliminated in the life which awaited them beyond history. No matter how insignificant the task which they performed for the Lord on earth, they knew that God would carry it on to

---

[70]*CR* 52:405–406.

[71]*CR* 31:840; 52:365; 55:274.

[72]*CR* 55:320: "As there is nothing in this world but what is fading, and as it were for a moment, he hence concludes that they who seek their happiness from it make a wretched and miserable provision for themselves, especially when God calls us to the ineffable glory of eternal life; as though he had said, 'The true happiness which God offers to his children is eternal; it is then a shameful thing for us to be entangled with the world, which with all its benefits will soon vanish away.' I take 'lust' here metonymically, as signifying what is desired or coveted, or what captivates the desires of men. The meaning is that what is most precious in the world and deemed especially desirable is nothing but a shadowy phantom." Cf. *CR* 37:12–13; 52:300.

[73]*CR* 52:144–145: "For unless we are stirred up to the hope of eternal life, the world will quickly draw us to itself. For it is only confidence in the divine goodness that induces us to serve God, and it is only the expectation of final redemption that keeps us from giving way. Let everyone, therefore, who would persevere in a course of holy life apply his whole mind to an expectation of Christ's coming. It is also worthy of notice that he uses the expression 'waiting for Christ' instead of the hope of everlasting salvation. For, unquestionably, without Christ we are ruined and thrown into despair, but when Christ shows himself, life and prosperity do at the same time shine forth on us. Let us bear in mind, however, that this is said to believers exclusively, for as for the wicked, as he will come to be their Judge, so they can do nothing but tremble in looking for him." Cf. *CR* 52:79, 300, 391.

[74]*CR* 50:55.

fulfillment. Wernle has well written that this tension between heaven and earth served as the mainspring of Calvin's ethics.[75] It is just this tension which gives zest to Calvin's whole worldview.

At this point Calvin's whole understanding of Christian action stands in contrast to many modern attempts at Christian social action which have confined human attention to the needs of earth. In prosperous days it was easy to maintain the zest of Christian action by an appeal to the needs of earth; but in more recent times, when eschatology has become a more relevant fact, Calvin's eschatological understanding of Christian action becomes increasingly important.

In sum, the importance of eschatology for the Christian life is threefold. First, it means that progress is real. It is not merely a phantom of earthly existence which sooner or later, individually or collectively, faces the brute fact of death. True progress is undergirded by the will of God.[76]

The Christian life, according to Calvin, stands under the claim of the eternal will of God, which does not rest until it has obtained its goal. The eschatological promise is: "I am holy, and you shall be holy."[77] Thus that progressive movement which characterizes the Christian life, the reconstruction of the image of God in human beings, does not end in futility, but in triumph. The resurrection is the completion of our salvation.[78] This is to say that in the resurrection true obedience to the divine claim becomes a reality.[79]

Thus eschatology is the solution of the problem of the law and the gospel for Calvin. As previously indicated, the law is abrogated only in regard to its rigor. The divine claim on human life as expressed in the law remains. At the resurrection the sanctified give perfectly free obedience to God, and the fellowship is fully restored. Gospel and law are one.

Second, the eschatological perspective frees human life from all the tyrannies of earthly existence. The calamities and adversities which assail human beings cannot harm that obedience and fellowship which constitute the essence of life. This freedom is not based on a denial of the value of the things and affairs of the historical process. On the contrary, it is based on the affirmation that the growth of fellowship with God is the center of history. History loses

---

[75] Paul Wernle, *Calvin*, vol. 3 of *Der evangelische Glaube nach den Hauptschriften der Reformatoren* (Tübingen: J. C. B. Mohr [Paul Siebeck], 1919), p. 352.

[76] *CR* 58:19–20.

[77] Cf. Peter Barth, "Was ist reformierte Ethik?" *Zwischen den Zeiten* 10 (1932), 420.

[78] *CR* 49:545–546.

[79] Cf. P. Barth, op. cit.

its meaning for Calvin only when it is divorced from its center. In other words, the events of history are significant as they contribute to or hinder a person's relationship with God. Only when history is interpreted apart from fellowship with God are calamities and afflictions able to destroy the meaning of life. Because this is not the case with Calvin, he can even ascribe a positive function to afflictions in promoting the Christian life. Such is the creative freedom of the eschatological perspective.

Finally, the eschatological perspective provides a vantage point from which history can be judged. Christian action in history can never become mere secular social planning, no matter how noble the motivation may be. Christian action always takes place in the light of eternity. Its goal is not simply a better society in terms of human welfare, but a society which stands in living obedience to God's word. Human welfare is a concomitant of obedience to the will of God.

The eschatological perspective means that all of human existence is under the claim of the eternal will of God, not under the claim of some ideal or ideology. The fact that human performance in history stands under the claim of the eternal will of God excludes all compromise with sinister ideologies. On the human level it is impossible to find either a criterion of judgment or a scale of values sufficiently lofty to condemn wholly the more subtle forms of collective selfishness and pride or to impel one to resist these ideologies to the point of death. The eschatological perspective provides both the standard of judgment and the compulsion to resist, even at the cost of life itself.[80]

The eschatological character of Calvin's theology, as already indicated, inheres primarily in the claim of the eternal will of God on human life. The meditation on the future life is fundamentally fellowship with God, and its eschatological character can be best understood from the viewpoint of Calvin's interpretation of the relation of the law and gospel. In the eschatological future human fellowship

---

[80]*CR* 40:635: "When we are allowed to be at ease, we ought to apply our minds to meditation on a future life, so that this world may become cheap to us, and we may be prepared when necessary to pour forth our blood in testimony to the truth."

CR 41:5: "Hence we must bravely undergo all dangers whenever the worship of God is at stake. This temporary life ought not to be more precious to us than that most sacred of all things—the preservation of God's honor unstained."

CR 41:28: "Daniel therefore rested in the help of God, but he closed his eyes to the event and was not remarkably anxious concerning his life. . . . Even if he had to die a hundred times, yet he never would have failed in his confidence, because our faith is extended beyond the boundaries of this frail and corruptible life, as all the pious know well enough."

with God reaches its full development, and the law and the gospel become one.

Calvin reveals little interest in the actual events which shall bring history to its conclusion or in the furniture of heaven. "Very few persons are concerned about the way that leads to heaven, but all are anxious to know, before the time, what passes there."[81] He called millenarian speculations a fiction too puerile to require or deserve refutation.[82] Nevertheless, he considered the resurrection of the body, the second coming of Christ, and the judgment essential to a true understanding of eschatology.

The resurrection of the body is an example of the completeness of salvation. Christ is the author of complete salvation of the body as well as the soul.[83] So far as I know, Calvin does not expressly say that this carries the meaning that historical existence (insofar as it is true to that which constitutes its meaning—growth in fellowship with God) is brought to completion in the resurrection; but this is certainly in harmony with his teaching.

Calvin knew the difference between resurrection and the philosophic concept of immortality, and he was also aware of the difficulties which the former doctrine involved for the human mind. In order to surmount the difficulties involved, Calvin pointed to the resurrection of Christ and to the power of God.[84] In the resurrection all those qualities of the earthly body which are of a corruptible nature or of the fading nature of this world will be changed.[85]

There are frequent references to the second coming of Christ in Calvin's writings.[86] He felt that this fact was an important stimulant for the Christian life, for the heavenly life which we now contemplate with the eyes of faith will be manifested then.[87] Christ's coming will represent both the redemption and the judgment of history. In the case of believers Calvin wrote:

> Looking for Christ's coming must both restrain the importunate desires of . . . flesh, and support . . . patience in all . . . adversities; and lastly, it must refresh . . . weariness. . . . It brings to the wicked nothing but dread, horror, and great fearfulness. . . . [They shall] be compelled to behold him sitting on his tribunal seat, whom now they will not vouchsafe to hear speak.[88]

---

[81] 3.25.11.
[82] 3.25.5.
[83] 3.25.3.
[84] Ibid.
[85] 3.25.8. Cf. *CR* 14:333.
[86] *CR* 45:657, 671, 679, 676, 686, 776; 52:424; 48:14; 49:544, 565; 55:274.
[87] *CR* 45:685.
[88] *CR* 48:14. Cf. *CR* 52:424.

Calvin had little sympathy with efforts to date the second coming or with speculation about its nature.[89] In general, people are guilty of two errors of a very different nature: haste and slothfulness.

> We are seized with impatience for the day of Christ already expected; at the same time we securely regard it as afar off. As, then, the apostle has before reproved an unreasonable ardor, so he now shakes off our sleepiness, so that we may attentively expect Christ at all times, lest we should become idle and negligent, as is usually the case. For whence is it that flesh indulges itself except that there is no thought of the near coming of Christ?[90]

We must stand in continual expectancy of the coming of Christ, but expectancy is no substitute for patient and relentless warfare against evil. In general, Calvin was so keenly aware of the immediate and continual claim of the eternal will of God on human life that he did not need to create a sense of urgency by overemphasizing the events of eschatology.

As for the judgment, Calvin was primarily concerned with the fact, not with the descriptive details. "No description can equal the severity of the Divine vengeance on the reprobate, their anguish and torment are figuratively represented to us under corporeal images; as darkness, weeping, and gnashing of teeth, unextinguishable fire, a worm incessantly gnawing the heart.[91]

In sum, Calvin maintains the tension between history and the transhistorical by the double affirmation that the essence of life consists in fellowship with God and that the historical process can contribute to and destroy this fellowship. The eschatological hope is the conviction that the eternal will of God will carry to completion the work which it has begun and thereby solve the problem of law and gospel in human life. What begins in forgiveness ends with sanctification of human life and the renovation of all things.

---

[89]3.25.11.
[90]*CR* 55:476.
[91]3.25.12.

Chapter 5

The Christian Life
in Relation to Church
and Society

John Calvin was convinced that human life was true to its origin and to its destiny only when it was lived in community with other people. Schism from the social solidarity of humankind was anathema to him. This emphasis on the communal character of human existence is found in all of his writings. In the *Institutes* he wrote: "As man is naturally a creature inclined to society, he has also by nature an instinctive propensity to cherish and preserve that society."[1]

The Genesis commentary contains the assertion that a person is a social animal who desires mutual intercourse with other people.[2] The same truth is reiterated in the sermons. "We all come from one source, and we ought to tend to one end, and to one God who is the father of all. . . . It is impossible to deny that all men are our neighbors, because God has joined and united us by one common nature."[3]

The entrance of sin into human existence has partially vitiated the human capacity and propensity for communal life. Sin destroys fellowship and in its place produces hatred and violence. Nevertheless, the communal character of human existence is not completely destroyed.[4] Calvin's repeated reference to *humanitas* both as an ideal and as a standard of judgment is sufficient evidence of this.[5]

Calvin's primary concern and point of departure is not the natural community of humankind, but that community of the elect which is called forth by God's gracious activity in restoring to human beings what they had lost by their sin. This community is the practical locus

---

[1] 2.2.13.
[2] *CR* 23:96.
[3] *CR* 28:16.
[4] Cf. 2.2.13.
[5] E.g., *CR* 23:486, 487, 495, 513, 568, 575, 617; *CR* 24:22, 33, 79, 117.

of the Christian life, and the members of this community are the subjects of the so-called Calvinistic ethics.[6] Just as the Christian life is called forth by the work of the Holy Spirit, so it takes place in that community which the Holy Spirit creates—the church. Nevertheless, the life of the Christian in the church cannot be detached from life in the larger community of humankind as a whole. Each community has its origin in the paternal love of God, and for this reason the church cannot turn its back on the larger human community. Consequently the Christian life must be understood not merely in relation to its primary locus in the Christian community but also in its relation to the whole of humankind.

A. The Church and Its Relation to the Christian Life

In the third book of the *Institutes* Calvin discussed the work of the Holy Spirit in the heart of an individual person. His primary concern was the individual's relationship to God. In the fourth book he turned to the church as one of the "external aids [which contribute] to the production of faith . . . and its increase and progressive advance even to its completion."[7] The transition from the problem of the individual's relation to God to the subject of the religious community is not abrupt and detached. Calvin did not distinguish between an individual Christianity and a communal Christianity. Neither individuality nor community is the primary fact in either book. The primary fact is the redemptive grace of God which calls the individual to a new life, which is always life in community. The church is the creation of grace, but paradoxically God's redemptive grace ordinarily acts within the community which it creates. This means that the church is no simple association of human beings, for the divine grace which creates and sustains it gives to it a special character. The importance of the church for the Christian life is at least threefold. In the first place, the divine acts which constitute the church originate, sustain, and direct the Christian life. In the second place, the church is the communion of saints in which the Christians are united not only with Jesus Christ, the Head of the church, but also with one another. Finally, the church provides the governmental and disciplinary environment which is suitable for the work of the Holy Spirit.

---

[6] Peter Barth, *Das Problem der natürlichen Theologie bei Calvin* (*Theologische Existenz heute*, no. 18; Munich: Chr. Kaiser, 1935), p. 39: "The subject of Calvinistic ethics is always the congregation of Christ in faith open for God's Word."
[7] 4.1.1.

1. The Church as the Creative Act of God

The premise that the ground of the church's existence lies outside of itself is basic in John Calvin's doctrine of the church. The church obtains the right to existence not by virtue of any quality inherent in itself but solely by virtue of faith in the promise of God, given in Jesus Christ. The origin of the church was the free grace of God which effected the restoration of humankind after Adam's fall.[8]

> And certainly the source and origin of the church is the free love of God; and whatever benefits he bestows on his church, they all proceed from the same source. The reason, therefore, why we are gathered into the church and are nourished and defended by the hand of God is only to be sought in God.[9]

The tract on *The Necessity of Reforming the Church* points out the same fact. "The restoration of the church is the work of God, and no more depends on the hopes and opinions of men than the resurrection of the dead or any other miracle of that description."[10] Nevertheless, the power of God which creates the church does not nullify the work of human beings. God uses the work of believers in the building of his church, and Calvin never hesitates to exhort them to the performance of their tasks in its establishment.

> Properly speaking, it is he [God] alone that builds his church; yet he uses the work of men, and will have many builders associated with him, that the edifice of his church may arise in some measure by the labor of men; as also he ascribes the praise of its prosperity and success to them. Meanwhile, we offer nothing which he himself has not bestowed; just as the Israelites gave nothing but what had been derived from his bounty alone. Therefore, he distributes the gifts of his Spirit in certain measures (1 Cor. 12:7) so that as each has received more or less, he may employ it on the building of the church. But this should be the best incentive to activity, that none is so poor or humble but that his offering is acceptable and pleasing, however small it may be, and almost worthless in the eyes of men.[11]

In sum, the church is not merely an association of human beings or even an ideal. It is a special kind of community, created by the

---

[8]*CR* 23:11: "After Adam had by his own desperate fall ruined himself and all his posterity, this is the basis of our salvation, this the origin of the church, that we, being rescued out of profound darkness, have obtained a new life by the mere grace of God."
[9]*CR* 31:439.
[10]*CR* 6:510.
[11]*CR* 24:402.

grace of God. For this reason it is not to be confused with any human enterprise.[12]

Calvin seeks to give expression to the divine basis of the church's existence in at least four ways. First, the church is the community of the elect. The Geneva Catechism defines the church as "the body and society of believers whom God hath predestined to eternal life."[13] The definition of the church in terms of election is especially strong in the *Institutes* of 1536,[14] and it is repeated in all subsequent editions. The final edition declares unequivocally that the foundation of the church is the secret election of God.[15] God alone "knoweth them that are his." For this reason the church shall remain secure even though the whole machinery of the world shall go to pieces.[16]

Second, the church's existence is predicated on the forgiveness of sin. God receives and adopts persons into his church by the forgiveness of sin, and he preserves and keeps them in it by the same mercy. "As we carry about with us the relics of sin, therefore, as long as we live, we shall scarcely continue in the Church for a single moment, unless we are sustained by the constant grace of the Lord in forgiving our sins."[17]

Third, the marks by which the church is identified are not found in its own qualities but in the divine acts which create and nourish it. The church is not known by its organization or by its moral quality but by the presence of the word and sacraments. "Wherever

---

[12]The Barthian interpreters of Calvin have emphasized this aspect of the church. Alfred de Quervain, *Calvin, sein Lehren und Kämpfen* (Berlin: Furche, 1926), p. 31: "The Church of Jesus Christ is a fact for Calvin, no ideal. In spite of her pollution—he knows it, he does not deny it—she remains the creation of God. She does not live of her own strengths, but through the grace of him who again and again by the power of his word awakens her to life: through him who makes the dead alive and speaks to the non-being as being." Cf. W. Niesel, "Wesen und Gestalt der Kirche nach Calvin," *Evangelische Theologie* 3 (1936), 309–310.

Peter Barth goes beyond Calvin in emphasizing the existential character of the church and does not sufficiently notice Calvin's emphasis on the governmental and disciplinary character of the church. He objects to the idea that the church is a ship or ark to which people can retire in peace amid the storm of the world: "Always anew the congregation faces the decision for faith or for unbelief. Always anew possibilities for obedience, for trial, for growth open up, opposite which there are just as many opportunities for disobedience, for failure, for falling, for stagnation. In each new situation it will become clear anew whether there is a congregation growing in obedience toward God, strengthening, maybe even ready for suffering. There is never a resting in oneself. The congregation exists only in the action of obedience-in-faith toward God, who through his Word calls from death to life, from vanity to his service." ("Calvins Verständnis der Kirche," *Zwischen den Zeiten* 8 [1930], 231.)

[13]*CR* 6:40. Cf. *CR* 58:38.
[14]Cf. pp. 122–123 in Chapter 3.
[15]4.1.2.
[16]4.1.3.
[17]4.1.21.

we find the word of God purely preached and heard, and the sacraments administered according to the institution of Christ, there, it is not to be doubted, is a church of God."[18]

Calvin interpreted the word and sacraments in terms of the life-giving grace and power of God. God, the Author of preaching, connects the Spirit with the preaching and promises that it shall be followed by success.[19]

> These [the word and sacraments] can nowhere exist without bringing forth fruit and being prospered with the blessing of God. I assert, not that wherever the word is preached the good effects of it immediately appear, but that it is never received so as to obtain a permanent establishment without displaying some efficacy.[20]

The word of God is the living deed of God's grace which calls the church into being.[21] The church has its life and the possibility of inner and outer growth only in the fact that it hears the voice of its Lord, that it confesses to him, that it decides for him and serves his glory.[22]

In the sacraments also the primary fact is the act of God. It is true that people "testify [of their] piety towards him, in his presence and that of angels, as well as before men" by participating in the sacraments,[23] but this is of secondary importance. "The office of the sacraments is precisely the same as that of the word of God; which is to offer and to present Christ to us, and in him the treasures of his heavenly grace; but they confer no advantage or profit without being received by faith."[24] The sacraments

> only perform their office aright when they are accompanied by the Spirit, that internal Teacher, by whose energy alone our hearts are penetrated, our affections are moved, and an entrance is opened for the sacraments into our souls. If he be absent, the sacraments can produce

---

[18]4.1.9. Cf. "Augsburg Confession" (Article 7), in Philip Schaff, *The Creeds of Christendom* (New York: Harper & Brothers, 1919), 3:11–12.

[19]4.1.6.

[20]4.1.10.

[21]Peter Barth, op. cit., pp. 228–229: "For Calvin it is underivable certainty that God alone, through the Word of his revelation, throughout all times calls into life his congregation. Through his Word God has created for himself a congregation under the Old Covenant. Through the medium of the proclamation of the gospel, through the witness of the apostles and the prophets about Christ, God has once founded the Christian church. . . . For Calvin it is never a matter of the dead written letter, of the paper Bible codex, but rather one of the living and always acute judgment, commandment, and promise of God, of the living and present Lord of his world, heard through the manifold biblical witnesses. From his Word, the church has diverged. Therefore she has fallen into confusion, need, and shame. Now, God through His Word wants to make her rise anew."

[22]Ibid., p. 232.

[23]4.14.1.

[24]4.14.17.

no more effect upon our minds than the splendour of the sun on blind eyes, or the sound of a voice on deaf ears.[25]

The sacraments, according to Calvin, are of vital importance for the Christian life. They increase, nourish, and strengthen faith.[26] They help to produce that progress in piety which characterizes the Christian life.[27] For these reasons Calvin wanted the Lord's Supper celebrated at each Sunday service.[28]

Baptism is the initiatory sacrament by which human beings are admitted to the society of the church. Yet its importance is much more than a badge of admission, for it confers at least three lasting benefits. It is a symbol and token of the forgiveness of sins.[29] It shows Christians their mortification in Christ and also their new life in him.[30] Finally, it affords a certain testimony that Christians are not only ingrafted into the life and death of Christ, but that they are also so united to Christ as to be partakers of all his benefits.[31]

The Lord's Supper is particularly related to growth in the Christian life. Having begotten us as members of the society of his church,

> he [God] acts towards us the part of a provident father of a family, in constantly supplying us with food, to sustain and preserve us in that life to which he has begotten us by his word. Now, the only food of our souls is Christ; and to him, therefore, our heavenly Father invites us, that being refreshed by a participation of him, we may gain fresh vigour from day to day, till we arrive at the heavenly immortality.[32]

By the terms "eating" and "drinking" Christians are taught that they are quickened by a real participation in Christ, that the life which they receive from him does not consist in mere knowledge.[33] The sacrament is a testimony to the participants that they are incorporated into one body with Christ so that whatever is his they are at liberty to call their own.[34] By the sacrament the Christian is nourished, refreshed, strengthened, and exhilarated.[35] No person in the whole world is ever so perfect that he or she does not need to be aided and advanced by the Lord's Supper.[36]

---

[25] 4.14.9.
[26] 4.14.16.
[27] 4.14.8.
[28] *CR* 10(a):7.
[29] 4.15.1.
[30] 4.15.5.
[31] 4.15.16.
[32] 4.17.1.
[33] 4.17.5.
[34] 4.17.2.
[35] 4.17.3.
[36] *CR* 49:803.

Calvin's insistence on the real presence of and the genuine participation in the body and blood of Christ stands in apparent opposition
to the equally emphatic statement that the body of Christ is in
heaven.[37] The solution of the problem is found in the work of the
Holy Spirit.[38]

> Let our faith receive, therefore, what our understanding is not able to
> comprehend, that the Spirit really unites things which are separated
> by local distance. Now, that holy participation of his flesh and blood,
> by which Christ communicates his life to us, just as if he actually
> penetrated every part of our frame, in the sacred supper he also testifies
> and seals; and that not by the exhibition of a vain or ineffectual sign,
> but by the exertion of the energy of his Spirit, by which he accom-
> plishes that which he promises.[39]

The divine character of the church is also revealed in a fourth way
by its relation to the kingdom of God. Calvin did not have a fully
developed doctrine of the kingdom of God in the modern sense. The
kingdom consists, he said, in the doctrine of the gospel and is spread
by the preaching of the word, made effective by the power of the
Holy Spirit.[40] It is spiritual in nature and is utterly opposed to earthly
kingdoms. The notion of a millennial kingdom on earth is emphatically rejected.[41] At times Calvin spoke of the kingdom of God in
terms that are identical with those which he used to describe the
meditation on the future life.[42] In general, he simply defined the
kingdom of God as the reign of God.

> We must first attend to the definition of the kingdom of God. He is
> said to reign among men when they voluntarily devote and submit
> themselves to be governed by him, placing their flesh under the yoke
> and renouncing their desires. Such is the corruption of our nature that
> all our affections are so many soldiers of Satan, who oppose the justice
> of God and consequently obstruct or disturb his reign. By this prayer
> we ask that he may remove all hindrances and may bring all men

---

[37]4.17.26.

[38]Wilhelm Niesel, *Calvins Lehre vom Abendmahl* (Munich: Chr. Kaiser, 1930), p. 93:
"Through the Holy Spirit, Christ in the Supper descends to us, and lifts us to himself. Thus
the Holy Spirit is the bond which connects us with Christ. But Calvin says even more. The
Holy Spirit not only connects us with the Exalted Lord, but he unites us with him. Therefore
Calvin calls the Holy Spirit not only the bond connecting us with Christ but also the channel
through which all that Christ is and has gets to us, so that we with body, soul, and spirit
become one with him."

[39]4.17.10.

[40]*CR* 45:139: "We must observe the designation which Mark gives to the gospel, 'the kingdom
of God'; for hence we learn that by the preaching of the gospel 'the kingdom of God' is set
up and established among men, and that in no other way does God reign among men."

[41]*CR* 48:10–11.

[42]*CR* 45:197; 46:82; 47:138, 403–404; 48:10–11.

under his dominion, and may lead them to meditate on the heavenly life.

This is done partly by the preaching of the word and partly by the secret power of the Spirit. . . . We therefore pray that God would exert his power, both by the word and by the Spirit, that the whole world may willingly submit to him. The kingdom of God is opposed to all disorder and confusion: for good order is nowhere found in the world except when he regulates by his hand the schemes and dispositions of men. Hence we conclude that the commencement of the reign of God in us is the destruction of the old man and the denial of ourselves that we may be renewed to another life.[43]

The kingdom will be perfected at the last advent.[44] The function of Christ in the preservation and salvation of the church shall be fully discharged, and he shall deliver the kingdom back to his Father.[45] The administration of the kingdom in perfect glory after all enemies have been subdued will be different from what it is at present. Nevertheless, Calvin did not hesitate to speak of Christ as the eternal King.[46] The change in administration is not repugnant to the Kingship of Christ. As King, Christ is not only the Lord of the faithful, who yield voluntary obedience to him, but he is also the judge of all evil. The judgment he administers is somewhat visible now, but it shall be consummated at the last judgment.[47]

Calvin does not hesitate to include the church within the kingdom of God.[48] He frequently substitutes the name of the one for the other.

The kingdom of heaven means the renovation of the church, or the prosperous condition of the church, such as was then beginning to appear by the preaching of the gospel. In this sense, Christ tells us that he who is least in the kingdom of God is greater than John (Luke 7:28). The meaning of that phrase is that God, restoring the world by the hand of his Son, has completely established his kingdom. Christ declares that when his church shall have been renewed, no teachers must be admitted to it but those who are faithful expounders of the law and who labor to maintain its doctrine entire.[49]

---

[43]*CR* 45:197.
[44]3.20.42.
[45]2.15.5. Cf. *CR* 55:19; 4.1.20.
[46]2.15.5; *CR* 46:81, 83; 55:19.
[47]2.15.5.
[48]The kingdom of God appears to have a broader meaning than the church and the kingdom of Christ. The kingdom of God is eternal. The church is completely subsumed in the kingdom of God when Christ delivers up his kingdom. Cf. 2.15.5. Calvin's writings are not specific on this point.
[49]*CR* 45:172–173. Cf. 3.20.42: "God therefore erects his kingdom on the humiliation of the whole world, though his methods of humiliation are various; for he restrains the passions of some, and breaks the unsubdued arrogance of others. It ought to be the object of our daily

Yet Calvin's inclusion of the church within the kingdom of God does not mean that he identifies the eternal kingdom of God with any particular historical entity.[50] As has already been noted, Calvin does not define the church in terms of any historical organization, but in terms of the deeds of God in history which call people into a living fellowship with God and with one another in the communion of saints. It is the invisible church which is the kingdom of God. Thus the church as an earthly institution cannot be identified with this kingdom.

The inclusion of the church within the kingdom of God has important bearing on the idea of progress in the Christian life, in both its individual and its social aspects. Although the kingdom cannot be finally identified with any human enterprise, there does exist in and through history an eternal kingdom which gathers up the faith-obedience of human beings and carries it to completion beyond history.[51] The reign of God is exercised in history and is brought to completion beyond history. Calvin exhorts his hearers and readers to the progressive realization of God's kingdom in history.[52] His insistence that the kingdom is not earthly does not nullify the existence of the kingdom in and through history. It simply means that the kingdom does not find its fruition in history and in the form of an earthly power. The historical deeds which belong to the reign of God have real significance, for they belong to a reality which is in history but also beyond history.

The identification of the church and the kingdom of God also brings to focus another doctrine which is prominent in Calvin's whole conception of the church, as well as of the Christian life—the Kingship of Christ.

> The church of the Lord is only rightly formed when the true David rules over it; that is, when all with one consent obey Christ and submit to his bidding. . . . When we believe the gospel, we choose Christ for our king, as it were, by a voluntary consent.[53]

---

wishes, that God would collect churches for himself from all the countries of the earth, that he would enlarge their numbers, enrich them with gifts, and establish a legitimate order among them; that, on the contrary, he would overthrow all the enemies of the pure doctrine and religion, that he would confound their counsels, and defeat their attempts. Whence it appears that the desire of a daily progress is not enjoined us in vain; because human affairs are never in such a happy situation, as that all defilement of sin is removed, and purity can be seen in full perfection. This perfection is deferred till the last advent of Christ, when, the apostle says, 'God will be all in all.' "

[50]Cf. 4.7.29.
[51]*CR* 52:92.
[52]3.20.42.
[53]*CR* 42:221. Cf. 4.3.1; *CR* 48:90; 49:380; 52:139.

"It is the prerogative of Christ to preside over all councils, and to have no mortal man associated with him in that dignity. . . . He really presides only where he governs the whole assembly by his word and Spirit."[54]

The distinction which Calvin makes between the visible and the invisible church does not mean that there are two churches, one in which Christ truly reigns and another in which Christ shares his sovereignty with the forces of evil. There is only one church, and in this church Christ alone rules. This true church, however, is known only to God. Human knowledge is limited by time and space, while the saints of all times and places belong to the church. Furthermore, human knowledge sees only the surface and does not penetrate into the heart. Thus only God can know who are truly his.[55] Yet we can know that this true church exists on earth by virtue of such signs as the word and the sacraments, even though they cannot define its bounds exactly. Therefore, it is necessary to believe in the church which is known only to God, and to honor and maintain communion with the church which is visible to people.[56]

The Kingship of Christ as exercised in the church means that he is the Lord of the Christian life. It also means that Jesus Christ protects and undergirds the Christian life.[57]

In sum, the church is called into being, is sustained, and is ruled by the activity of God. It is this same activity which calls the Christian life into being and nourishes its growth. For this reason the church is the locus of the Christian life.

2. The Communion of Saints

The church as community stands in paradoxical relatedness to those gracious acts of God which create the church. On the one

---

[54]4.9.1.

[55]Because we cannot fully know the members of the church, charity must be exercised in determining church members. Those "who by a confession of faith, an exemplary life, and a participation of the sacraments profess the same God and Christ with ourselves" ought to be acknowledged as members of the church (4.1.8).

[56]4.1.7.

[57]*CR* 46:83: "Now, our Lord Jesus Christ (as he says it) is the strongest. And this is why he exerts his dominion in order to sustain us: when we are under his protection, we can spite the devil, sin, and death, and we will proceed in our calling, knowing that we will be sustained by him. . . . Our Lord's kingdom is permanent. And even when our hope has surmounted the world, it will extend even further. That is to say that in the midst of death our Lord Jesus Christ is still King, and being King, he will show that he has what is needed to sustain those whom he has taken into safekeeping, and that he has promised to lead them to the last day in complete felicity, joy, and glory. This, then, is what is meant by the permanence about which he spoke."

hand, these acts of grace create community, but on the other, they ordinarily take place only within the community.[58] The basic point, however, is not chronological order but apprehension of the fact that the church is something more than an aggregation of people.

There can be no doubt that the communal nature of the church was important for Calvin. The phrase "communion of saints" ought not to be neglected, he wrote, for "it excellently expresses the character of the Church."[59] According to Calvin, there are three things which deserve attention about the communion which is the church. The first is that Christ is the head of the body which is the church.

> As the root conveys sap to the whole tree, so all the vigor which we possess must flow to us from Christ. . . . All the life or health which is diffused through the members flows from the head; so that the members occupy a subordinate rank. The second is that by the distribution made, the limited share of each renders the communication between all the members absolutely necessary. The third is that without mutual love, the health of the body cannot be maintained. Through the members, as canals, is conveyed from the head all that is necessary for the nourishment of the body. While this connection is upheld, the body is alive and healthy. Each member, too, has its own proper share, according to the effectual working in the measure of every part.[60]

The analogy of the human body, which Calvin used frequently, reveals the organic nature of this communion. The church is more than an aggregation of people. Christians do not constitute a "civil society, but, being ingrafted into Christ's body, are truly members one of another."[61]

> It is usual, however, for any society of men, or congregation, to be called a body, as one city constitutes a body, and so, in like manner, one senate, and one people. Menenius Agrippa, too, in ancient times, when desirous to conciliate the Roman people, when at variance with the senate, made use of an apologue, not very unlike the doctrine of Paul here. Among Christians, however, the case is very different, for they do not constitute a mere political body, but are the spiritual and

---

[58]This paradox can be seen in 4.1.20 and 21. Here there is the assertion that by remission of sins persons are not only adopted into the church but also preserved and sustained in it. On the other hand there is the statement: "The heavenly Jerusalem, therefore, ought first to be built, in which this favour of God may be enjoyed, that whoever shall enter it, their iniquity shall be blotted out. Now, I affirm that this ought to be built, not that there can ever be any church without remission of sins, but because God has not promised to impart his mercy, except in the communion of saints."

[59]4.1.3.

[60]*CR* 51:203.

[61]*CR* 49:505.

mystical body of Christ, as Paul himself afterward adds. The meaning therefore is, "Though the members of the body are various and have different functions, they are, nevertheless, linked together in such a manner that they coalesce in one. We, accordingly, who are members of Christ, although we are endowed with various gifts, ought, notwithstanding, to have an eye to that connection which we have in Christ."[62]

Christ, as the head of the body, is the source of the church's strength and distinctive character. Membership in the church means a genuine participation in his life, death, and resurrection. No fact is more important for Calvin's doctrine of the church than this mystical or personal union of the believer with Christ, but it is equally important that this union shall not be understood in any substantial sense.[63] The Holy Spirit is the bond of union, yet he is not merely a bond which unites the believer to Christ; he is a life-giving Spirit through whom the believer receives the grace of Christ.[64]

Another important point is the interdependence of all the members of the body of Christ. No one has so much of Christ as to be able to get along without one's brother or sister.

> No one has so much as to have enough within himself, so as not to require help from others. For this is what he means by these words, "distributing to everyone severally as he will." The Spirit of God, therefore, distributes gifts among us in order that we may all contribute to the common advantage. To no one does he give all, lest anyone, satisfied with his particular portion, should separate himself from others and live solely for himself.[65]

The benefits conferred on an individual member must be reckoned as gain to the whole church.[66] God confers his gifts not that each can enjoy his own separately, but that each can help another.[67]

It is essential that members of the body of Christ work together, just as it is necessary in the case of members of the human body.[68] Likewise, there is the same type of variety in the church which one finds in the human body. It would be disastrous for the church, just as it would be for the body, if all members were identical. It takes eyes, feet, hands, and many other members to constitute one body. The true genius of the church consists in the fact that it is one body but many members.

---

[62]*CR* 49:501.
[63]3.11.5.
[64]3.1.1 and 2.
[65]*CR* 49:500. Cf. *CR* 51:192: "No member of the body of Christ is endowed with such perfection as to be able, without the assistance of others, to supply his own necessities."
[66]*CR* 52:188. Cf. *CR* 50:101.
[67]*CR* 49:501.
[68]*CR* 49:503.

The symmetry of the church consists, so to speak, of a manifold unity, that is, when the variety of gifts is directed to the same object—as in music there are different sounds, but suited to each other with such an adaptation as to produce concord. Hence it is befitting that there should be a distinction of gifts as well as of offices, and yet all harmonize in one.[69]

Calvin gave practical implementation to the communal character of the church by the office of deacon, whose task was to provide for the sick and needy in the congregation.[70] In general, the Christian must be especially solicitous for the household of faith, although the needs of the larger community of humankind must not be neglected.[71]

The strongly organic character of Calvin's doctrine of the church stands in opposition to all schism. The church is one as Christ is one. Against the Anabaptists Calvin wrote:

This should serve as a warning to us that when under the guise of a zeal for perfection, we are not able to bear any imperfection either in the body or in the members of the church, it is the devil who inflames us with pride and seduces us by hypocrisy in order to make us abandon the company of Jesus Christ, knowing well that he has won all when he draws us from it. For there is no remission of sins or salvation elsewhere, when we would have above all an appearance of sanctity greater than that of angels, if through such a presumption we come to separate ourselves from the Christian company and become devils.[72]

The environment which nourishes the Christian life is the communion of saints.

3. The Church as Government and Discipline

John Calvin was convinced that the communion of saints does not exist on earth by virtue of the sheer spontaneity of Christian experience.[73] The fact of sin even in the lives of the regenerate was sufficient to account for this. "Our ignorance . . . , slothfulness, and . . . the

---

[69]*CR* 49:497.

[70]*CR* 10(a):23–25, 101–103. Cf. Émile Doumergue, *Jean Calvin, les hommes et les choses de son temps* (Lausanne: Georges Bridel & Cie., 1899–1927), 5:262, on the importance of this office in the church at Strasbourg.

[71]*CR* 52:78, 442.

[72]*CR* 7:77.

[73]*CR* 11:281: "Immediately after I had offered my services to the Senate, I declared that a church could not hold together unless a settled government should be agreed on, such as is prescribed to us in the word of God, and such as was in use in the ancient church."

vanity of our minds require external aids . . . to the production of faith in our hearts."[74] Furthermore, there was the scriptural injunction that all things in the church must be done decently and in order. This required some sort of government, for "in every society of men, we see the necessity of some polity in order to preserve the common peace, and to maintain concord."[75] No doubt Calvin's judicial training influenced him in this direction, as the comparison of the church to a well-regulated state would indicate.[76] At any rate he considered government and discipline a very important, though not the decisive, aspect of the church's existence on earth.

The government of the church, Calvin maintained, stands under the sole Lordship of Jesus Christ. Concerning his own exposition of the doctrine he wrote: "Hitherto we have treated of the mode of government in the Church, as it has been delivered to us by the pure word of God, and of the offices in it, as they were instituted by Christ."[77] Even the details of church life, which are determined by custom, modesty, and humanity itself and not by scriptural text, are subject to the general rules God has given in the scripture.[78] Calvin's purpose is clearly to maintain the sovereignty of Jesus Christ in the government of his church, and his writings reveal little doubt in his own mind that he succeeded in this aim.

One important function of the church was instruction. Although knowledge of the Christian religion was not sufficient in itself to produce the Christian life, it was one of those external aids which was not neglected at Geneva. Catechetical instruction was emphasized in addition to the worship services of the church.[79]

For the purposes of this study the power of the church in jurisdiction and discipline is also of primary importance. "As the saving doctrine of Christ is the soul of the Church, so discipline forms the ligaments which connect the members together, and keep each in its

---

[74]4.1.1.
[75]4.10.27.
[76]4.11.1.
[77]4.4.1.
[78]4.10. 30–31.
[79]Calvin once wrote to Somerset: "The church of God will never preserve itself without a catechism, for it is like the seed to keep the good grain from dying out, and causing it to multiply from age to age. And therefore, if you desire to build an edifice which shall be of long duration, and which shall not soon fall into decay, make provision that the children may be instructed in a good catechism, which may show them briefly, and in language level to their tender age, wherein true Christianity consists. This catechism will serve two purposes, to wit, as an introduction to the whole people, so that everyone may profit from what shall be preached, and also to enable them to discern when any presumptuous person puts forward strange doctrine." (*CR* 13:71–72.)

proper place."[80] The purpose of discipline is threefold. In the first
place, it maintains the honor of God. The church is the body of
Christ and must not be contaminated with foul and putrid members.
In the second place, discipline keeps the good from contamination
by the bad, and finally it leads the guilty to repentance.[81] Church
discipline, therefore, provides the suitable environment for the work
of the Spirit in human hearts. It is, in other words, an aid in bringing
to everyday expression the sonship to which people have been adopted by God in Jesus Christ. The question which arises is whether
this discipline actually develops the spirit of sonship and fellowship
with God or whether it really erects a heteronomous and abstract
entity between human beings and living fellowship with God. In
other words, was Choisy right in claiming that Calvin's church had
more of the character of a legal institution than the body of
Christ?[82]

In answering this question the previous sections on the church as
the creative act of God and as the communion of saints must be kept
in mind. Calvin's emphasis on the existential character of the church
is part of the truth which Choisy ignored. However, when Calvin
turned to church government and discipline, his tendency seemed to
be in the opposite direction. He insisted that discipline must be
exercised in love, and no doubt he sought to achieve this ideal. Yet
the records of the Consistory reveal an impersonal quality which is
the antithesis of love.[83] He also qualified the power of discipline by
the doctrine that the church does not have authority to condemn a
person to eternal death. Excommunication is a judgment passed only
on a person's conduct and manner of life, for the person is in the
power and hands of God alone.[84] Yet this qualification is also partially nullified by the authority which Calvin did ascribe to the
judgment passed on manner and conduct of life.

> The Lord testifies that such judgment of believers is no other than the
> promulgation of his sentence, and that what they do on earth shall be
> ratified in heaven. For they have the word of God, by which they
> condemn the perverse . . . and they cannot err or dissent from the
> judgment of God, because they judge only by the Divine law, which
> is not an uncertain or earthly opinion, but the holy will and heavenly
> oracle of God.[85]

---

[80]4.12.1.
[81]4.12.5.
[82]Eugène Choisy, *La théocratie à Genève au temps de Calvin* (Geneva: C. Eggimann & Cie.,
1897), p. 258.
[83]Cf. pp. 53–54 in Chapter 1.
[84]4.12.9; 4.12.10; 4.11.2.
[85]4.11.2.

This statement reveals an important fallacy or contradiction in Calvin's thinking. It is based on the assumption that since we have the word of God as a standard of judgment, we shall unerringly apply it in cases of discipline. The doctrine of the fall and of original sin as expounded in book II of the *Institutes* excludes the possibility of such confidence in the use of human reason and judgment. Calvin's practical confidence in the competence of reason once the biblical premise is assumed in matters of discipline and doctrine belies his own assertions about the sinfulness of the regenerate as well as the unregenerate.

A second factor which must be considered in this regard is the high position Calvin gave to ministers. They are God's delegates, instruments in the performance of his work, interpreters of his secret will, and his personal representatives.[86] Criticism of ministers was sufficient offense to call for a reprimand by the Consistory.[87] Great importance was attached to the word as preached by human beings. Pastors were as the mouth of God.[88] Since Christ has instituted human beings to be the organs of his Spirit, one must receive the doctrine which is preached by them if one wishes to be taught of the Lord.[89] Calvin's purpose was for the living authority of Jesus Christ to be mediated through the ministry of people. Actually he provided the occasion for the elevation of the fallible pronouncements of human beings to the position of infallible commands of God.

Thus, although Calvin was no doubt correct in his assumption that some form must be given to the spiritual government of Jesus Christ, and although he certainly had good historical precedent for his emphasis on polity and discipline, he nevertheless laid the groundwork for a legal institution to take the place of the body of Christ and for the heteronomous authority of a fallible consistory to assume the prerogatives of the living authority of Jesus Christ in his church. Choisy was correct in his judgment that the living authority of Jesus Christ was eclipsed in Calvin's church, but he erred in ignoring the strong emphasis Calvin also placed on the existential character of the church. The Reformer's error lay not in his intention but in a faulty ecclesiastical and theological implementation of that intention. The problem cannot be solved by weighing the evidence of one side

---

[86] 4.3.1.

[87] *CR* 21:303, 413, 417.

[88] *CR* 29:705: "Prophetae igitur et doctores sunt in ecclesia Dei tanquam os ipsum Dei."

[89] *CR* 51:361: "As when there are beautiful streams which deliver water in abundance, one goes to them to satisfy thirst, thus did our Lord, who wanted us to be exposed to his Word here on earth, when he made men as organs for his Spirit. Since it is thus, therefore let us learn to hold on, and if we are taught by God, let us receive the doctrine which is preached to us through the mouths of men." Cf. *CR* 24:156.

against that of the other, but by finding some explanation of the presence of both tendencies in Calvin's thought and polity.

In sum, the church is the mother of the faithful. In her bosom

> it is God's will that all his children should be collected, not only to be nourished by her assistance and ministry during their infancy and childhood, but also to be governed by her maternal care, till they attain a mature age, and at length reach the end of their faith. . . . The Church is the mother of all those who have him [God] for their Father.[90]

Outside the bosom of the church there can be no hope of the remission of sins or of any salvation.[91]

> The church is the common mother of all the godly, which bears, nourishes, and brings up children to God, kings and peasants alike; and this is done by the ministry. Those who neglect or despise this order choose to be wiser than Christ. Woe to the pride of such men! It is, no doubt, a thing in itself possible that divine influence alone should make us perfect without human assistance. But the present inquiry is not what the power of God can accomplish, but what is the will of God and the appointment of Christ. In employing human instruments for accomplishing their salvation, God has conferred on men no ordinary favor. Nor can any exercise be found better adapted to promote unity than to gather around the common doctrine—the standard of our General.[92]

In theory at least, Calvin does not claim these privileges of the church exclusively for any one particular historical organization.[93] For this reason he could quote with apparent approval this sentence from the pen of Augustine: "According to the secret predestination of God, there are many sheep without the pale of the Church, and many wolves within."[94] In his reply to Sadolet Calvin defined the church in strikingly nonecclesiastical terms:

> Now, if you can bear to receive a truer definition of the church than your own, say, in the future, that it is the society of all the saints, a society which, spread over the whole world and existing in all ages, yet bound together by the one doctrine and the one Spirit of Christ,

---

[90] 4.1.1.

[91] 4.1.4.

[92] *CR* 51:199.

[93] Cf. 4.7.29: "To confine Christ, and the Holy Spirit and the church, to one particular place, so that whoever presides there, even though he be a devil, must nevertheless be deemed the vicar of Christ, and head of the church, because that place was formerly the see of Peter, I maintain to be not only impious and dishonorable to Christ, but altogether absurd and repugnant to common sense."

[94] 4.1.8.

cultivates and observes unity of faith and brotherly concord. With this church we deny that we have any disagreement. Nay, rather, as we revere her as our mother, so we desire to remain in her bosom.[95]

The importance of the church for the Christian life is threefold. In the first place, the church is important as the sphere in which God not only calls people to the Christian life but also nourishes them in it. Advancement in piety is not a human achievement. It does not depend on the determination of the human will, but on the life-giving word of God which can be heard and obeyed only in the church. Thus those who exclude themselves from the church separate themselves from the one power which can lead human beings to the good life. As Calvin wrote:

> We see that though God could easily make his people perfect in a single moment, yet it was not his will that they should grow to mature age, but under the education of the Church. . . . Hence, it follows, that all who reject the spiritual food for their souls, which is extended to them by the hands of the Church, deserve to perish with hunger and want.[96]

In the second place, no one has so much Christianity that he or she can get along alone. We need to be united not only with Christ, the Head of the body, but also with other people. Calvin thoroughly repudiated that religious individualism which believes that a person can truly progress in piety alone.

> Many are urged by pride, or disdain, or envy, to persuade themselves that they can profit sufficiently by reading and meditating in private, and so to despise public assemblies, and consider preaching as unnecessary. But since they do all in their power to dissolve and break asunder the bond of unity, which ought to be preserved inviolable, not one of them escapes the just punishment of this impious breach, but they all involve themselves in pestilent errors and pernicious reveries.[97]

Private worship is inadequate to maintain the spiritual level of the Christian life. The Geneva Catechism declared that "the people [should] meet to hear the doctrine of Christ, to engage in public prayer, and make profession of their faith."[98] In justifying the use of singing in public worship Calvin wrote:

> The principal use of the tongue is in the public prayers which are made in the congregations of believers; the design of which is, that with one

---

[95]*OS* 1:466.
[96]4.1.5.
[97]Ibid.
[98]*CR* 6:65.

common voice, and as it were with the same mouth, we may all at once proclaim the glory of God, whom we worship in one spirit and with the same faith; and this is publicly done, that all interchangeably, each one of his brother, may receive the confession of faith, and be invited and stimulated by his example.[99]

The church is also important for the Christian life in that it provides the discipline and government of life which aids growth in piety. John Knox correctly called Geneva a school of Christ,[100] for that was what Calvin intended it to be. The work of the Consistory provided a suitable environment for the work of the Holy Spirit. In Calvin's words, the discipline of the church is an "external aid" to the Christian life.[101]

B. Society in Its Relation to the Christian Life

Calvin makes very plain that every person has a real responsibility for society. The practice of self-denial which plays so large a part in the Christian life involves love for neighbor.[102] This responsibility arises out of the solidarity of humankind and out of the Christian gospel.

People are neighbors by the fact of creation. God could have covered the earth with a multitude of people, "but it was his will that [people] should proceed from one fountain, in order that [their] desire of mutual concord might be the greater and that each might the more freely embrace the other as his [or her] own flesh."[103] God created humankind to live peaceably with one another.[104] The whole human race is one body.[105] God has bound and united all people in one body in order that each one will be careful to serve his or her neighbors and maintain that community and sense of justice which does to others only what one wishes to be done to oneself.[106]

> To keep up the exercise of brotherly love, God assures us that all men are our brethren because they are related to us by a common nature. Whenever I see a man, I must, of necessity, behold myself as in a mirror, for he is my bone and my flesh. Now, though the greater part of men break off, in most instances, from this holy society, yet their

---

[99]3.20.31.
[100]David Laing, ed., *The Works of John Knox* (Edinburgh: John Stone & Hunter, 1855), 4:240.
[101]4.1.1.
[102]3.7.4ff.
[103]*CR* 23:28.
[104]*CR* 26:325.
[105]*CR* 26:229.
[106]*CR* 33:66–67.

depravity does not violate the order of nature, for we ought to rega
God as the author of the union.[107]

This neighborly love which our common humanity enjoins is genuine and warm.

> We know that men were created for this end, that they should love one another. Therefore, none will be counted guiltless of the crime of hatred before God, but he who embraces his neighbors with love. For not only will a secret displeasure be accounted as hatred, but even that neglect of brethren and that cold charity which ever reigns in the world. But in proportion as anyone is more closely connected with another, there must be the endeavor to adhere to each other in a more sacred bond of affection. Moreover, with respect to married persons, though they may not openly disagree, yet if they are cold in their affection toward each other, this disgust is not far removed from hatred.[108]

The Geneva Catechism declares that the word "neighbor" includes all people.

> *Master:* What do you understand by the term neighbor?
> *Scholar:* Not only kindred and friends, or those connected with us by any necessary tie, but also those who are unknown to us, and even enemies.
> *M:* But what connection have they with us?
> *S:* They are connected by that tie by which God bound the whole human race together. This tie is sacred and inviolable and no man's depravity can abolish it.[109]

"To make any person our neighbor . . . it is enough that he be a man, for it is not in our power to blot out our common nature."[110] Only excessive pride can cause a person to be ashamed to acknowledge as a neighbor one whom God accounts his child.[111] Respect of persons is inconsistent with the faith of Christ.[112] These affirmations of a

---

[107] *CR* 45:187–188. Cf. *CR* 33:308–309.

[108] *CR* 23:405. Cf. *CR* 27:641; 51:211.

[109] *CR* 6:77.

[110] *CR* 45:613. Cf. *CR* 24:724: "Not only those with whom we have some connection are called our neighbors, but all without exception; for the whole human race forms one body, of which all are members, and consequently should be bound together by mutual ties; for we must bear in mind that even those who are most alienated from us should be cherished and aided even as our own flesh, since we have seen elsewhere that sojourners and strangers are placed in the same category and Christ sufficiently confirms this in the case of the good Samaritan." Also cf. *CR* 28:16.

[111] *CR* 52:447.

[112] *CR* 55:398.

common humanity stand in opposition to all pride of race and class. Although Calvin did not face the acute race and class tensions of modern times, he did speak out repeatedly against all attempts to evaluate people on the basis of race or position. God, he said, respects the purity and innocence of the heart, not such things as kindred, country, dignity, and riches which people esteem highly.[113] Whatever difference there may have been between Jew and Greek before the coming of Christ, that difference has been abolished by Christ.[114]

> We should not regard what a man is and what he deserves: but we should go higher—that it is God who has placed us in the world for such a purpose that we be united and joined together. He has impressed his image in us and has given us a common nature, which should incite us to providing one for the other. The man who wishes to exempt himself from providing for his neighbors should deface himself and declare that he no longer wishes to be a man, for as long as we are human creatures we must contemplate as in a mirror our face in those who are poor, despised, exhausted, who groan under their burdens. . . . If there come some Moor or barbarian, since he is a man, he brings a mirror in which we are able to contemplate that he is our brother and our neighbor: for we cannot abolish the order of nature which God has established as inviolable.[115]

Likewise, rank and position do not alter a person's situation before the judgment and laws of God.[116] God has no respect of people in avenging murder. The murder of the slave is avenged even as is that of the master. The life of a person cannot be estimated in terms of money, and one cannot buy the right to kill a slave. "Indeed, it was a proof of gross barbarism among the Romans and other nations to give to masters the power of life and death; for men are bound together by a more sacred tie than that it should be permitted to a master to kill with impunity his wretched slave."[117]

In addition to a common humanity, God also created people for the sake of people.[118] He joined all together so that they should help one another.[119] Indeed, human beings are created so that they cannot get along by themselves. Mutual helpfulness is necessary to every person's well-being.[120]

---

[113]*CR* 49:36.

[114]*CR* 48:230; 27:321; 28:16; 48:278; 49:502.

[115]*CR* 51:105.

[116]*CR* 40:226.

[117]*CR* 24:624.

[118]*CR* 45:614.

[119]*CR* 33:313.

[120]*CR* 24:185: "Here, too, it is worthwhile to remark that no single mortal can be sufficient to do everything, however many and various may be the endowments wherein he excels.

Human beings are united not only by a common flesh, but also by the image of God, which is imprinted on all. In his sermons, as in other writings, Calvin was careful to point out the double basis of social responsibility. The following passage is typical:

> When the prophet Isaiah wishes to convince men of their inhumanity, he says: You will not despise your flesh. I should contemplate myself as in a mirror in the many human creatures who are in the world. That is one thing. But there is still more: it is that the image of God is imprinted on every man. Not only do I despise my flesh when I wish to oppress someone, but I violate the image of God which is in me. Thus, therefore, let us note well that God wished through this passage to show to those who are of authority and reputation, to those who are richer than others, and who are in some position of honor, that they ought not to abuse those who are in their power, ought not to torment them beyond measure, that they should always remember that we are all descended from the race of Adam, that we have a common nature, and that the very image of God is imprinted on us. That is what we have to note: and above all now, that we have our Lord Jesus Christ who descended here below to be crushed by all for the purpose of condemning all pride, of showing that there is no means of serving God except through humility: and he has made us members of his body, both slaves and those who are masters and superiors— there is no distinction among them.[121]

"The image of God ought to be particularly regarded as a sacred bond of union; but for that very reason no distinction is here made between friend and foe, nor can the wickedness of men set aside the right of nature."[122]

Of especial significance is Calvin's assertion that the invisible God "represents himself to us in the brethren, and in their persons demands what is due to himself."[123] Murder, for example, is a violation of the image of God.[124] One who hurts a neighbor also hurts God.[125]

Calvin occasionally appeals to the fact of redemption as a demand

---

... In order, therefore, that everyone should confine himself within his own bounds, let us learn that in the human race God has so arranged our condition that individuals are only endued with a certain measure of gifts, on which the distribution of offices depends. For as one ray of the sun does not illuminate the world, but all combine their operations as it were in one, so God, that he may retain men by a sacred and indissoluble bond in mutual society and good will, unites one to another by variously dispensing his gifts and not raising up any out of measure by his entire perfection."

[121]*CR* 26:304. Cf. *CR* 26:351, 305, 226–227, 325; 27:204; 33:660; 51:19; 55:402; 52:78.
[122]*CR* 50:251.
[123]Ibid.
[124]*CR* 26:227–228.
[125]*CR* 27:542.

for community. If Christ redeems with his blood the weak and ignorant, then we should not despise or neglect those for whom Christ did so much.[126]

The second basis for the social responsibility of the Christian is the very nature of the gospel itself. Social action flows from true religion as a stream from its fountain. "The commandment to love our neighbors . . . is like the first [commandment] because it depends on it."[127] Apart from its true source in religion, social responsibility is impossible.

> Since every man is devoted to himself, there will never be true charity toward neighbors unless where the love of God reigns; for it is a mercenary love which the children of the world entertain for each other because every one of them has regard to his own advantage. On the other hand it is impossible for the love of God to reign without producing brotherly kindness among men.[128]

> Since love is from the Spirit of God, we cannot truly and with a sincere heart love the brethren, except the Spirit puts forth his power. In this way he testifies that he dwells in us.[129]

Thus Calvin was fully convinced that religion is the source of all true social action, and that any effort to develop social responsibility apart from religious foundations is based on a superficial understanding of the radical evil which is in human beings. Even apart from their existing sinfulness, any purely human effort to develop social responsibility would constitute a perversion of their creation in the image of God. Fellowship with God is the fundamental fact in human life, and every effort to bypass this fact ends in disaster. Faith determines ethics.

Calvin was equally convinced that every religion is false which does not issue forth in social action and responsibility. "We cannot worship God in a right manner if we do not observe the Second Table

---

[126]*CR* 49:435. Cf. *CR* 49:265; 26:304.

[127]*CR* 45:612.

[128]Ibid.

[129]*CR* 55:355. Cf. *CR* 49:429–430; 49:253–254; 26:309; 23:533; 31:144; 55:312. Cf. *CR* 44:487: "There is no justice where there is no obedience rendered to God. The first thing then in a good and upright life is to serve God, for it would be but of little benefit to be harmless toward men when his right is denied; and we know that God is not rightly served except according to what his law prescribes. We must then always come to this—that men must obey God if they desire to form their life aright."

CR 40:426: "It is clear from this that we fear God when we live justly with our brethren, for piety is the root of charity. Although many profane persons seem blameless in their life and manifest a rare integrity, yet no one ever loves his neighbor from his heart unless he fears and reverences God."

and abstain from all dishonesty and violence, for he who defrauds or injures his neighbors does violence also to God."[130] Those who do not make progress in neighborly love should be concerned about the validity of their religious profession.

> There is not growing among us the real fruit of the gospel unless we exercise mutual love and benevolence and exert ourselves in doing good. Though the gospel is at this day purely preached among us, when yet we consider how little progress we make in brotherly love, we ought justly to be ashamed of our indolence. God proclaims daily that he is reconciled to us in his Son . . . , that he renders him propitious to us, for this end, that we may live as brethren altogether. We indeed wish to be deemed the children of God, and we wish to enjoy the reconciliation obtained for us by the blood of Christ; but in the meantime we tear one another, we sharpen our teeth, our dispositions are cruel. If then we desire really to prove ourselves to be the disciples of Christ, we must attend to this part of divine truth, each of us must strive to do good to his neighbors. But this cannot be done without being opposed by our flesh, for we have a strong propensity to self-love and are inclined to seek too much our own advantage.
>
> We are also reminded that it is not enough for anyone to refrain from doing harm, unless he be also occupied in doing good to his brethren. . . . Unless, then, we endeavor to relieve the necessities of our brethren and to offer them assistance, there will not be in us but one part of true conversion, as the case is with many who are not indeed inhuman, who commit no plunder, who give no occasion for complaint, but who live to themselves and enjoy unprofitable leisure.[131]

Calvin repeatedly asserts that a person's obedience to the Second Table of the law is the true test of religion.

> And this is the sum of the Second Table of the law, in keeping which we give proof of our piety, if we have any. For this reason the prophets always draw our attention to that table, because by means of it our real

---

[130]*CR* 37:378. Cf. *CR* 37:331: "In vain do men serve God if they only offer to him trivial and bare ceremonies. . . . This is not right and proper worship of God, who rigidly commands and enjoins us to lead an upright and innocent life with our neighbors, willingly to give ourselves and our labors to them, and to be ready to assist them readily and cheerfully whenever it is necessary. . . . It would not be enough to perform acts of kindness toward men if our disposition toward them were not warm and affectionate."

Cf. *CR* 52:309: "He says that those who do not care about any of their relatives, and especially about their own house, have denied the faith. And justly; for there is no piety toward God when a person can thus lay aside the feelings of humanity. Would faith, which makes us the sons of God, render us worse than brute beasts? Such inhumanity, therefore, is open contempt of God and denying of the faith."

[131]*CR* 43:347.

character is better known and true uprightness is ascertained; for hypocrites, as we have formerly seen, often practice deceit by ceremonies.[132]

Because man has been created a "social animal," desiring spiritual intercourse and bearing the image of God, and by the very nature of true religion, the possibility of any private Christianity is precluded. The true Christian life must be lived among people and with a profound sense of social responsibility. The practice of self-denial involves love for neighbor.[133] Except for the special section in the *Institutes* on the state, Calvin does not give any systematic treatment of human responsibility to society. Yet his writings in general and his sermons in particular continually refer to various aspects of this responsibility. Likewise, the annals of Geneva reveal that Calvin was genuinely concerned about the general political and economic welfare of the citizens of that city. It now remains to point out more concretely some of the social responsibilities which rest on the Christian. In order to summarize Calvin's scattered remarks, it is convenient to speak of the Christian as a neighbor, as a citizen, and as a witness to the faith.

Calvin never allowed his parishioners in Geneva to forget that all people are neighbors. As has been pointed out, he believed strongly that God created human beings for fellowship with one another. Consequently it is not surprising that in his sermons and other writings he continually refers to the general duty of neighborliness. The following passage from the commentary on 1 John 3:17 is a good summary of what he meant by the term:

> Let this then be the first proposition, that no one truly loves his brethren except he really shows this whenever an occasion occurs; the second, that as far as anyone has the means, he is bound so far to assist his brethren, for the Lord thus supplies us with the opportunity to exercise love; the third, that the necessity of everyone ought to be seen to, for as anyone needs food and drink or other things of which we have abundance, so he requires our aid; the fourth, that no act of kindness, except accompanied with sympathy, is pleasing to God. There are many apparently liberal persons who yet do not feel for the miseries of their brethren. But the apostle requires that our hearts should be opened, which is done when we are endued with such a feeling as to sympathize with others in their evils, not otherwise than as though they were our own.[134]

---

[132]*CR* 37:294. Cf. *CR* 26:301, 309; 28:163; 36:44, 45; 43:462–463; 42:394; 45:119, 325, 539; 40:674; 51:19, 47; 55:228, 315, 338, 340.

[133]3.7.4ff.

[134]*CR* 55:340–341.

The godly "should not live to themselves and to the promotion merely of their own interests, but should endeavor to promote the common good of all according to their opportunities, and as far as they are able."[135] Christians must not merely live at peace with people, but they must aid, as far as they can, the miserable who are unjustly oppressed, and they should endeavor to resist the wicked lest they should injure human beings as they wish.[136]

In his insistence on the virtue of neighborliness, Calvin remained a realist. Neighborliness does not require the abolition of either the magistrate or the law courts.[137] Christians have a perfect right to seek justice through the regular processes of law, but they are not at liberty as either plaintiff or defendant to hate their neighbors or to seek revenge. Judicial processes must be conducted in a Christian spirit.[138]

Calvin was particularly concerned that people live as neighbors in the business and economic affairs of life. He repeatedly speaks out against fraudulent business practices. God's blessing does not rest on efforts to seek gain by plunder and evil methods.[139] He deplores the fact that these methods are common.[140] Fraudulent weights and unfair business practices destroy society.[141]

> Now, if the laws of buying and selling are corrupted, human society is in a manner dissolved; so that he who cheats by false weights and measures differs little from him who utters false coin; and consequently one who, whether as a buyer or a seller, has falsified the standard measure of wine, or corn, or anything else is accounted criminal.[142]

He strongly condemns "respectable" people who use tricks to take advantage of the simple.[143]

> Not only are those thieves who secretly steal the property of others, but those also who seek for gain from the loss of others, accumulate wealth by unlawful practices, and are more devoted to their private advantage than to equity. . . . He pronounces all unjust means of gain to be so many thefts. . . .

---

[135]*CR* 31:380.
[136]*CR* 24:612. Cf. *CR* 27:69.
[137]4.20.17–21.
[138]*CR* 23:557; 28:213ff; 49:246–248, 391.
[139]*CR* 27:197.
[140]Ibid.
[141]*CR* 28:235.
[142]*CR* 24:675.
[143]*CR* 36:42.

In order that we may not be condemned as thieves by God, we must endeavor as far as possible that everyone should safely keep what he possesses and that our neighbor's advantage should be promoted no less than our own.[144]

Calvin never hesitated to denounce fraudulent and oppressive business transactions in his sermons.[145] This indicates that he regarded economic injustices as a serious matter both for the Christian community and for the Christian individual.

Current wages and prices did not escape the scrutiny of his eye. If a merchant charges more than a piece of goods is worth, he steals.[146] Calvin denounced the rich for seeking means of denying the poor their full wage.[147] The employer must not take advantage of the employee's need.[148] Wages should be paid promptly.

> Consequently, if a rich man keeps a poor and wretched individual, whose labor he has abused, in suspense, he deprives him as it were of life in depriving him of his daily food. The sum is that humanity is so to be cultivated that none should be oppressed or suffer loss from default of payment.[149]

Servants should at least be paid enough to live frugally, and they should be paid voluntarily. Proper payment of servants is a strict duty.[150]

Calvin does not seek to destroy the master-servant (in modern terminology employer-employee) relationship. His endeavors were directed at its proper regulation. Masters are not obligated to give servants equal status and condition, but they are obligated to deal

---

[144]*CR* 24:669.

[145]*CR* 27:197; 28:111–124.

[146]*CR* 26:348.

[147]*CR* 28:162, 187.

[148]*CR* 28:189: "If I bargain with someone to serve me, then the day will cost so much: but that day will be so diminished that a poor man, after having done all he can, will have nothing with which to feed himself. And why? I see that this man has nothing to do, he has no means of working, he has to manage by his hands. I could therefore have him for what I want. This is what the rich do sometimes; they look for occasions to cut back half of the wages of the poor so that they (the poor) do not know how to get by. They may offer all that they have (themselves) and they only ask to be able to earn a living, on condition that they find out where; a wealthy man will look at this, this one is deprived of everything, I can have him for a piece of bread. Because in spite of his hunger, he will have to work for me, I will pay him only half wages, and still he will have to be content. Therefore, when we use someone with such reasoning, and even if we have not withheld the salary, there is still cruelty and we have cheated a poor man. This deception will not profit before God, even if we have paid out money from the first day."

[149]*CR* 24:670–671.

[150]*CR* 24:672.

with their servants in humanity and clemency.[151] Calvin considered the abolishment of chattel slavery a notable achievement, but the new status did not free the master from responsibility for the treatment of his servants.[152]

Calvin was a strong supporter of honest labor by precept as well as example. Human beings were created to labor.[153] Labor in itself is impotent to provide the goods of life. These depend on the blessing of God. Consequently, people are exhorted to labor in humility and trust.[154] "Nothing is more unseemly than a person who is idle and good for nothing, who profits neither himself nor others and seems born only to eat and drink."[155] Calvin had no sympathy with the money changers who sit in idleness.

> It is also a very strange and shameful thing that while all other men obtain the means of their subsistence with much toil, while husbandmen fatigue themselves by their daily occupations, and artisans serve the community by the sweat of their brow, and merchants not only employ themselves in labors but also expose themselves to many inconveniences and dangers, that money-mongers should sit at their ease without doing anything and receive tribute from the labor of all other people.[156]

---

[151]*CR* 50:101.

[152]*CR* 27:346–347: "There is no longer servitude such as there once was between Jews and all pagans. In some places this servitude still exists, as in the countries of the Orient, Greece, and in barbarous places. It is such that it would be for the better if the usage were abolished, as it is among us; and this is indeed praiseworthy. But if we must look at ourselves, as our Lord admonishes us by his law, then those who are in service to us would be treated humanely by us. We should support them, and not disappoint them with their wages, and we should not consider such strictness as to have everything we can take from them. But there should be equity, that we ourselves be moderate and not wait for someone to impose on us a law which constrains us, but that each rule himself."

[153]*CR* 28:380. Calvin makes clear that work is not punishment, although sin has made work less pleasant. Cf. *CR* 23:72ff.; 26:296: "It is true that we are born to this and we know that God does not expect us to be lazy, living in this world. He gave man feet and hands. He gave them skill. And even before sin, it is said that Adam was put in the garden to cultivate it. However, work which men now take on is chastisement for sin. . . . And even before sin came into this world and we were thus condemned by God to painful and hard work, it was already necessary for men to exert themselves to some work. And why? Because it is against our nature to be like a useless tree trunk. Thus it is quite certain that we need to apply ourselves to some type of labor our whole life long."

[154]*CR* 28:379–380.

[155]*CR* 52:164. Cf. *CR* 10(b):64: "If those idle bellies with you, who chirp together so sweetly in the shade, were only as well disposed as they are talkative, they would instantly flock hither to take on themselves a share of the labor, to which we must be inadequate, since there are so few of us."

[156]*CR* 31:148.

Although Calvin was generous with the poor, he condemned beggars, whom he called wicked rascals. He strongly advocated the prohibition of mendicants.[157] He was opposed to excessive religious holidays other than Sundays, and he maintained the right of people to work on the extra holidays which were observed if they so chose.[158] He spoke out against the rich who exploited the enforced idleness of the poor,[159] and on at least one occasion took positive steps to provide work for the unemployed in Geneva.[160]

Calvin did not consider riches as necessarily evil, nor did he consider poverty as especially conducive to Christian living. Riches in themselves and from their nature are not to be condemned. Indeed, it is a great blasphemy against God if one condemns the rich, for riches proceed from God.[161] Nevertheless, it is certain that prosperity corrupts more people than all the other afflictions in the world.[162] Poverty also carries many temptations.

> It is true that poverty brings many temptations, for when a man is in need, then he considers, What is to become of me? and the devil urges him to defiance, induces him to murmur against God, for we see that many vex themselves and it seems to them that God had done them wrong. They do not know which way to turn, and then they conclude, Since I am not able to earn my living through my labor without doing wrong to another, I must proceed otherwise.[163]

Indigence, however, is no more an excuse for malice and theft than riches are an excuse for greed.[164] Nevertheless, the Christian must always be generous to those who are in need.[165] God accepts alms given to the poor as sacrifices to himself.[166] Charity must not be calculating and niggardly, but free and spontaneous.[167] It must be combined with fair business practices also.

> Uprightness and righteousness are divided into two parts: first, that we should injure nobody; second, that we should bestow our wealth and abundance on the poor and needy. And these two ought to be joined

---

[157]*CR* 27:340–341. Cf. Martin Luther, "An Open Letter to the German Nobility," *Works of Martin Luther* (Philadelphia: A. J. Holman Co., 1915), 2:115–118, 134–135.

[158]*CR* 21:211; Aimé-Louis Herminjard, ed., *Correspondance des Réformateurs dans les pays de langue française* (Geneva: H. Georg, 1877), 5:4.

[159]*CR* 28:189.

[160]Cf. Amédée Roget, *Histoire du peuple de Genève* (Geneva: John Jullien, 1870), 2:150.

[161]*CR* 33:36–37.

[162]*CR* 33:68.

[163]*CR* 33:35.

[164]*CR* 28:137–138; 58:88.

[165]*CR* 28:136, 194.

[166]*CR* 27:339.

[167]*CR* 50:96.

together, for it is not enough to abstain from acts of injustice if you refuse assistance to the needy, nor will it be of much avail to render your aid to the needy if at the same time you rob some of that which you bestow on others.[168]

Furthermore, the poor receive the special care of God.

The proud, indeed, never think of this, that the poor, whom they afflict and despise, are of such estimation in the sight of God that he feels himself insulted and injured in their persons; for they do not imagine that the blows aimed at them are struck against heaven any more than if they trampled a little dust or clay under their feet. But God bestows on his servants the inestimable reward of taking their cause into his own hand.[169]

Nevertheless, it is a foolish prodigality to scatter at random what the Lord has given one.[170] Indiscriminate charity creates beggars, who are a menace to society.[171]

Calvin did not consider prosperity or poverty to be of primary importance for human life. The one matter of fundamental significance is fellowship with God. The real task of the Christian life is to use whatever condition God places one in for the advancement of piety and fellowship with him. God assigns people their respective stations in life, and he does it for very good reasons.

Why, therefore, does God permit there to be poor ones here on earth except that he wishes to give us an occasion for doing good? Thus let us not attribute it to fortune when we see one person is rich and another poor, but let us recognize that God disposes it thus and that it is not without cause. It is true that we cannot always see why God has enriched one and has left another in his poverty. We do not have the discretion necessary for that. And thus God wishes that we lower our eyes often in order to honor him, because he governs men by his will and according to his counsel, which is incomprehensible to us. . . . God distributes inequally the decaying goods of this world in order to probe the courage of men; it is a test which he makes.[172]

By far the most publicized economic pronouncement Calvin made concerns usury.[173] In this matter he recognized that a change in

---

[168]*CR* 37:329.
[169]*CR* 31:71.
[170]*CR* 45:186.
[171]*CR* 27:340.
[172]*CR* 27:337–338.
[173]It is important to note that Calvin did not indiscriminately endorse usury. The following exceptions are found in one of his most important pronouncements on the subject:

CR 10(a):248–249: "Now I come to the exceptions: . . . Since almost all look for a little word to delight in excessively, it is fitting to add this preface: that when I permit some usury, I do not deem all usury lawful. And I disapprove if someone proposes to make a living by profiting from usury. Furthermore, I concede nothing except in setting forth certain exceptions. The economic conditions required a change in the position of the church. As previously noted, he refused to be bound by biblical literalism.[174] In regard to the Christian life, Calvin's position on usury is important as an illustration of the attitude which should exist in business matters. Money makes money, and for this reason interest is permissible. Yet this fact can never be a pretext for the exploitation of the poor. When usury contravenes equity and neighborly love, it is wrong.[175] Calvin warned that the tendency of usury is always to oppress one's neighbor.[176] In other words, the spirit of neighborly love must dominate such business transactions as the lending of money. For this reason he refused to set any one rate as legitimate interest.[177] Each case must be judged separately, and in the case of the poor and needy all interest is wrong when it oppresses people.[178] On the other hand he was open to the possibilities that interest may serve human good in a new economic situation.

The Christian life also involves a distinctive attitude toward property. Calvin was a vigorous advocate of the right of private property.[179] With equal emphasis he opposed every notion of absolute ownership. We own nothing fee simple. Everything is a sacred trust from the one true Owner—God.[180] This principle of stewardship has far-reaching social consequences, as Calvin himself pointed out.

---

first is that one not take usury from the poor, and that no one, being in a bad situation through indigence or afflicted by some calamity, be forced into it. The second exception is that he who lends not be so occupied with the gain that he neglects necessary duties; nor, wishing to keep his money secure, that he scorns his poor brothers. The third exception is that nothing intervene which is not in accord with natural conduct and that one look closely at the thing according to Christ's rule: that is, do as you wish men to do, etc.; it will be found to fit everywhere. The fourth exception is that he who borrows make as much profit from the borrowed money. In the fifth place, that we not value things according to common custom and take that which is allowable for us, or that we not measure what is right and equitable by the iniquity in the world, but that we take as a guide the word of God. In the sixth place, that we do not look only at the private comfort of those with whom we do business, but also that we consider what is expedient for the public. It is obvious that the usury which the merchant pays is a public pension. We must, therefore, see to it that this contract be useful rather than detrimental. In the seventh place, that we not exceed the limits that public laws of the region allow, even though these laws do not always suffice because they often allow what they cannot correct or repress. We must therefore choose fairness which gets rid of what is superfluous. But it is not that I want to value my opinion about you, because I want nothing more than that all be so humane that there would be no need to say any more of this."

[174] *CR* 10(a):247–248: "I now conclude that it is necessary to judge usuries not according to some certain and particular statement of God, but according to the rule of fairness."

[175] *CR* 24:680ff.

[176] *CR* 40:432.

[177] *CR* 28:111–124.

[178] *CR* 10(a):248.

[179] *CR* 7:214; 45:120; 47:418; 50:100–101.

[180] *CR* 27:324; 26:503–504; 33:100.

> He reminds us what we ought to bear in mind when we do good to our neighbors, for nothing is more fitted to correct our murmurings than to remember that we do not give our own, but only dispense what God has committed to us.[181]

> By commanding them to break bread to the hungry, he intended to take away every excuse from covetous and greedy men, who allege that they have a right to keep possession of that which is their own. "This is mine and therefore I may keep it for myself. Why should I make common property of that which God has given me?" He replies, "It is indeed yours, but on this condition, that you share it with the hungry and thirsty, not that you eat it yourself alone." And indeed this is the dictate of common sense, that the hungry are deprived of their just right if their hunger is not relieved.[182]

Calvin's actual participation in the political and economic affairs of Geneva is certainly as impressive as anything he ever wrote. It makes his own sense of social responsibility indubitably clear. In addition to the task of organizing the Geneva church, Calvin gave considerable attention to the civil and judicial laws of the city.[183] No matter was too insignificant for his interest. On one occasion he brought to the attention of the authorities a new type of heating stove which saved considerable fuel.[184] When the economic and social conditions of Geneva were at a low ebb, Calvin did not hesitate to appear before the council and request that employment be provided for the poor.[185] After making this request he continued to prosecute the matter actively.[186]

The actual economic and political measures by which Calvin implemented his understanding of human responsibility are not too important in themselves. He did not revolutionize society by any brilliant economic theory.[187] His importance for our times lies in his refusal to set up any artificial dichotomy between a person's relation to God and a person's relation to other people. True religion always reveals itself in neighborly love. Consequently the Christian cannot separate religion from economic and social affairs, for these are important mediums for the expression of faith.

In addition to the responsibilities of neighborliness, the Christian also bears the responsibility of a subject to the state. The Christian

---

[181]*CR* 55:276.
[182]*CR* 37:329.
[183]*CR* 10(a): 125–146.
[184]*CR* 16:498. Cf. Roget, op. cit., 5:58.
[185]Doumergue, op. cit., 5:679.
[186]Ibid.
[187]Cf. J. T. McNeill, *Christian Hope for World Society* (Chicago: Willett, Clark & Co., 1937), p. 111.

subject's first duty "is to entertain the most honourable sentiments of [the magistrates'] function, which [he knows] to be a jurisdiction delegated to them from God, and on that account to esteem and reverence them as God's ministers and vicegerents."[188] In other words, the state is God's ordinance.

Christians must be careful to avoid two errors with regard to the state. On the one hand, they must not attempt to "subvert this ordinance established by God."[189] The church does not supplant the state, and only those who "foolishly imagine a perfection which can never be found in any community of men" believe that the state can be dispensed with. To entertain such a thought is inhuman barbarism, for the state is as "necessary to mankind as bread and water, light and air, and far more excellent."[190] On the other hand, the flatterers of princes do not hesitate to oppose the authority of the state to God.[191] The purity of faith requires that both errors be resisted.

The state is a remedy for human perversity.[192] If human beings had continued in that integrity in which God created them, the state, at least as a coercive order, would not have been required.[193] The

---

[188]4.20.22.

[189]4.20.1.

[190]4.20.3.

[191]4.20.1.

[192]It is difficult to determine Calvin's exact views on the origin of the state. Insofar as the state is coercive, sin is certainly the occasion of its existence, although God's will is the effective cause. Would the state have existed as an association of men if sin had not entered human history? H. Strohl has strongly maintained that Calvin did not exclusively justify the existence of the state on the fact of sin. A power which organizes the social life is made necessary by the simple fact that men are not pure spirits. Strohl based his argument on the *Institutes*—4.20.1–6. (*Bulletin de la Société de l'histoire du protestantisme français*, 84 [1935], 171–172.) Strohl's opinion that the nature of man calls for the existence of the state has been rejected by other Calvin scholars. Cf. Marc-Édouard Chenevière, *La pensée politique de Calvin* (Geneva: Éditions Labor et Fides, 1937), pp. 115–119; Doumergue, op. cit., 5:399–400; J. Bohatec, *Calvins Lehre von Staat und Kirche* (Breslau: M. & H. Marcus, 1937), pp. 169–173; Peter Barth, *Das Problem der natürlichen Theologie bei Calvin* (*Theologische Existenz heute*, no. 18; Munich: Chr. Kaiser, 1935), pp. 57–60.

[193]*CR* 27:409: "If we remained in the integrity of nature, as God created it, the order of justice, as it is called, would not be at all required, inasmuch as each would carry the law in his heart, so that no restraint would be necessary to keep us in order. Each would know his rule and we would all live in accord, which would be good and just. And furthermore, justice is like a remedy for the corruption that is in man. Each and every time one speaks of the police here on earth, know that here we have a mirror of our perversity, in the same proportion that we are led to follow fairness and reason by force. Because those who lead are those who have sword in hand, and for what purpose? To repress those who rise up by riots and wrongful acts. And where does that propensity come from if not from men who should themselves look for what is good and just, but who pervert it, and who try to put everything in confusion, unless they are stopped. Now this is a great shame, seeing that God created us in his image, that he has given us mastery and superiority over all creatures, that because of our evil, it is necessary that

authority of the magistrates, however, is not derived from human perversity but from the ordinance of God.[194] The magistrates have their command from God. Calvin does not hesitate to give them the highest titles. They are God's representatives and his vicegerents.[195] Great kings are nothing but the hands of God.[196] "No doubt ought . . . to be entertained by any person that civil magistracy is a calling not only holy and legitimate, but far the most sacred and honourable in human life."[197] The state, therefore, is not merely a remedy for sin; it is a divinely ordained remedy.[198]

Despite Calvin's high regard for the state, he zealously fought for and guarded the independence of the church from state control. The state has no right to make laws concerning religion and the worship of God.[199] The sword belongs to the state, but the task of preaching the gospel belongs to the church.[200] In the field of polity he sought to secure the independence of the church by means of the Consistory. He found it necessary to leave Geneva in 1538 when the state denied the independence of this body in church discipline and worship. On his return in 1541 Calvin immediately began to work for a church which would be independent of state control.[201] The fact that he spent two thirds of his ministry in Geneva fighting an uphill battle for a church independent of state control should not be overlooked. However, in demanding the independence of the church in the performance of its task of preaching and discipline, he did not ask for special privileges for the clergy. The liberty and dignity of the church do not consist in the exemption of the clergy from common judicature and laws, as the Roman ecclesiastics imagined.[202]

---

we be thus forced. Choose among men the one the most scorned: yet he carries in him the image of God and that mark of superiority. So it is such that we must be subjects, and this because of our vice, as I have already said. Know then that it is not without cause that God established the order of justice here on earth; but that he has looked at the corruption in us." Cf. *CR* 27:446–447.

[194] 4.20.4: "This is just as if it had been affirmed, that the authority possessed by kings and other governors over all things upon earth is not a consequence of the perverseness of men, but of the providence and holy ordinance of God, who has been pleased to regulate human affairs in this manner; forasmuch as he is present, and also presides among them, in making laws and in executing equitable judgments." Cf. *CR* 52:152.

[195] 4.20.4.

[196] *CR* 35:152.

[197] 4.20.4.

[198] Cf. Doumergue, op. cit., 5:400.

[199] 4.20.3.

[200] 4.11.3.

[201] *CR* 10(a):15–30; 11:431–432.

[202] 4.11.15. Cf. *CR* 53:223–224: "As we know that God has separated these two things, the state of police here on earth and the spiritual kingdom of his church. These are the magistrates who rule, they are seated in the seat of justice, God has given them swords to rule his people. Now

Doumergue has aptly observed that Calvin advocated the distinction of church and state and not the separation of the two.[203] There is one Lord Jesus Christ, and he is Lord of church and state. Calvin wanted a Christian state.

> This civil government is designed, as long as we live in this world, to cherish and support the external worship of God, to preserve the pure doctrine of religion, to defend the constitution of the Church, to regulate our lives in a manner requisite for the society of men, to form our manners to civil justice, to promote our concord with each other, and to establish general peace and tranquillity.[204]

In the letter in which Calvin dedicated the *Institutes* to Francis he wrote: "Where the glory of God is not made the end of the government, it is not a legitimate sovereignty, but a usurpation."[205] Furthermore, the only stable power in the world is that which is founded on Christ.[206]

---

in the same way as pastors and ministers of God's word are members of the body, they must be subject to the magistrates; but this does not overturn the authority of the doctrine they profess, and they shouldn't preside in virtue and the name of God over all earthly eminence as it is said in Jeremiah: I have appointed you over kingdoms and over all principalities. As for the ministers of God's word in their own selves, as men, they must be subject to the laws and be obedient to the magistrates and honor and revere them."

[203]Op. cit., 5:408.

[204]4.20.2. Cf. *CR* 52:140–141: "This is why he established kings and magistrates, and police; it is first of all 'that we will live,' says St. Paul, 'in complete piety.' What does this word 'piety' mean? It is the honor of God when there is a pure and holy religion between us. By this the magistrates are sanctioned when they use the sword against those who disturb the church, against all heretics, and those who sow error and false opinions, and those capricious ones who are led by Satan's spirit, who today want to give unpunished license to those who overthrow the truth, to those who break the union of faith, and the peace of the church, such that they show quite well that they battle against God and that it is Satan who drives them to it. For we hear what the Holy Spirit says through the words of St. Paul: that is to say, that God orders the magistrates to keep the pure religion. . . . Now here is the living God, who appoints a poor mortal creature, and sits him down and says, 'I want you to represent me, but on this condition: that I be served and honored.' For God does not want to give up his right, that is, that he forfeits anything, nor that he does any harm to his glory, nor that he lessen it. And here is mortal man who will suffer that God's truth be vilified, that he be mocked, and that the way he has ordered to rule among men be abolished. Is this tolerable? Thus let the magistrates know well what condemnation there will be on their heads, and the horrible vengeance which awaits them, unless they decide to make an effort to keep the honor of God, which consists in pure religion's having position and strength among men."

[205]*OS* 3:11. Cf. *CR* 13:282 (Letter to Sigismund Augustus, King of Poland): "Your kingdom is extensive and renowned, and abounds in many excellencies; but its happiness will then only be solid, when it adopts Christ as its chief ruler and governor, so that it may be defended by his safeguard and protection; for to submit your scepter to him is not inconsistent with that elevation in which you are placed; but it would be far more glorious than all the triumphs of the world."

[206]*CR* 18:617: "For God shows how all earthly power which is not founded on Christ must fall; and he threatens speedy destruction to all kingdoms which obscure Christ's glory by

Calvin's ideal was a Christocracy, though the execution of that ideal was no doubt imperfect.[207] The term "theocracy" is also applicable to Calvin's purpose in Geneva if it means the reign of God through Jesus Christ in the whole of society.[208] Thus it is grossly incorrect to say that Calvin stood for a secularized state. He exempted the state only from the control of an ecclesiastical hierarchy, not from the sovereignty of God.[209] Church and state should work together under a common Lord and for a common purpose.[210] The tasks assigned are different, and neither has the right to usurp the powers of the other.[241]

The difficulty in Calvin's solution of this vexing problem of the relation of church and state lies in the practical problem of determining what is the will of God. His solution can work easily only if there is some agreement as to what God's will is. Calvin frequently proceeds on the assumption that the will of God can be easily determined from a study of the Bible. He does not always take into consideration the possibility that equally sincere and honest persons may differ in their interpretation of scripture. Likewise, he too easily

---

extending themselves too much. And those kings whose sway is most extended shall feel by sorrowful experience how horrible a judgment will fall on them unless they willingly submit themselves to the sway of Christ."

[207]Choisy has written: "[Calvin] puts the Bible in place of papal hierarchy. He does not believe in hierarchy ("un hierocrate"), but in the Bible ("un bibliocrate"). There was no clerical theocracy. There was a theocracy in what is meant by the 'Word of God,' biblical theocracy, read and interpreted not as human witness of divine action in history, but as a rule of doctrine and conduct" (op. cit., pp. 52–53).

[208]J. Bohatec prefers "Pneumatocracy." Cf. Bohatec, "Die Souveränität Gottes und der Staat nach der Auffassung Calvins," *Second International Conference of Calvinists* (Amsterdam: Martinus Nijhoff, 1935), p. 99.

[209]4.20.9.

[210]*CR* 29:659–660: "Quamobrem agnoscamus ita Deum mundi huius gubernacula regere, ut reges et principes ac magistratus esse velit, et alios primariae dignitatis viros qui caeteris praesint et gladium gerant, quo utantur sicut ipsis Deus praeceperit. Ac vicissim aliud etiam a Deo spirituale regimen constitutum sciamus in ecclesia, nimirum verbi sui praedicationem, cui omnes subiiciantur, et adversus quod nulla rebellio toleretur: sed ut cuiusvis conditionis homines sese illi regendos tanquam oves pastori permittant, cuius unius vocem audiant, et quocunque vocaverit sequantur. Duo itaque illi ordines a Deo constituti non inter se repugnant; ut ignis et aqua inter se sunt contraria; sed ut dixi, res sunt adeo coniunctae ut una sublata, alia vehementer laboret. Non secur ac si quis oculum cuipiam effodiat, ex cuius effossione vehementer alterum affici, atque etiam reliqua totius corporis membra, necesse est; aut detruncato ex corpore brachio, alterum valde laborare, et proinde solum non posse utriusqua labori sufficere."

[211]Doumergue has summarized the relation of church and state in the following manner: "The Christian state is a creation of God, just as is the Christian church: two creations of the same God. These two creations can therefore be autonomous and independent, without ceasing to concur in a common activity. The church is not Christian because the state forces it to be: no Caesar-papacy (césaropapie)! The state is not Christian because the church forces it to be: no theocracy!" (op. cit., 5:411).

assumes that ministers speak for God. The possibility that even good ministers are sometimes wrong is not sufficiently recognized. He fails to see that the dialectical tension of opposing views is sometimes nearer to the truth than dogmatic pronouncements. These are factors which made for difficulty in the actual realization of Calvin's program. Another fallacy is the tendency to regard force and coercion as effective factors in religious development. This tendency continually creeps out in Calvin's writings despite his own protests that force is ineffective in religious matters.

The important fact for this study, however, is that Calvin placed the totality of society under the sovereignty of God. He did not give up the medieval ideal of the *Corpus Christianum.* He only set about with great energy to make the *Corpus Christianum* and the *Corpus Christi* one and the same. The state, as well as the church, is an arm of the Lord, and the Christian must honor the magistrates as the Lord's vicegerents.

In addition to honoring the magistrates, the Christian must render obedience to them.

> Hence follows another duty, that, with minds disposed to honour and reverence magistrates, subjects approve their obedience to them, in submitting to their edicts, in paying taxes, in discharging public duties, and bearing burdens which relate to the common defence, and in fulfilling all their other commands.[212]

The duty of obedience flows naturally from the premise that the magistrate is the Lord's vicegerent. Calvin does not hesitate to add that it is impossible to resist the magistrate without, at the same time, resisting God.[213]

The duty of bearing "burdens which relate to the common defence" indicates that Calvin was no pacifist. He believed that war in defense of peace and justice was lawful according to natural equity and to the Holy Spirit in many passages in scripture.[214] Furthermore,

---

[212]4.20.23.

[213]Ibid. In interpreting these remarks it is important to remember that Calvin and the people whom he represented were held under the suspicion of sedition. In the Dedication of the *Institutes* to Francis, Calvin was obliged to refute the calumny that Protestants sought "to wrest the scepters of kings out of their hands, to overturn all the tribunals and judicial proceedings, to subvert all order and governments, to disturb the peace and tranquillity of the people, to abrogate all laws, to scatter all properties and possessions, and, in a word, to involve everything in total confusion" (*OS* 3:10). In 1560 Charles IX of France wrote a letter to the Council of Geneva charging that the Genevans were stirring up sedition in France: "Its . . . birth comes from the malice of some preachers and partisans of the Reform, most sent by you or the principal ministers of your city" (*CR* 18:338).

[214]4.20.11. Cf. *CR* 27:593–594: "And as a judge must punish a robber, also those who have power directed by God can take up arms against those who come to trouble them and their

he believed that it was legitimate to defend Christianity by arms.[215] Calvin typically does not give rules or guides to determine which wars are just. Here, as elsewhere, he was pragmatic and occasional rather than theoretical and universal in his prescriptions. Any lawful war must be waged, however, without passion, anger, or hatred and only when compelled by the strongest necessity. War is a measure of last resort and is only to be undertaken after all other methods failed.

> If arms are to be resorted to against an enemy, that is, an armed robber, they ought not to seize a trivial occasion, nor even to take it when presented, unless they are driven to it by extreme necessity. For, if it be our duty to exceed what was required by that heathen writer who maintained that the evident object of war ought to be the restoration of peace, certainly we ought to make every other attempt before we have recourse to the decision of arms. In short . . . , they must not suffer themselves to be carried away by any private motive, but be wholly guided by public spirit; otherwise, they grossly abuse their power, which is given them, not for their own particular advantage, but for the benefit and service of others.[216]

Even in just wars, cruelty must be repressed and bloodshed abstained from as much as possible.[217] All must strive for peace with all of their powers.[218] Calvin's own reticence about war is seen in his relations with the French Protestants. He counseled against war when a word from him would have been sufficient to set off a bloody struggle.[219] His attitude toward war presupposed his belief that human society is still far distant from the perfection which belongs to the peaceful reign of Christ. He believed that people should endeavor to make progress toward that perfection, but that it was fatal to assume the presence of this perfection when it was still far away.[220]

---

subjects; wars will therefore not only be allowed, but one would be forced to use them. . . . From this we can gather that it is lawful to fight in necessity, in that war would only be to bring peace, and to obtain it. . . . We know that today faithful princes have God's promise that he will be their guide in times of war. . . . But we also know that there is no just war if God is not the author of it. Because if we want to be armed with his strong hand, we must interpret his words, and his Spirit must preside in the advice that we take."
[215]*CR* 47:404.
[216]4.20.12.
[217]*CR* 24:632. Cf. *CR* 27:617: "God, therefore, wanted to declare here that his people must maintain, even in times of war, such humanity that they would pardon their enemies . . . , because these men, no matter who they are, are made in God's image. Then we must think about our nature; we must be removed from all reason if this does not restrain us, if we have no pity on those who are our flesh, our bones, and even carry the mark of our God, of him who made us all in his image."
[218]*CR* 26:54.
[219]*CR* 16:629–632; 18:84ff., 436–437.
[220]*CR* 27:593–594; 36:66.

Calvin knew full well that there are magistrates who are evil and who do not act as if they were the Lord's vicegerents.

> Some princes, regardless of every thing to which they ought to have directed their attention and provision, give themselves up to their pleasures in indolent exemption from every care; others, absorbed in their own interest, expose to sale all laws, privileges, rights, and judgments; others plunder the public of wealth, which they afterwards lavish in mad prodigality; others commit flagrant outrages, pillaging houses, violating virgins and matrons, and murdering infants; many persons cannot be persuaded that such ought to be acknowledged as princes, whom, as far as possible, they ought to obey.[221]

Should the Christian obey such princes? Calvin answers that the Christian must "submit to the government, not only of those princes who discharge their duty to us with becoming integrity and fidelity, but of all who possess the sovereignty, even though they perform none of the duties of their function."[222]

In the first place, an evil ruler may be the judgment of God.[223] Of greater importance is the fact that rulers of the most undeserving character who hold sovereign power really possess "that eminent and Divine authority, which the Lord has given by his word to the ministers of his justice and judgment."[224] Calvin proceeds to substantiate his principle by numerous examples from the Bible.[225]

This principle of obedience accounts for the conservatism which has characterized Calvinistic peoples. The ability of Calvinists to combine a revolutionary trait with their conservatism arises out of the single exception which Calvin allows to the duty of obedience, an exception which is more explicit in the *Institutes* of 1559 and the sermons on Samuel.

> But in the obedience which we have shown to be due to the authority of governors, it is always necessary to make one exception, and that is entitled to our first attention, that it do not seduce us from obedience to him, to whose will the desires of all kings ought to be subject, to whose decrees all their commands ought to yield, to whose majesty all their sceptres ought to submit. And, indeed, how preposterous it would be for us, with a view to satisfy men, to incur the displeasure of him on whose account we yield obedience to men![226]

---

[221] 4.20.24.
[222] 4.20.25.
[223] 4.20.29.
[224] 4.20.25.
[225] 4.20.26–28.
[226] 4.20.32.

This exception is not given a very large place in the *Institutes,* but it is very pronounced in some of the sermons. The authority of Jesus Christ ought to be valued not only more than all the liberty of this world but also more than all earthly kingdoms and empires.[227] In his commentary on Daniel 6:22 Calvin wrote:

> Fear God, honor the king (1 Peter 2:17). The two commands are connected together and cannot be separated from one another. The fear of God ought to precede, that kings may obtain their authority. For if anyone begins his reverence of an earthly prince by rejecting that of God, he will act preposterously, since this is a complete perversion of the order of nature. . . . We ought rather utterly to defy than to obey them whenever they are so restive and wish to spoil God of his rights and, as it were, to seize on his throne and draw him down from heaven.[228]

One of the most pronounced statements on the obligation to resist is found in a sermon on the same chapter:

> If, as St. Paul says, it be necessary for us to obey princes and our superiors who are established over us and yet see that they burden us in the flesh, that they use tyranny and cruelty against us, yet when they rise up against God, it is necessary that they be put down, and that one consider them no more than a pair of old shoes. Why? For there is the foundation which is quite ruined as today. If one regards the fashion of ruling this world, one will find great excess on the part of the princes—that they burden their subjects, that they are transported by ambition and greed so that they no longer know what they are— they are so intoxicated, so bewitched that it seems to them the world was created only for them; they abuse men without any humanity, but in all of that it is necessary for the subjects to humble themselves and that they know that it is for their sins they endure this, that they pray to God to give them patience and to enable them, moreover, to perform their duty. But when princes forbid that God be served and honored, when they command that one pollute himself in idolatry, when they will that one consent to all the abominations which are contrary to the service of God and yield himself to them, oh, they are not worthy to be called princes or to be given authority. And why? for (as I have already said) there is but one foundation for all the power the princes are to have—and we are to know that God has ordained them and if they wish to tear God from his throne, shall one have any regard for them? . . . God must have his sovereign position. All creatures should humble themselves before him, and when we disobey princes to obey God, they must not think we do wrong, for we are not

---

[227]*CR* 27:459–460.
[228]*CR* 41:25–26.

to consider men when we see it is a question of honoring God, of rendering to him that which belongs to him. And indeed those who wish to magnify the estate of princes, who flatter them to make them proud against God, are the ones who do the greatest harm—those who wish to acquire the grace and favor of princes, each devising some means to make his prince rise up in pride and presumption. You should set your hand strongly against them that you might resist such a thing.[229]

Calvin himself did not carry this principle of disobedience to many of its logical conclusions. He seems to limit it to acts of government which directly affect the formal worship of God. Yet the question must be raised, Is not the abuse of human beings made in the image of God an act against God as well as the prohibition of the worship of God? On the basis of Calvin's own principles, brutality and inhumanity must certainly be regarded as acts against God, but Calvin did not reach that conclusion on this particular point. In actual practice, however, he never hesitated to criticize in strong terms irresponsible acts of the Genevan government. One of the criticisms the government lodged against him was the fact that he meddled in politics.[230]

The *Institutes* summarized the obligations of citizens under the duties of honor and obedience. On the basis of random remarks and inference from Calvin's practice and doctrine, it is necessary to add a third duty—responsibility for the social welfare. This is illustrated by Calvin's remarks on the duties of the people in the election of magistrates and judges. He considered this duty a privilege, not a right, which should receive diligent attention.[231] Calvin himself did not hesitate to take part in the framing of political and judicial laws

---

[229]*CR* 41:415–416. Cf. *CR* 9:700; 22:74; 29:229; 30:72, 325.

[230]Doumergue, op. cit., 2:273: "Therefore on March 11, 1538, . . . (the Council) decided that 'the preachers must be warned not to get involved in politics, but to preach the gospel as God has commanded; . . . not to attend the small Council or the Two Hundred; yet to live by the Word of God according to the ordinances of the gentlemen of Berne.' " Cf. Herminjard, op. cit., 4:403–404.

[231]*CR* 27:467: "Now, as for the second reason too, note that if God favored a people to choose kings or princes and magistrates or judges, that people must see that God's rule was ordered for the salvation of humankind, not to be given to an unbeliever. Because when people choose either a king or a judge without knowing if he is a Godfearing man or not, they wittingly put the rope around their own necks. When they go to an election and choose magistrates who are either mortal enemies of the gospel, or hypocrites who want to pervert everything, or profane people who would be happy to trample religion underfoot, when they choose people such as that, is it not like opening the door to Satan that he may find a place among us?" Cf. *CR* 21:685; 27:41, 413–414, 458.

Doumergue has made a strong case for the democratic direction of Calvin's thought (op. cit., 5:440–447). Unquestionably, Calvin is more inclined toward a republican form of government in the sermons than the *Institutes* indicate.

for Geneva.[232] It is true that he energetically condemned "meddling" in governmental affairs.[233] However, in the light of his practice, this condemnation clearly does not include responsible criticism of and participation in the affairs of government. Calvin expected the Christian to be a Christian citizen, not merely a citizen.

Calvin gave institutional form to the Christian concern for social welfare in the revival of the office of deacon as the church's ministry of compassion. On New Testament grounds, Calvin believed that in the organized life of the church the deacon had the specific task of relieving human suffering, caring for the sick, and caring for those in physical need.

The Christian life in its social outreach also includes a missionary function. Calvin says little which in the modern sense would be labeled as missionary.[234] Nevertheless, he energetically asserts the obligation of all Christians to give a testimony to their faith. The *Ordonnances* of 1537 required this of every citizen of Geneva.[235] Calvin was unalterably opposed to secret professions of faith.[236] Christians must stand up and be counted. Furthermore, Christians must be prepared to give reasons for their faith to their adversaries.[237] Christians truly honor God when neither fear nor shame hinders them from making a profession of their faith.[238] When they depart from a plain and candid profession of Christ, they deprive him of the testimony to which he has a lawful claim.[239] There is no believer whom God does not require to be his witness.[240]

An obligation rests on Christians to help one another in the matter of salvation.

---

[232]Cf. *CR* 10(a):125ff.

[233]4.20.23.

[234]There is one passage which seems to indicate that the doctrine of predestination may have been a hindrance to missions: "In the first place, St. Paul said to Timothy, at the first part of the second chapter, that God wants all men to be saved. Already he who has troubled the church in this matter has put this question forward. That is where it was sufficiently answered by a congregation. And I bring up this particular question because it is the basis for the confusion, confusion which wants to mix up the doctrine of this church. There, it says, God wants every man to be saved, and arrive at the knowledge of the truth (says St. Paul). If God wants everyone to arrive at the knowledge of the truth, why doesn't he send the Word of the gospel to the Turks? Why does he allow the world to be blind for such a huge expanse of time? And as St. Paul speaks of it, in the 10th chapter of Acts, saying how did he let men err for such a long time? It therefore follows that St. Paul is not talking of each man, but of all conditions" (*CR* 8:112).

[235]*CR* 10(a):11–12.

[236]*CR* 41:10.

[237]*CR* 55:262; *OS* 1:458.

[238]Ibid.

[239]*CR* 45:743.

[240]*CR* 45:291.

> We are at the same time reminded that we ought to undertake the care of our brethren, for it would be a shame for anyone to be content with his own salvation and so to neglect his brethren. It is then necessary to join together these two things, to stir up ourselves to repentance, and then to try to lead others with us.[241]

> He who has a true zeal for honoring God does not think only of himself, but he considers all and looks for means as much as are possible to him to correct those who are debauched, to incite those who are cold and nonchalant, to strengthen those who are weak, to converse with those who are already in good course, and to advance them all the more. This is what all the faithful should consider.[242]

True Christians are not content to walk aright themselves, but they will also do their best to draw all people to the love of God.[243] Christians have an obligation even to the wicked, and this obligation cannot be discharged by withdrawal from their company. Calvin had little sympathy with that "excessive and fruitless fastidiousness" on the part of Christians which may alienate many from the Lord.[244] In the commentary on Matthew 28:19 he recognized the obligation to spread the doctrine of salvation in every part of the world.[245] God calls us to advance and magnify his gospel.[246]

Numerous factors contributed to the Reformers' apparent indifference to foreign missions.[247] In the first place, Protestant churches had little access to heathen lands. Furthermore, they were involved in a life-and-death struggle to maintain their existence. On one occasion, however, Calvin did respond to a request of Coligny for ministers for the French colony which he was establishing off the coast of Brazil. Although the ministers who went worked among the colonists, they also attempted to minister to the natives.[248] Thus, in the midst of the urgent needs of Europe, Calvin did not hesitate to give up these ministers to the work of the colony and to the needs of the natives.

The task of the Christian witness does not end with the proclamation of the gospel, for it also includes the maintenance of God's glory and truth.[249] This is a signal honor which God has bestowed on

---

[241]*CR* 42:320.
[242]*CR* 32:502.
[243]*CR* 33:181.
[244]*CR* 23:544.
[245]*CR* 45:822.
[246]*CR* 50:474.
[247]K. S. Latourette, *A History of the Expansion of Christianity,* vol. 3 (New York: Harper & Brothers, 1939), pp. 25–27.
[248]*CR* 16:433–443.
[249]*CR* 34:144.

Christians and is a privilege which should inspire them to show a constant and invincible zeal in maintaining the service and honor of God.[250] The sense of personal responsibility for public and private obedience to God and for the honor of God's name is one of the most important sources of the social activism of Calvinism. Christians are God's warriors.

Calvin's emphasis on the task of Christians as champions of God's glory accentuates the cleavage, which has been noted, in his interpretation of the meaning of the glory of God. While he asserted that God's glory is chiefly revealed in the forgiving love of the cross, he also used the analogy of an earthly king's honor to impress on his readers the significance of the concept. When God's glory was interpreted in this latter sense, the emphasis on believers as the champions of that glory led to at least two consequences which, in the light of the testimony of the total Christian community, must be judged as unfortunate. The first was a ruthlessness which denied the claims of love in the Christian community. God's glory became dangerously confused with the vanity of an earthly monarch.[251] Calvin concluded that God wants the magistrates to use the sword to maintain his honor and the unity of faith.[252] This interpretation of the glory of God had a tendency to exalt the place of governmental fiat and the use of force in religious matters despite Calvin's own avowals of the inwardness of all true religion. He cautioned against excessive zeal in religious matters,[253] but he did not always heed his own advice.

---

[250]*CR* 27:255–256.

[251]*CR* 27:434: "It is true that, at first glance, this would seem quite severe: as we see in complaining about God's exerting such strictness against those who through devotion do some act contrary to his truth. In the same way as we do not value God's honor as he deserves, we make a bigger story of a mortal creature than of the living God. For if someone plotted against his prince when he wanted to change the public condition, he would be condemned to death without difficulty. If someone conspired with the enemy of his prince, that he did him a favor, plotted with him, no one could excuse such disloyalty. Yet this is only applied to men. Now one turns away from serving God to go after idols: and it seems that this must be pardoned as if it were nothing. We show that it does not mean much to us that God's honor is diminished, that his integrity is violated."

Calvin apparently never saw any contradiction between God's forgiving love and the following assertion: *CR* 27:251: "Now, formerly we heard what was said about false prophets: that if someone bothered God's church, he would be stoned without any remission. Now God expresses yet more than he said. We should put away all natural affections when it is a question of honor. Let not the father spare the child, neither one brother another, nor the husband his own wife, and if there is a friend who is dear to him as his life, that he put him to death. And that is as it should be. All friendships in the world, do they not come from that natural order which was established by the Creator? We must always therefore (if we do not want to put the cart before the horse) begin with God."

[252]*CR* 27:247.

[253]*CR* 27:434; 47:300.

The tragedy of the Servetus incident and similar events cannot be erased from his record in Geneva.

A second unfortunate consequence of Calvin's interpretation of God's glory in terms of an earthly king's honor was the tendency to exalt theoretical worship of God above the service of people. Calvin asserted over and over again that true religion always expresses itself in love of neighbor, but the emphasis on the glory of God tended to obscure the truth that the invisible God represents himself to us in our fellow human beings. Likewise, it was easy to forget that God is glorified when people deny themselves to serve their neighbors, a truth which Calvin also asserted forcefully. Such an interpretation of the glory of God was certainly not universal in Geneva or in Calvin's writings, but the fact that there is evidence which points to a tendency in this direction is significant.[254]

The real importance of Calvin's teachings and administration in Geneva, however, is seen in the fact that under his tutelage the glory of God became a living faith for people in every walk of life. Calvin's errors are significant, but they are not the really distinguishing part of his ministry. Heretics were burned and sumptuary legislation was on the lawbooks before he ever arrived in Geneva.[255] He brought to Geneva a vitality and a spirit which had been lacking. This spiritual vitality which he nourished was the source of amazing social action for the achievement of a Christian society. Calvin's errors shall ever remain as a warning to all those who follow in his way, but the power which his preaching released must always encourage people to find in a living commitment to the *sola gloria Dei* the true dynamic for personal and social living.

A church coextensive with society was Calvin's hope for Geneva and for humankind. Yet he was no utopian. He had no illusions about the possibilities of historical existence. He did not even envisage a perfect church. Nevertheless, he apparently regarded a society dedicated to and striving toward the kingdom of God as a real possibility. His writings are not characterized by despair about society but by exhortations to a better society. In the attainment of this better society the church and the state are independent but cooperating arms of God. The church preaches the gospel, administers the

---

[254]*CR* 44:348: "If we rightly consider what it is to speak falsehood in the name of Jehovah, it will certainly appear to us to be more detestable than either to kill an innocent man, or to destroy a guest with poison, or to lay violent hands on one's own father, or to plunder a stranger. Whatever crimes then can be thought of, they do not come up to this, that is, when God himself is involved in such a dishonor, as to be made an abettor of falsehood." Cf. *CR* 27:263.

[255]Cf. Henri Naef, *Les origines de la réforme à Genève* (Geneva: A. Jullien, 1936), p. 216.

sacraments, maintains discipline, and thereby strengthens and nourishes the souls of people. The state preserves order, but its function is not merely negative. It maintains and supports the Christian religion in a way that does not usurp the authority of the church. There is one Lord, Jesus Christ, and he is the Lord of the state as well as of the church. He is *the* Lord.

What can be said for the relevance of Calvin's ideal for these days? Calvin was quite clearly a person of his age. It is neither possible nor desirable now to make the church coextensive with society by banishing all those who refuse to accept the Lordship of Jesus Christ. The Christian community is increasingly a minority group in a pagan civilization. Even if force were effective in religious matters, the church could not bring the same pressure to bear which it did in Geneva. The magistrates of that city were committed to the sovereignty of the word of God.

Calvin's essential contribution to the church and community lies in his keen awareness of the Lordship of Jesus Christ. He and he alone is the Lord. Every thought and deed of humankind stands under the claim of his authority. For this reason every human deed is important, decisive even for eternity. Furthermore, the authority of Jesus Christ is actively at work in the redemption and judgment of history. This is the basis of the implicit optimism which runs through Calvin's approach to the problems of society, for he saw every deed of faith-obedience taken up into the unconquerable purpose of the will of God.

The Lordship of Jesus Christ means that the church must be not only pure, acknowledging him as its only Lord, but also socially responsible. The community which God founded in the very act of creation is renewed in the gospel, which calls human beings to a fellowship with God which reveals itself in love for neighbor. The responsibility of the Christian community is not to wield the sword, but to preach the gospel, which is the proclamation of God's will for every area of life. The state and the economic order stand under the claim of God's will no less than the church, and the church must bear witness to that claim.

Social action is the truest test of religion, but it is never an end in itself. It has value only as it contributes to a greater value—fellowship with God in the kingdom of God. Historical deeds contribute to this fellowship, and for this reason social action is important. Yet it must not be forgotten that social action stands under the eschatological shadow. History may contribute to the highest human good, but it does not contain it. The fulfillment of life always lies beyond history.

Conclusion

We are now in a position to summarize and evaluate Calvin's view of the Christian life. To do so is not simple, because diversities and even inconsistencies are evident in his thinking. Prevailingly the Christian life is the expression of humankind's deeply mutual relationship with the living God, but on occasion theology and polity were allowed to become substitutes for the personal and living quality of faith.

The Christian life, according to Calvin, is the intensely personal and deeply mutual human response to the gracious activity of God on life. This response is enriched by the manifold variety of any personal commitment and reorients the totality of personal existence. Of primary significance, however, is the unity of the Christian life which inheres, not in an abstract principle or quality, but in the existential fact that a person "has to do with the living God every moment of his life."[1] The *sola gloria Dei* is the lifeblood of Christian living. "This is a very important consideration, that we are consecrated and dedicated to God; that we may not hereafter think, speak, meditate, or do anything but with a view to his glory. . . . We are God's; to him therefore, let us live and die."[2]

Calvin interpreted the Christian life in the light of the Reformation's emphasis on the immediacy of a person's relationship to the living God. The Christian is immediately accountable not to a hierarchy, not to a carefully reasoned set of rules governing conduct, but to the personal will of the Lord of heaven and earth. The Christian life is not the achievement of some ideal or the imitation of some code of morality. It is not a puritanical legalism. It is a living and personal response to the grace of the living and personal God.

Calvin summarized the activity of God which calls forth the

---

[1] 3.7.2.
[2] 3.7.1.

Christian life by the word "adoption." God chooses to reclaim prodigal people by his fatherly love. He elects to restore us to fellowship with himself by gently drawing us to him. He lays aside his authority and power and approaches us in love to evoke from us free rather than constrained service. "No one can with alacrity render service to God except he be allured by his paternal goodness."[3] The diverse human response to God's grace is summarized by the word "sonship." God chooses children, not slaves. "The symmetry and agreement between the righteousness of God" and the obedience of human beings is the spontaneous expression of love and thanksgiving to God. Gratitude is the dominant motive of the Christian life.

On analysis the Christian's deeply mutual relationship to God involves the dialectic of claim–obedience, grace–gratitude, power–trust, promise–hope, paternal love–community. Such an analysis is not precisely correct, for in actual experience the human response to God is one complex whole, and the various factors in the relationship are so interrelated that any separation does violence to their meaning. An abstract analysis is helpful only in pointing out the various facets of the Christian life.

The Christian life flows from God's activity on personal existence as a stream from a fountain. Calvin's so-called ethics are organically related to his theology. For example, cross bearing is unintelligible apart from God's activity which theology describes as providence. Self-denial is socially responsible because God has created all people in the divine image. Predestination, which faith writes into the hearts of believers, issues forth in the confidence and trust which provide the milieu of Christian living. In sum, the Christian life is the human response to God's gracious deeds.

The achievement of the Christian life is the reconstruction of the image of God which was defaced by the fall. This means that human existence is reoriented in such a manner that we can know God and reflect the glory of God. The Christian life is growth in fellowship with God.

On the human level the Christian life has two general characteristics. It is typified in the first place by a vigorous emphasis on moral and spiritual growth, and in the second place by communal life. Christians are crusaders against public and private evil. They are engaged in a continual warfare. The method they use in the conquest of evil and in the regulation of their lives is self-denial, cross bearing, and meditation on the future life. The Christian is a vindicator of the honor of God, and fights against sin not only in private life but also in society. The Christian witnesses that Jesus Christ is acknowledged

---

[3]*CR* 43:265.

as the Lord of all of life. The most frequent metaphors Calvin uses in regard to the Christian life are those of warfare and conquest. In short, the Christian is heroically engaged in the conquest of sin, not to save one's own soul, but to glorify God.

Calvin's concern that the Christian progress in the moral life is one of the most significant characteristics of his doctrine. The Christian belongs to the army of God and is commissioned to fulfill God's purposes in the historical process. The certainty of the final victory is nothing less than the eternal will of God. For this reason Calvin's doctrine of the sinful nature of humankind did not issue in any form of quietism. Human life as well as society is renewable. So far as I know, Calvin never regarded the fight against evil as a hopeless struggle.[4] His sermons abound in spirited exhortations which are indicative of hope rather than despair about the plight of humankind and society. Calvin was no utopian, but he believed not only in the individual's progress in the moral life but also in the kingdom of God's advance in and through history largely by the instrumentality of the visible church, which, though not identical with the kingdom of God, for practical purposes constitutes the army of God commissioned to conquer the world.

History, in which God's purposes are at least in part worked out, is therefore of vital significance for the Calvinist. Eschatology intensifies this significance because the deeds of history are either brought to completion or to judgment in eternity. The kingdom of God, which is never fully realized on earth, is completed beyond history. The eschatological orientation of the doctrine of the Christian life is not the expectation of a sudden and imminent return of Christ, but the continual impingement and demand of eternity on time. There is little, if any, evidence that Calvin had any notion that the world would shortly come to an end, as was the case with Luther. Yet the vivid awareness that every personal decision has significance for eternity vitalized Calvin's theology and ethics.

In addition to the emphasis on moral and spiritual growth, the human response which constitutes the Christian life is also typified by its communal character. The Christian life takes place in the Christian community and involves social responsibility. Its source and strength are derived from the body of Christ. The deeds of God which call the church into being also evoke and nourish the Christian life. The communion of saints undergirds and strengthens individual Christians, who never have so much of Christ that they do not need

---

[4]There are pessimistic judgments of the plight of the world in Calvin's writings as in 4.9.8; but these judgments do not seem to have decreased Calvin's optimism about the possibilities of Christian activity in society.

the fellowship of the Christian community. The discipline and government of the church provide a suitable environment for the work of the Holy Spirit. In sum, the practical locus of the Christian life is the church. However, the social responsibility which the Christian life involves reaches beyond the Christian community to the whole of humankind. The Christian life expresses its love for God by love for people made in God's image. A person cannot be a child of God without being in community with all who bear the image of God, an image which sin can shatter but cannot destroy. The invisible God is present in one's fellow human beings. Furthermore, the Christian life involves the responsibilities of Christian citizenship and of witnessing to the gospel and to the honor of God.

The question now arises as to whether Calvin's doctrine is a practical concern of our times and possesses more than historic interest. The answer is not theoretical, for the relevance of Calvin's theology to the needs of the current time is attested by the fact that one of the most vital theological movements of our day claims Calvin as its teacher. The Crisis theologians have found Calvin's emphasis on the immediate and responsible relationship of every believer to God especially meaningful to the needs of modern people.[5] His understanding of what it means to have to do with the living God is one of the most vivid in all of history. Since the days of Kant this teaching of Calvin has been obscured by the tendency to interpret religion in people-centered terms and to establish it on the basis of morality. The dramatic revelation of human wickedness in this generation and the rise of totalitarianisms which coerce obedience to a pattern of life that is anti-Christian have convinced many people that such an understanding of religion and morality is inadequate. Totalitarian oppression reveals the strength of a Christian life which has its source and end in God. Thus Calvin's radically theocentric interpretation of the Christian life speaks to the needs of our day. The *sola gloria Dei* stands over against current religious apathy as well as the religious and secular totalitarianisms. Although no word from the past can be repeated in exactly the same form to a later generation, the insights of Calvin's theology may be the inspiration of a theological proclamation which will do for our generation what Calvin did for his. The very existence of a vigorous Crisis theology is clearly indicative of the relevance of Calvin's theology at this point.

Although the Crisis theologians have interpreted Calvin's doctrine of the *sola gloria Dei* for our times, they have neglected his doctrine

---

[5]Emil Brunner, *Das Vermächtnis Calvins. Vortrag bei der Calvinfeier im Grossmünster am 28. Juni 1936* (Bern: Gotthelf).

of hope for human history, which surely speaks to our needs. His analysis of the human plight is certainly as radical as any which would be made today; yet it did not issue in quietism or despair. Calvinism is characterized by the conviction that human beings can progress in Christian life through the grace of God. Calvin regarded theology as a practical science and considered as heresy any doctrine which did not edify. Moreover, Calvinism is militant in its attack on evil. Christians are God's warriors. They confidently attack the citadels of evil because they believe that their cause is undergirded by the eternal will of God. Even though the outward appearance of the church is weak, the Christian has the promise of God that the seed of Abraham will multiply and replenish the earth, which is of greater significance than the appearance of things. Thus Calvinism can speak a relevant word to the quietism and despair of this generation.

A third contribution Calvinism can make to our times is its emphasis on the sovereignty of the word of God. This does not mean a literalistic bibliocracy but a fresh recognition of the fact that the claim of God, mediated through the Bible, is coextensive with life. According to Calvin, the Christian does not think, speak, meditate, or do anything but with a view to the glory of God. Calvin could not conceive in the sixteenth century what is taken for granted in the twentieth century—a secular state and society. His ideal for Geneva was a church which was at least coextensive with society. Here again his answer cannot be repeated in its sixteenth-century form, but it may be the inspiration of a creative solution of the problem today.

The very fact that Calvin's doctrine of the Christian life is significant for our times makes it all the more necessary to detect those fallacies which obscured his profoundest insights. His development of this doctrine is subject, I think, to two major criticisms. The first is his failure to maintain consistently the immediacy of the human response to God's gracious activity which gave vitality to the doctrine. The second reservation in regard to Calvin's doctrine is the failure to give love a place of priority in the Christian community.

The immediacy of the human response to God's grace is sometimes obscured or perverted by speculative theological abstractions, laws, and ecclesiastical discipline. In the course of this study we have observed a number of inconsistencies in Calvin's interpretation of the doctrine of the Christian life which are relevant at this point. Among the more important are the following:

1. The glory of God is said to be principally revealed in the forgiving love of God as manifest in the cross of Jesus Christ; yet it is sometimes compared to the honor of an earthly prince, which is the very antithesis of forgiving love.

2. The glory of God is vigorously asserted to be the fulfillment of human welfare; it is also said to involve the annihilation of our humanity.

3. The law is presented as the embodiment of the personal claim of God, but it is sometimes made an abstract substitute for that claim.

4. The Bible is declared to be the personal address of God which finds its fullest expression in Jesus Christ, but Calvin also used the Bible as if it were a codebook of doctrine and morality, all of which was equally valid.

5. The meaning of predestination is said to be revealed in Jesus Christ, and a knowledge of predestination is described as a testimony of our adoption. Yet predestination is also defined in mechanical terms as a decree by which God has determined what he would do with every individual, including the reprobation of infants.

6. The church is defined as the community of believers who hear God's word and as the context in which God's gracious acts call people to the Christian life, but Calvin at times turns the church into a legal institution which possesses and disposes God's truth and, in a measure, his grace.

These contradictions reveal the conflict between Calvin the exegete of scripture and Calvin the systematizer of scripture, giving the data of scripture an ordered, coherent form. In almost every case they have resulted from his systematic rationalization of the anomalies of revelation and Christian experience. They represent speculative additions to the biblical data in spite of Calvin's avowed loyalty to scripture and his disavowal of the scholastic theological method. In every case they obscure the deeply personal and mutual relationship of humankind to God which Calvin declared to be fundamental in the Christian life. The failure to recognize these inconsistencies in Calvin's thought certainly in part accounts for the important cleavage which exists among competent scholars as to whether Calvin was some sort of scholastic or a true disciple of Luther in his apprehension of the existential quality of the Christian life.

The problems which these contradictions raise cannot be solved by adding up the available data and then concluding that the side which has the greater weight of evidence represents Calvin's true opinion. Although this may be true in certain cases, such a procedure would be based on the presupposition that these inconsistencies are occasional aberrations which do not occupy a serious place in Calvin's thought. The frequency with which they occur and the thorough way in which they penetrate Calvin's thought indicate that another approach must be taken. The objectification of the human relationship to God into abstract precepts, formulas, and institutions belongs to

Calvin's thought as surely as does his emphasis on the Christian's deeply mutual fellowship with God. The fact that Calvin was unaware of the objectification of this fellowship which took place in his polity and theology is all the more reason that subsequent Calvinists must look for the source and cause of this contradiction.

No doubt many factors contributed to Calvin's objectification of the Christian life. He was a trained jurist. He was frequently preoccupied with the demands of polemics and with the tasks of an ecclesiastical administrator. Logical and practical considerations continually pressed on him. However, a more insidious and significant cause is found in his theological methodology.

The significance of Calvin's methodology in this regard becomes clearer when we identify three presuppositions which dominated it in many instances, though not in every case. The first presupposition was a formal biblicism. Calvin set out to make his theology and polity a consistent and complete representation of the biblical materials. This procedure was predicated on three ideas about the Bible: (1) There is nothing in the Bible which is not useful for salvation; (2) there is nothing useful to salvation which is not in the Bible; and (3) the essence of the Bible is clear and plain. Furthermore, Calvin did not have the benefits of modern historical criticism, and he did not always make use of his own avowed principles of interpretation. In theory he distinguished between the Old and New Testaments and asserted that God's full disclosure of himself has taken place in Jesus Christ. In actual practice, however, these distinctions were frequently forgotten in his expositions of the scripture.

The second factor which entered into this scholastic methodology was implicit confidence in the competence of reason to theologize on the basis of the biblical materials. In the second book of the *Institutes* Calvin left no doubt about the sinful corruption of reason, and everywhere he rejected reason as an avowed source of theology. He knew also that reason is finite, limited by time, space, and competence. However, reason did become a source of his theology through speculation about the biblical materials. So far as I know, Calvin did not betray any doubt as to the full competence of reason in the systematization and rationalization of the biblical materials. A factor which may have contributed to this confidence in reason was his doctrine of providence. Whether this doctrine led to the practical reversal of his opinion about the sinful corruption of reason is not of too great significance, for the results are the same in any case.

On the basis of the presupposition that the Bible supplies infallible material for theology and that reason is competent to manipulate and theologize about those materials, Calvin was convinced that he possessed *the* truth. When he was involved with Trolliet about the doctrine of predestination, he told the Council at Geneva, "So far as I am concerned, my masters, I am quite certain in my conscience that that which I have taught and written did not arise out of my own head, but that I have received it from God, and I must stand firmly by it if I am not to be a traitor to the truth."[6] Calvin was convinced that he had the right to punish heretics because he possessed the "infallible truth." He objected to punishment of heretics by Roman Catholics on the ground that they did not have the truth and would therefore punish innocent persons.[7] Beza's judgment that Calvin's theology never changed may be relevant here.[8] These facts are indicative of a notion of truth which is rigid and absolute and of a failure to see that the dialectical tension of opposing views may be nearer the truth than dogmatic pronouncements. This static and impersonal notion of truth has not only led to acrimony among theologians who believed that truth could be absolutely possessed in precise formulas and argued about who possessed it, but it has also obscured Calvin's own emphasis on the personal and deeply mutual relationship of humankind to God, which expresses itself in the Christian life.

Furthermore, this understanding of Christian truth tends to eliminate all mystery from faith and to destroy religious paradox as a means of expressing the content of faith. While formal paradoxes may be retained, all mystery is taken from them, and they become a logically satisfying and speculative unraveling of humankind's relationship to God.[9]

The true significance of Calvin's conviction that he possessed the truth in regard to creeds, polity, and discipline can be assessed only in the light of his intense desire to bring human beings into a personal and ethically fruitful relationship with the living God and also in the light of his conviction that external aids contribute to moral and spiritual growth. Calvin had learned from Martin Luther, his spiritual father, the importance of humankind's existential relationship

---

[6]*CR* 14:382.

[7]*CR* 27:253: "And today, when papists say heretics must be punished, it is true, we confess that they deserve it. But we must arrive at this point which is contained herein: that is to say, we knew who the God is that we served, and we were assured that it is not for fortune that our religion has been announced, but that we hold the infallible truth that God has given to us, and that his name has been announced to us and by his authority: that it is in him that our faith is founded. Now, the papists are stupefied here because it seems to them that in closing their eyes they will be able to execute their anger and fury against the innocent." In assessing the significance of this statement, it must be remembered that much of Calvin's theology proclaims the impotence of force in religious matters.

[8]*CR* 21:170.

[9]Emil Brunner, *The Divine-Human Encounter,* tr. Amandus W. Loos (Philadelphia: Westminster Press, 1943), pp. 123–126; Gustaf Aulén, *The Faith of the Christian Church,* tr. Eric H. Wahlstrom and G. Everett Arden (Philadelphia: Muhlenberg Press, 1948), pp. 94–105.

to God, and his theology and polity were intended to be means of implementing this relationship, not of denying it. Luther's writings of 1520 emphasized the spontaneity of the Christian life and even suggested that love does not need any instruction.[10] Calvin agreed with this emphasis, but he felt a greater need for external aids such as the creed, the law, the Bible, and church discipline. Yet at this point it must be remembered that Luther gave a larger place to music and art than Calvin did, though these external aids did not affect our particular subject as directly as those aids which Calvin emphasized. The purpose of the external aids was to nourish and guide the spontaneity of the Christian life and not to supplant it. As far as we can judge, Calvin's emphasis on the particular external aids mentioned above apparently did help to intensify the vital experience which Luther cherished, for the actual history of the Reformed community has displayed greater vigor and enthusiasm than the Lutheran community. It is true that in the total development of the Reformed community in the West the accidental factors of history may have contributed heavily to its activism, but during Calvin's own administration in Geneva the Reformer's emphasis on the *sola gloria Dei* and on external aids to moral and spiritual growth appear to have been more significant than accidental factors. The rise of scholasticism on Lutheran soil may have been due in part to the need for more external aids than Luther's early writings provided. External aids can deepen the personal quality of the Christian life as long as they are the framework and environment in which the experience takes place. They destroy the personal and responsive character of the Christian life only when they become abstract and legalistic substitutes for the living claim of God on human life. Calvin never intended this to happen, but his theological methodology, which provided the basis for excessive confidence as to the divine authority and infallibility of the external aids, made it easy for this very perversion of his doctrine to take place.

Calvin's demand for Christian growth both in public and in personal life, together with his understanding of the place of external aids in the Christian life and his theological method, made it very difficult for him to give love a place of priority in the Christian community. "The most perfect school of Christ since the apostles" was built at the expense of Christian love. The sovereignty of God's law sometimes eclipsed the sovereignty of his love. In Calvin's writings the response of obedience receives more attention than the response of love to God's claim on personal existence. In the polity of the Genevan church obedience in the legalistic sense and faith in

---

[10]*Works of Martin Luther* (Philadelphia: A. J. Holman Co., 1915), 1:190–191.

the fideistic sense came to have priority over the Christian grace of love. For this reason Servetus could be destroyed with no rending of the conscience. The problem in Calvin's thought is revealed in his commentary on Paul's letter to the Corinthians where he had to struggle with the apostle's assertion that love is greater than faith.[11] This failure to give love its due priority in the Christian community must be regarded as a serious weakness of Calvin's interpretation of the Christian life.

It was Calvin's deliberate intention to build his theology on a Lutheran foundation. He always spoke of Luther in terms of genuine respect, though he was not slavishly dependent on him.[12] It is difficult to point out with precision the ways in which Calvin differed from the German Reformer. Yet it seems that there is a difference of emphasis at least on the following points which affect the doctrine of the Christian life:

1. Calvin placed greater emphasis on such external aids as creeds, the law, the Bible, and church discipline as means of nourishing the Christian life than Luther did.

2. He also placed greater emphasis on the working out of God's purposes in private and public life. This emphasis, combined with the different interpretation of eschatology mentioned previously, gave to the Calvinist a greater appreciation of the historical process than was true in the case of the Lutheran.

3. Calvin's emphasis on the *sola gloria Dei* also tended to minimize introspection and to emphasize the fulfillment of God's purposes in private and public life. The fact that Calvin interpreted God's glory not only in terms of the forgiving love of the cross but also in terms of an earthly king's glory is important in this regard.

These three points of emphasis constitute a significant difference between Calvinism and the Lutheranism of 1520 and, together with accidental factors of history, account, at least in part, for the divergent roles which Calvinism and Lutheranism have played in subsequent history. In the course of history Calvin's unique emphases have at times both deepened and destroyed the distinctive Lutheran theology of 1520. For this reason Calvinism is healthiest when read in the context of its Lutheran origins.

In summary, the evidence accumulated in this study of Calvin's doctrine of the Christian life has thrown light on one of the major problems of Calvin research. For almost a century Calvin studies have been stymied by the fact that equally competent scholars have interpreted Calvin in diametrically opposing ways. The existence of

---

[11] *CR* 49:515–516.
[12] *CR* 11:774.

these contradictory interpretations of Calvinism has concerned scholars since the first part of the twentieth century. Bauke concluded that they were due to the failure to distinguish between the form and the content of Calvin's thought. Doumergue traced their source to the failure to detect what he called Calvin's *méthode des contrariétés*. More recently, Wilhelm Niesel has concluded that the problems of Calvin research can be solved by the recognition of the Christocentric character of Calvin's theology. Although these attempts to unravel the problem of Calvin research have value, they have certainly not settled the problem; for we still are confronted with a diversity of interpretations.

The evidence which has been accumulated in this study points to a significant cause of this diversity. Calvin's fame for logical clarity and systematization has obscured the presence of ambiguities and complexities in his thought. His theology is not as fully integrated as the outward appearance of coherence and consistency has led many to believe. Consequently, attempts to interpret Calvin's theology in terms of one consistent pattern, as has been the case with most interpretations, run into serious difficulties. Although there may be a number of causes for the absence of complete coherence in Calvin's thought, one very significant cause is to be found in his theological methodology, which subordinates "system," or the ordering of theology, to scripture.

From this study we are able to appraise in a measure the relationship of Calvinism to fundamentalism as represented in such competent scholars as Warfield, Machen, and others who now participate in the American Calvinistic Congress. Fundamentalism has interpreted Calvin in terms of its theology and has claimed exclusive rights to him.[13] This type of orthodoxy, however, is unacceptable to all those who have been influenced in any significant way by theological liberalism, which despite its present decadence made permanent contributions to the history of Christian thought that cannot now be set aside. Thus the fundamentalist claim to exclusive possession of the historic Calvin is significant, for if it is true, Calvinism is wholly irrelevant to the search of a vast number of present-day Christians for an answer to the human plight. Some Calvin scholars who have been influenced by the dialectical theologians deny Calvin's positive relationship not only to fundamentalism but also to seventeenth-century Reformed theology, as in the Westminster Confession of Faith. On the basis of the evidence in this study, this position is unsatisfactory. It fails to recognize that there are tendencies in Cal-

---

[13]Clarence Bouma, "Calvinism in American Theology Today," *Journal of Religion* 27 (1947), 34–54.

vin's thought which lead to Westminster and which in part substantiate the fundamentalist claim. Calvin's tendencies in theological methodology, which did not consistently dominate his own thinking, have been exalted into a rigid dogma by the fundamentalists. On the other hand, evidence has also pointed out the personal core of Calvin's thought which does not fit into the fundamentalist system. Thus present-day Christians can regard Calvin as their teacher without becoming fundamentalists. Historically, it is an anachronism to call Calvin a fundamentalist, and there is abundant warrant for conjecturing that he would not be a fundamentalist if he were alive today. Yet it is neither historically correct nor practically advisable to follow the lead of the Crisis theologians and to overlook Calvin's affinities with present-day fundamentalism. His contribution to our day can be preserved only by recognizing those affinities and correcting them in the light of the wider knowledge of the Christian community.

The evidence accumulated in this study has also helped in the understanding of Calvin's doctrine of the Christian life by pointing out its source in the intensely personal and deeply mutual relationship of the Christian to God. The inner unity of the Christian life and of Calvin's theology as a whole is not some abstract principle but the vital fact that we have to do with the living God every moment of our life. The Christian life is not the achievement of an ideal or slavish obedience to a code of morals. It is the living and spontaneous human response to God's grace. The evidence which has been presented in these pages also contributes to the understanding of the development of Calvinism in history by pointing out the role of external aids, the emphasis on moral and spiritual growth, and the doctrine of hope for people in history in Calvin's interpretation of the Christian life.

Calvin's doctrine of the Christian life represents a magnificent effort to give expression to what it means to have to do with the living God every moment of one's life. No interpretation of the *sola gloria Dei* has been more vivid and dynamic than Calvin's. For this reason he speaks to the needs of this generation, which, at least until recently, has been more frequently concerned about the glory of humankind than that of God and which has fallen victim to many false gods and vicious ideologies. Yet if Calvinism is to render its full service to our day, it must be interpreted in the context of the shared faith of the total Christian community. On the basis of Calvin's own principles, no human statement of Christian faith can ever be final and absolute. Every statement of doctrine must be continually reformed by the Christian community's apprehension of the word of God as revealed in Jesus Christ.

Bibliography

Books

Aulén, Gustaf. *The Faith of the Christian Church.* Tr. Eric H. Wahlstrom and G. Everett Arden. Philadelphia: Muhlenberg Press, 1948.

Autin, Albert. *L'institution chrétienne de Calvin.* Paris: Société Française d'Éditions Litteraires et Techniques, 1929.

Bainton, Roland H. "Sebastian Castellio and the Toleration Controversy of the Sixteenth Century," in *Persecution and Liberty* (Essays in Honor of George Lincoln Burr). New York: Century Co., 1931.

Barth, Karl. *Die Kirchliche Dogmatik.* Munich: Chr. Kaiser, 1932ff. Vol. II, Part 2.

————. *Nein! Antwort an Emil Brunner. Theologische Existenz heute,* no. 14. Munich: Chr. Kaiser, 1934.

————. *The Word of God and the Word of Man.* Tr. Douglas Horton. Grand Rapids: Zondervan Publishing House, 1935.

Barth, Peter. "Die Biblische Grundlage der Prädestinationslehre bei Calvin," in *De l'élection éternelle de Dieu.* Edited by Martinus Nijhoff. Geneva: Éditions Labor et Fides, 1936.

————. "Calvin," in *Die Religion in Geschichte und Gegenwart.* Tübingen: J. C. B. Mohr (Paul Siebeck), 1927.

————. *Das Problem der natürlichen Theologie bei Calvin. Theologische Existenz heute,* no. 18. Munich: Chr. Kaiser, 1935.

Bauke, Hermann. *Die Probleme der Theologie Calvins.* Leipzig: J. C. Hinrichs, 1922.

Baumgartner, A. J. *Calvin hébraïsant et interprète de l'Ancien Testament.* Paris: Fischbacher, 1889.

Benoit, Jean-Daniel. *Calvin directeur d'âmes.* Strasbourg: Éditions Oberlin, 1947.

Beyerhaus, Gisbert. *Studien zur Staatsanschauung Calvins, mit besonderer Berücksichtigung seines Souveränitätsbegriffs.* Berlin: Trowitzsch & Sohn, 1910.

Bohatec, Josef. *Calvins Lehre von Staat und Kirche.* Breslau: M. & H. Marcus, 1937.

————. "Die Souveränitat Gottes und der Staat nach der Auffassung Calvins" in *Second International Conference of Calvinists.* Amsterdam: Martinus Nijhoff, 1935.

Breen, Quirinus. *John Calvin: A Study in French Humanism.* Grand Rapids: Wm. B. Eerdmans Publishing Co., 1931.

Brown, William Adams, "Calvin's Influence Upon Theology," *Three Addresses Delivered by Professors in Union Theological Seminary.* New York, 1909.

Brunner, Heinrich Emil. *Die Christliche Lehre von Gott.* Zurich: Zwingli, 1946. Dogmatik, vol. 1.

———. *The Divine-Human Encounter.* Tr. Amandus W. Loos. Philadelphia: Westminster Press, 1943.

———. *Justice and the Social Order.* Tr. Mary Hottinger. New York: Harper & Brothers, 1945.

———. *Man in Revolt.* Tr. Olive Wyon. New York: Charles Scribner's Sons, 1939.

———. "Nature and Grace" in *Natural Theology.* Tr. Peter Fraenkel. London: Geoffrey Bles (Centenary Press), 1946.

———. *Das Vermächtnis Calvins. Vortrag bei der Calvinfeier im Grossmünster am 28. Juni 1936.* Bern: Gotthelf, 1936.

Brunner, Peter. *Vom Glauben bei Calvin.* Tübingen: J. C. B. Mohr (Paul Siebeck), 1925.

Calhoun, R. L. *Lectures on History of Christian Doctrine.* New Haven, Conn.: Printed for private distribution, 1948. Vols. 2 and 3.

Calvin, John. *Commentaries.* Edinburgh: Calvin Translation Society, 1844–56.

———. *Épître à tous amateurs de Jésus-Christ.* Ed. Jacques Pannier. Paris: Fischbacher, 1929.

———. *Épître au roi.* Ed. Jacques Pannier. Paris: Fischbacher, 1927.

———. *Institutes of the Christian Religion.* Tr. John Allen. 2 vols. Philadelphia: Presbyterian Board of Publication, 1936.

———. *Institution de la religion chrétienne.* Ed. Jacques Pannier. 4 vols. Paris, 1936–39.

———. *Letters.* Ed. Jules Bonnet. Philadelphia: Presbyterian Board of Publication, 1858. 4 vols.

———. *Opera Quae Supersunt Omnia.* 59 vols., contained in *Corpus Reformatorum.* Ed. Guilielmus Baum, Eduardus Cunitz, Eduardus Reuss. Brunswick: C. A. Schwetschke & Filium, 1863–97.

———. *Opera Selecta.* Ed. Petrus Barth and Guilielmus Niesel. Munich: Chr. Kaiser, 1926. Vols. 1, 3–5.

———. *Tracts.* Tr. Henry Beveridge. Edinburgh: Calvin Translation Society, 1844–51. Vols. 1–3.

Calvinreden aus dem Jubiläumsjahr 1909. Tübingen: J. C. B. Mohr (Paul Siebeck), 1909.

Calvinstudien. Ed. J. Bohatec. Leipzig: Rudolf Haupt, 1909.

Camfield, F. W. *Revelation and the Holy Spirit.* London: Elliot Stock, 1933.

Castellio, Sebastian. *Concerning Heretics.* Ed. Roland Bainton. New York: Columbia University Press, 1935.

Chenevière, Marc-Édouard. *La pensée politique de Calvin.* Geneva: Éditions Labor et Fides, 1937.

Choisy, Eugène. *La théocratie à Genève au temps de Calvin.* Geneva: C. Eggimann & Cie., 1897.

Clavier, Henri. *Études sur le Calvinisme.* Paris: Fischbacher, 1936.

The Constitution of the Presbyterian Church (U.S.A.), Part I, *Book of Confessions.* New York and Atlanta: Office of the General Assembly, 1983.

Dakin, Arthur. *Calvinism.* London: Duckworth, 1941.

Davies, Rupert Eric. *The Problem of Authority in the Continental Reformers: A Study in Luther, Zwingli and Calvin.* London: Epworth Press, 1946.

Dewey, John. *A Common Faith.* New Haven, Conn.: Yale University Press, 1934.

Dominicé, Max. *L'humanité de Jésus d'après Calvin.* Paris: Éditions "Je Sers," 1933.

Doumergue, Émile. *Le caractère de Calvin.* Paris: Éditions de Foi et Vie, 1921.

———. *Jean Calvin, les hommes et les choses de son temps.* 7 vols. Lausanne: Georges Bridel & Cie., 1899–1927.

Engelland, Hans. *Gott und Mensch bei Calvin.* Munich: Chr. Kaiser, 1934.

Foster, Herbert Darling. *Collected Papers.* New York: Privately printed, 1929.

Fröhlich, Karlfried. *Gottesreich, Welt und Kirche bei Calvin.* Munich: E. Reinhardt, 1930.

———. *Die Reichgottesidee Calvins.* Munich: Chr. Kaiser, 1922.

Fuhrmann, Paul T. *God-Centered Religion.* Grand Rapids: Zondervan Publishing House, 1942.

Gauteron, Ellis. *L'autorité de la Bible d'après Calvin.* Montauban, 1902.

Gloede, Günter. *Theologia naturalis bei Calvin.* Stuttgart: W. Kohlhammer, 1935.

Göhler, Alfred. *Calvins Lehre von der Heiligung.* Munich: Chr. Kaiser, 1934.

Harkness, Georgia. *John Calvin, the Man and His Ethics.* New York: Henry Holt & Co., 1931.

Hastie, William. *The Theology of the Reformed Church.* Edinburgh: T. & T. Clark, 1904.

Hepp, V. "De Soevereiniteit Gods," in *Second International Conference of Calvinists.* Amsterdam: Martinus Nijhoff, 1935.

Herminjard, Aimé-Louis (ed.). *Correspondance des Réformateurs dans les pays de langue française.* 9 vols. Geneva: H. Georg, 1866–1897. Vols. 4, 5.

Holl, Karl. *Gesammelte Aufsätze zur Kirchengeschichte.* Vol. 1. Tübingen: J. C. B. Mohr (Paul Siebeck), 1923–28.

———. "Johannes Calvin" in *Calvinreden.* Tübingen: J. C. B. Mohr (Paul Siebeck), 1909.

Hoogstra, Jacob (ed.). *The Sovereignty of God.* Grand Rapids: Zondervan Publishing House, 1941.

Hunt, R. N. Carew. *Calvin.* London: Centenary Press, 1933.

Imbart de la Tour, P. *Calvin et l'Institution Chrétienne.* Vol. 4 of *Les origines de la Réforme.* Paris: Firmin-Didot & Cie., n.d.

Jacobs, Paul. *Prädestination und Verantwortlichkeit bei Calvin.* Kassel: J. G. Oncken Nachf., 1937.

Kampschulte, F. W. *Johann Calvin, seine Kirche und sein Staat in Genf.* Leipzig: Duncker & Humbolt, 1869.

Kromminga, D. "And the Barthians," in *The Sovereignty of God.* Ed. Jacob Hoogstra. Grand Rapids: Zondervan Publishing House, 1941.

Laing, David (ed.). *The Works of John Knox.* Edinburgh: John Stone and Hunter, 1855. Vol. 4.

Lang, A. *Johannes Calvin.* Leipzig: Verein für Reformationsgeschichte, 1909.

Latin Works of Huldreich Zwingli. Tr. S. M. Jackson. Philadelphia: Heidelberg Press, 1922. Vol. 2.

Latourette, Kenneth Scott. *A History of the Expansion of Christianity.* Vol. 3. New York: Harper & Brothers, 1939.

Lecerf, A. *Introduction à la dogmatique reformée.* Paris: 1931. Vol. 1.

Lefranc, Abel. *La jeunesse de Calvin.* Paris: Fischbacher, 1888.

Lobstein, Paul. *Études sur la pensée et l'oeuvre de Calvin.* Neuilly: Éditions de "La Cause," 1927.

Luther, Martin. *Bondage of the Will.* Tr. Henry Cole. London: T. Bensley, 1823.

Lüttge, Willy. *Die Rechtfertigungslehre Calvins und ihre Bedeutung für seine Frömmigkeit.* Berlin: Reuther & Reichard, 1909.

Mackinnon, James. *Calvin and the Reformation.* London: Longmans, Green & Co., 1936.

McNeill, J. T. *Christian Hope for World Society.* Chicago: Willett, Clark & Co., 1937.

Meeter, H. H. *Calvinism.* Grand Rapids: Zondervan Publishing House, 1939.

Mülhaupt, Erwin. *Die Predigt Calvins, ihre Geschichte, ihre Form und ihre religiösen Grundgedanken.* Berlin: Walter de Gruyter & Co., 1931.

Naef, Henri. *Les origines de la réforme à Genève.* Geneva: A. Jullien, 1936.

Niebuhr, Reinhold. *Moral Man and Immoral Society.* 1947 ed. New York: Charles Scribner's Sons, 1932.

Niesel, Wilhelm. *Calvins Lehre vom Abendmahl.* Munich: Chr. Kaiser, 1930.

———. *Die Theologie Calvins.* Munich: Chr. Kaiser, 1938.

Nijhoff, Martinus (ed.). *De l'élection éternelle de Dieu.* Geneva: Éditions Labor et Fides, 1936.

Pannier, Jacques. *Calvin à Strasbourg.* Strasbourg: Alsacienne, 1925.

———. *Recherches sur la formation intellectuelle de Calvin.* Paris: Alcan, 1931.

———. *Recherches sur l'évolution religieuse de Calvin jusqu'à sa conversion.* Strasbourg: Librairie Istra, 1924.

Parker, T. H. L. *The Oracles of God.* London: Lutterworth Press, 1947.

Quervain, Alfred de. *Calvin, sein Lehren und Kämpfen.* Berlin: Furche, 1926.

Reyburn, H. Y. *John Calvin.* London, 1914.

Ritschl, A. *A Critical History of the Christian Doctrine of Justification and Reconciliation.* Ed. and tr. H. R. Mackintosh and G. B. Macaulay. New York: Charles Scribner's Sons, 1900.

Ritschl, Otto. *Dogmengeschichte des Protestantismus.* Vol. 3. Leipzig: J. C. Hinrichs, 1908–27.

Roget, Amédée. *Histoire du peuple de Genève.* Geneva: John Jullien, 1870.

Schaff, Philip. *The Creeds of Christendom.* New York: Harper & Bros., 1919. Vols. 2 and 3.

Scheibe, Max. *Calvins Prädestinationslehre.* Halle: M. Niemeyer, 1897.

Schulze, Martin. *Meditatio futurae vitae: ihr Begriff und ihre beherrschende Stellung im System Calvins.* Leipzig: T. Weicher, 1901.

Schweizer, Alexander. *Die Glaubenslehre der evangelisch-reformirten Kirche dargestellt und aus den Quellen belegt.* Zurich: Orell, Füssli & Co., 1844. Vol. 1.

Second International Conference of Calvinists. Amsterdam: Martinus Nijhoff, 1935.

Seeberg, Reinhold. *Lehrbuch der Dogmengeschichte.* Vol. IV/2. Leipzig: A. Deichert, 1920.

———. *Textbook of the History of Doctrines.* Tr. Charles E. Hay. Vol. 2. Philadelphia: Lutheran Publication Society, 1905.

Strathmann, Hermann. *Calvins Lehre von der Busse in ihrer späteren Gestalt.* Gotha, 1909.

———. "Die Entstehung der Lehre Calvins von der Busse," in *Calvinstudien.* Ed. J. Bohatec. Leipzig: Rudolf Haupt, 1909.

Thomas Aquinas. *Summa Theologica.* Tr. English Dominican Province. London: Burns, Oates & Washbourne, 1937.

Troeltsch, Ernst. *The Social Teaching of the Christian Churches.* Tr. Olive Wyon. New York: Macmillan Co., 1931. Vols. 1, 2.

Walker, Williston, *John Calvin, the Organizer of Reformed Protestantism.* New York: G. P. Putnam's Sons, 1906.

Warfield, Benjamin Breckinridge. *Calvin and Calvinism.* London: Oxford University Press, 1931.

Wencelius, Léon. *L'esthétique de Calvin.* Paris: Société d'Édition "Les Belles Lettres," 1937.

Wernle, Paul. *Calvin.* Vol. 3 of *Der evangelische Glaube nach den Hauptschriften der Reformatoren.* Tübingen: J. C. B. Mohr (Paul Siebeck), 1919.

Works of Martin Luther. Philadelphia: A. J. Holman Co., 1915. Vols. 1–3.

Articles

Barth, Peter. "Calvins Verständnis der Kirche," *Zwischen den Zeiten* 8 (1930), 216–233.

———. "Fünfundzwanzig Jahre Calvinforschung 1909–1934," *Theologische Rundschau* (1934).

———. "Was ist reformierte Ethik?" *Zwischen den Zeiten* 10 (1932), 410–436.

Baur, F. C. "Über Prinzip und Charakter des Lehrbegriffs der reformirten Kirche in seinem Unterschied von dem der lutherischen, mit Rücksicht auf A. Schweizer's Darstellung der reformirten Glaubenslehre," *Theologische Jahrbücher* 6 (1847), 333.

Bouma, Clarence, "Calvinism in American Theology Today," *Journal of Religion* 27 (1947), 34–54.

Köstlin, D. J. "Calvin's Institutio nach Form und Inhalt," *Theologische Studien und Kritiken* 41 (1868).

Lang, A. "The Reformation and Natural Law," *Princeton Theological Review* 7 (1909), 177–218.

Lecerf, A. "De l'impulsion donnée par le Calvinisme à l'étude des sciences physiques et naturelles," *Bulletin de la Société de l'Histoire du Protestantisme Français* 84 (1935), 192–201.

———. "L'exposition Jean Calvin et la Réforme française," *Bulletin de la Société de l'Histoire du Protestantisme Français* 84 (1935).

Maury, Pierre, "La théologie naturelle d'après Calvin," *Bulletin de la Société de l'Histoire du Protestantisme Français* 84 (1935), 267ff.

McNeill, J. T. "Natural Law in the Teaching of the Reformers," *Journal of Religion* 26 (1946), 182.

Niesel, Wilhelm. "Calvin und Luther," *Reformierte Kirchenzeitung* 81 (1931), 195–196.

———. "Calvin wider Osianders Rechtfertigungslehre," *Zeitschrift für Kirchengeschichte* 46 (1927), 410–430.

———. "Wesen und Gestalt der Kirche nach Calvin," *Evangelische Theologie* 3 (1936), 309–310.

Pannier, Jacques. "L'autorité de l'Écriture sainte d'après Calvin," *Revue de Théologie et des Questions Religieuses* (1906), 377.

Schneckenburger, Matthias. "Die neueren Verhandlungen, betreffend das Prinzip des reformirten Lehrbegriffs," *Theologische Jahrbücher* 7 (1848), 74.

———. "Recensionen: Schweizer, *Die Glaubenslehre der evangelisch-reformirten Kirche*," *Theologische Studien und Kritiken* 20 (1847), 960–961.

Strohl, H. "Récentes études sur la théologie de Calvin," *Revue d'Histoire et de Philosophie Religieuses* 6 (1926), 544–552.

———. "L'exposition Jean Calvin et la Réforme française," *Bulletin de la Société de l'Histoire du Protestantisme Français* 84 (1935), 171–172.

Torrance, T. F. "Predestination in Christ," *Evangelical Quarterly* 13 (April 15, 1941), 109.

Ullmann, E. G. "Zur Charakteristik der reformirten Kirche. Mit Beziehung auf neuere litterarische Erscheinungen," *Theologische Studien und Kritiken* 16 (1843), 749ff.

Unpublished Material

Bainton, Roland H. Manuscript on the life and work of Servetus. [See Roland H. Bainton, *Hunted Heretic: The Life and Death of Michael Servetus, 1511–1553*. Boston: Beacon Press, 1953.]